excellence in

Leadership
and
Management

How to be the best and how to get the best from people

excellence in

Leadership and Management

How to be the best and how to get the best from people

Stuart Emmett, with Nigel Wyatt

Contents

About this book

Much has been written on leadership and management topics, unfortunately though, we continue to find that many managers and leaders have never actually studied or examined or reflected in any practical way at all, on what they actually do, beyond, having perhaps refreshed and updated their specialist technical skills.

Indeed in the author's work on supply chain, procurement, inventory logistics and finance topics, a common and recurring discovery is that, whilst hard, quantifiable skills are often practiced using computer software and systems, the softer subjective skills like negotiating, motivating, leading and managing people are often found to be lacking.

We regularly find a lack of in-depth knowledge in these soft skill areas, and, more than often, we also find very few worthwhile corrective and productive practical applications.

It seems to us that many organisations just do not get the best from their people; and we ask ourselves, "Is there something wrong somewhere"?

This question, whilst being a simple one, has a complex answer: collective social and organisational cultures are all intermingled into a complex web that includes topics like individual personal styles, personality, feelings and beliefs.

Some guidance however on what is required can be found by a listing by the UK National Occupational Standards (NOS) covering management and leadership, where the following competences are revealed:

A.   Managing self and personal skills
B.   Providing direction
C.   Facilitating change
D.   Working with people
E.   Using resources
F.   Achieving results

These standards provide a useful framework for management and leadership and we have expanded them further below. Whilst this book is not meant to exactly match the above NOS details; we can see in overview, the following links to this book contents:

Chapter topics	Chapter essentially covers	NOS
Management and Leadership	What is it all about?	A-F
Management Vision and Strategy	What direction are we going in?	B/F
Managing Me	What do I need to do to me?	A/F
Managing People	How can I get the best from people?	D/F
Managing Finance	What is involved in Finance?	E/F
Managing Performance	How can I get the best performance?	E/F

Managing Customers	How can I give exceptional service to customers internal or external?	D/F
Managing and Improving Systems	How can I make improvements, continually?	F
Management of Change	What is involved in change?	C/F

We hope this book will provide a practical application approach for those leaders and managers who need a refresher or development in these skills; after all, any organisation is good as its people, therefore getting the best from people and being the best leader/manager is interlinked and connected.

We have endeavoured not to include anything in this book that if used, would be injurious or cause financial loss to the user. The user is, however, strongly recommended before applying or using any of the contents, to check and verify for themselves the effects of the applications within their occupational activities, and perhaps also with their organisational policy/requirements. No liability will be accepted by the authors for any of the contents.

Author Introduction

Stuart Emmett

My journey to today, whilst an individual one, did not happen without the involvement of other people. On this journey of lifelong learning and meeting people, the original source of an idea or information may have been forgotten. If I have omitted in this book to give anyone credit they are due, I apologise and hope they will contact me so we can correct the omission in hopefully, a future edition.

To all those who had contact with me please be assured you will have contributed to my learning, growing and developing. If you ask me how, then I will tell you! Whilst thanking you all, my hope is that I have given something positive back to you. I am pleased to acknowledge that my learning still continues; indeed writing this book has certainly contributed to my learning and development, and I am grateful to Nigel Wyatt for his work on the Finance section.

I have a background in freight, warehousing, shipping, and international trade and have resided in both the UK and in Nigeria. Since 1998 I have been an independent mentor/coach, trainer and consultant trading under the name of Learn and Change Limited. I currently enjoy working all over the UK and on four other continents, principally in Africa and the Middle East, but also in the Far East and South America.

Additional to undertaking training, I have been involved with one to one coaching/mentoring, consulting, writing, and assessing along with examining for professional institutes' qualifications and as an external MSc examiner.

I'm married to the lovely Christine, and have two adult children, Jill and James; James is married to Mairead. We are additionally the grandparents of three girls (the totally gorgeous Megan, Molly and Niamh).

More about me can always be found out by visiting my web site: www.learnandchange. com. I welcome any comments.

Nigel Wyatt

I am a qualified accountant and former university lecturer. Over the last twenty years I have been running a consultancy specialising in financial training (www. MagentaNetwork.co.uk). I work with a wide range of clients in Europe, Asia and the Middle East, delivering training in variety of locations including nuclear power stations and even a royal palace.

I live with my wife and three children in Stony Stratford, Milton Keynes, UK.

1: A Leader or a Manager?

The modern era has spawned a raft of new terminology – and the 1990s in particular saw a shift away from established terms that had become outdated, to newer, more 'team'-orientated terms. An example of this is the shift away from the term 'manager' to the term 'leader' – a shift that indicated and emphasised the involvement of the person in question with their team, rather than just focussing on their title.

Thus, the title 'Team Leader' is now more commonly used, and we rarely find the term 'Team Manager' or 'Team Supervisor'. The term 'supervisor' has been changed to 'Team Leader'; similarly many former 'General Managers' have been renamed as 'Directors'.

Terminology shift is therefore a reality in the business world, and in an attempt to examine the differences between leaders and managers, the following was compiled from an internet discussion group's comments.

Leaders	Managers
About people	About systems
Innovates	Administers
Original	Copies
Develops	Maintains
Inspires trust	Controls
Eye on the horizon	Eye on bottom line
Challenges	Accepts status quo
Does right things	Does things right
Achieves tasks by working with a team, empowering, supporting, advising	Achieves tasks with people by effective efforts of the people is responsible for
Being paradigm	Doing paradigm
"What do we want to do?"	"How are we going to do it"
Success means need both and you cannot have one without the other, it is a question of "style"	Success means need both and you cannot have one without the other, it is a question of "style"
You can tell them by their followers	They only need "doers"
Different aspects of the same role	Different aspects of the same role
More on direction, vision, mission	More on doing things with other people
"Soft" tasks, such as motivation, communicating.	"Hard" tasks that is measurable such as SMART objectives, KPIs.
Inspires	Requires
Values	Rules

Vision and future	Objectives and present
Coaching	Instructing
Pulling	Pushing
Involving	Telling
Empowering	Delegating

We also have John Adair's useful view from his Action Centred Leadership model, in which leadership is "To Achieve a Task and Build a Team and Develop Individuals."

This definition is useful as it covers not only the job task to be done, but also shows that this can only be achieved by people – who participate both as individuals and also within teams. These three aspects – Task/Team/Individuals – can be expanded, showing that the following is involved:

Achieve the Task
- defines the job
- plans the work objectives
- organises
- directs
- controls

Build the Team
- sets team standards
- maintains discipline
- builds team spirit
- encourages and motivates
- communicates
- determines methods and procedures

Develop the Individuals
- attends to "welfare"
- encourages and motivates
- communicates
- builds status
- determines roles and responsibilities
- sets individual targets

The value of Adair's approach is that the effective leader must have all three in equal balance, and cannot be biased towards one aspect than another.

Thus, if leadership and management are all about 'getting people to do things', then the 'do things' equates to 'the Task', which can, however, only be achieved by people, either in their capacity as Individuals, or as Team members.

This view of people as both individual and team members is important, as people will often behave differently in these different roles.

> **Quotes on leadership and management**
>
> *"We want about 5 per cent leaders and the rest to be very good managers."*
> – Alan Leighton. Chairman Royal Mail in Motor Transport 28 November 2002.
>
> *"You can be a terrific manager but a poor leader."*
> (From: Pagonis *"Moving Mountains"*)

Leaders and managers are ultimately all about getting the best performance possible from all of the available people and the available resources; we most deliberately do not use the expression 'human resources' as this devalues the individual aspects within the equation (an aspect we will discuss soon).

Getting the best performance means:
- Improving individual, team and organisation performance
- Motivating, developing and releasing potential
- Reflecting and supporting the organisation culture, strategy and style
- Communicating to people what is expected, what they are rewarded for, how they should deliver results and what results the organisation wants
- Striving for consistency in the way people are treated, the way people operate, and within the culture, purpose and strategy of the business itself

Getting the best performance means the following is unhelpful, as leadership/management is not about the following:
- Unclear direction(s)
- Weak values
- Vague and unrealistic objectives
- Variable appraisals/reviews
- Poor performance and motivation

- Inadequate training and development
- Bureaucracy
- Poor communications

Five practices have to be acquired to be effective:
1. Effective executives know where their time goes...
2. Make outward contributions...
3. Build on strengths....
4. Concentrate on superior performance...
5. Make effective decisions

Peter Drucker

Meanwhile the following gives another 'extremes' view on differences found between managers/leaders.

Managers	Leaders
Handle tactics, drive forward using authority	Handle strategy, drives forward by using inspiration and goodwill
Make the provision and the "how"	Make the vision and the "why"
Work is managed to a satisfactory performance	People are led and influenced beyond simple legitimate authority
Plans the pace and reacts	Direct and are proactive
"Fire-fighting"	"Fire-lighting"
Work with boundaries/limits and demand respect	Work with hopes and dreams and command respect
Mainly is short-term	Mainly with the medium/longer term
Inspire stability within the "status quo"	Inspire innovation and change

Perhaps the following transactional and transformational roles represent a better view:

Feature	Transactional	Transformational
Vision	Goals and objectives for immediate results	Long-term vision
Control	Structures and processes created; solves problems	Creates climate of trust and empowers people to control themselves; manages problem solving
Outlook	Maintain and improve the current situation	Changes the current situation
Style	Plans, organises, directs and controls people	Coaches and develops people

Culture	Guards and defends	Challenges and changes
Power	From position and authority within the organisation	From influencing a network of relationships

Maybe here, one is a manager and the other a leader? However, organisations need both leaders and managers – try to imagine an organisation without all of the above characteristics in their people. We have presented many different and varied views here, so let us now try and differentiate them simply.

Management definitions
- Getting people to do things right
- Using resources to achieve objectives
- Planning-organising-directing-controlling, as detailed in the following diagram:

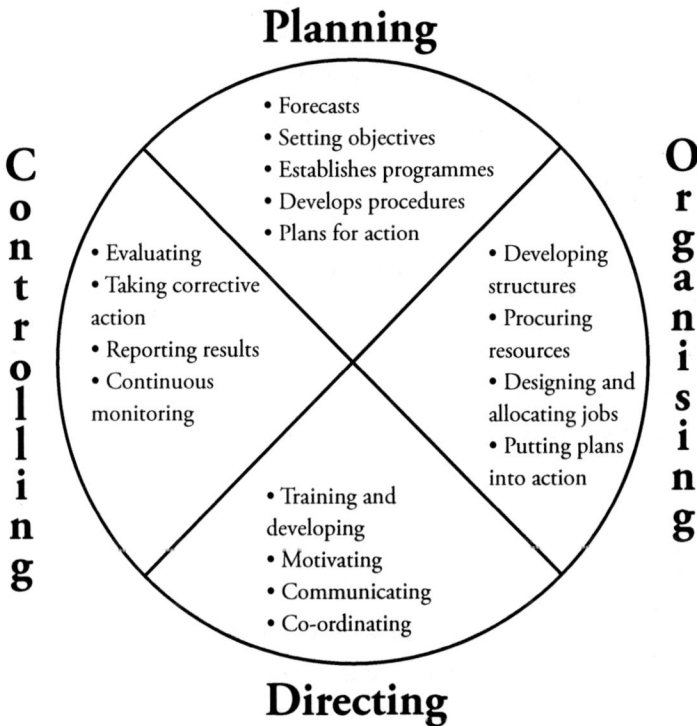

Planning

C o n t r o l l i n g

- Forecasts
- Setting objectives
- Establishes programmes
- Develops procedures
- Plans for action

- Evaluating
- Taking corrective action
- Reporting results
- Continuous monitoring

- Developing structures
- Procuring resources
- Designing and allocating jobs
- Putting plans into action

- Training and developing
- Motivating
- Communicating
- Co-ordinating

O r g a n i s i n g

Directing

Leadership Definitions
- Getting people to do the right things
- Sets strategic objectives and helps others achieve those objectives
- Is defined by the followers

Therefore, it would seem that:

- Managers do things right; leaders do the right things.
- Where managers direct and control, leaders inspire and enable others.

It seems a pity that the current evolution of the two terms is only another step towards making the role of the leader the one that is preferred, and the one that holds the greater status. This should really not be the case, as any organisation is a collection of people and there is the view that leaders need to serve people (and not the other way round). Maybe, however, this view of having a more servant role is perhaps not one that is seen as "sexy" or deserving of higher status in the more financially-driven organisations?

It should also never be the case that managers are assumed not to be able to display the characteristics of leaders. Indeed, many of us will have met managers who do use many of the above identified leadership characteristics, and rightly so. Additionally, as discussed, leaders are not just the 'top team'. Leaders need followers, who may also be managers, but then these managers will need to lead their own people (and will be seen by their people as a leader); and so the cycle develops.

Some myths on leadership
- It is a rare skill (no, they are commonly found)
- Leaders are born (no, they can be made)
- Leaders are only found at the top (no, they can be found at all levels)
- Leaders are heroes (no, they are human and are just the same as everyone else)

In **The Leadership Gospels** *(Emmett, 2008)*, the following leadership qualities were identified, and can be applied to this title as well.

Leadership Keys
- Leadership and change are directly connected
- Leaders bring in a new order and shift the paradigm
- Leaders need a "servant heart" that gives, rather than takes
- Leaders must be clear on whom/what they are and stand for, as it is this inner side will drive what they say and do (rubbish in equals rubbish out).
- Leaders have to attract followers
- Leaders will not always find a "fit" with every person, and will be often criticised.
- Leaders use a vision/mission statement, and in this case, having financial success as the main vision should be seen as problematic.

Leadership Style
- Leaders show by example: "come with me and I will teach you" and in effect, they will also recruit their own replacement.
- Leaders have a bold and decisive presence: they practice "walking in front" and literally will pull and lead people. They will not be a bully that forces people, or pushes and "kicks from behind."
- Leaders correct mistakes with people one on one; if the mistakes cannot be rectified then they need to "go public." If it still cannot be rectified, then they need to treat the person as not being a part of the "team."
- Leaders use strong and direct communication and say it like they see it. This means accepting that inevitably, some will think they are being rude. To communicate most effectively, face-to-face contact is needed, as it is body language that really communicates (eye contact being the most revealing part of body language).
- Leaders trust: often this is the absolutely essential quality. This means an acceptance that any lack of trust will usually destroy relationships.

Leadership Roles
- Planning is essential – leaders ensure plans are both made and carried out.
- Leaders know their people, and recognise that people will use different methods. Therefore, some methods in certain circumstances may be more appropriate than others.
- Leaders select the appropriate number of people for the team
- Leaders give clear directions to the team
- Leaders need to give power and authority to the leadership team
- Followers need motivating to do things, and when people have a compulsive inner drive, they can be unstoppable, as the only motivation that will ever last is one that satisfies a core/internally held value/belief.

Leadership Essentials
- People make the financial differences in any organisation. Therefore, people, and not money, must be established as the main driver of any organisation
- Culture counts: 'the way we do things round here' must be consciously considered and the right choices made.
- Leaders need followers (who may be managers) and then these managers will need to lead their own people (and will be seen by their people as a leader) and so forth.

The concept of the "servant leader" has also been noted in **Leadership by the Book** *(Blanchard, Hybels and Hodges, 2004)* as follows:

Personal Aspects	Most Leaders	Servant leaders
Motivation	Driven to lead	Called to lead
Satisfaction	Power/status. Being in charge. Possessions. Ownership.	Growth of others. Serving others. Sharing. Stewardship.
Origin of rewards	External	Internal
Feedback from others	Not liked. Viewed as threatening.	Liked. Viewed as helping.
Aim	Please self. "Me"	Please others. "We"
Goals/focus	Results/KPIs	Process/methods

Meanwhile, let us remind ourselves that ultimately both managers and leaders are both looking to carry out and maintain peak performance, as shown below:

Checklist: Maintaining Peak Performance

Direction
- Have vision, goals, commitment and purpose to self and to others.
- Work on the "being" as well as the "doing"
- Individuals need to clear out any external obstacles (e.g. people to deal with, systems to check)
- Clearing out the internal obstacles (e.g. fears, doubts, self limiting beliefs), for "as a person thinks then so they are"

Power
- Drive and energy mentally, emotionally, physically, spiritually
- Identify what drains and holds you and others back
- Identify what energises and moves you and others forward

Truth
- Being true to own beliefs, values and honesty in dealing with others
- In giving feedback to self and from others

Values
- Be clear on the basic and bottom lines below which you not go. These provide the fall back and the support to everything you do

Skills
- Having and developing the right tools and creativity

What makes a "good" organisation?

This is a difficult question to answer, as what is good for one person, will perhaps not be so for another. With this in mind, the following represents views of good organisations and does provide a basis for an interesting comparison to your own personal views and experiences.

Characteristics of Unhealthy and Healthy Organisations

	Unhealthy	Healthy
Leadership	Top-down control of decisions	Decision-making at all levels
	Frequent bottlenecks	Organisational level not a factor
	Manager is like a prescriptive parent	Leadership is flexible and shifting
	Control and justification	Freedom and trust
	Excessive justifications required	High degree of autonomy
Commitment	Nobody volunteers	Everyone pitches in
	Nobody cares when things go wrong	Optimistic about problem solving
	Mistakes and problems hidden	People signal awareness of problems
	Investment in objectives comes only from the top level	Objectives widely shared by all levels

	Managers get minimum cooperation	Noticeable sense of team work
	People feel locked in jobs	People involved by choice
	People are stale, bored, security-oriented	People are excited, motivated, energized
Interpersonal issues	Needs and feelings are side issues and marginalised	Problem solving includes personal needs
	Judgement at lower levels is not respected	Judgement at lower levels is respected
	Marksmanship and image building	Relationships are honest
	People feel alone	People care about one another
	Undercurrent of fear	Confidence and assurance
Problem solving	Innovation in hands of a few	Everyone anticipates the future
	Organisational charts dominate	Informal, non territorial and cross functional
	Pleasing management top priority	Boss is frequently challenged

(From: *"Organisation Development"* Lenny T. Ralphs (1996))

Another view of what makes a good organisation comes in the following from the *Sunday Times* of some years ago.

The best organisation

The best organisation is one which:

- Puts something back into the local community
- Treats customers well
- Has positive leadership

- Makes the world a better place
- Has a good work-life balance
- Open management
- Will help in times of personal crisis

The people in such an organisation:
- Laugh a lot with colleagues
- Have colleagues who care
- Are the least exhausted at work
- Have job satisfaction
- Love working for the organisation

Of course an organisation is judged by its people, and the following comparison between a good and a bad boss is useful:

	The good boss	The bad boss
Time management	Good planner	Leaves to the last minute
Decision-making	Decisive	Keeps changing decisions and at worst, procrastinates
Direction/guidance	Praises	Criticises
Attitude	Positive	Negative and stressed
Personal development of others	Supports	No interest
Team	Defends the team	Over commits the team
Delegation	Does	"Dumps"
Style	"Sells" (and most staff will support colleagues)	"Tells" (and most staff will criticise colleagues)
Problem handling	Faces up to problems	Hides from problems
Staff view	Below average absenteeism	30% take "sickies" 60% looking for new job

People in an organisation are part of the undeclared assets/resources of the organisation. As mentioned earlier, unfortunately the term 'human resources' has other implications.

Human Resources

Despite the almost universal use of this word, people are the most important aspect of organisations – they make everything else work and happen. They are clearly not just 'resources' like money, machinery, time etc. therefore people are not 'human resources'. The following quotation is a reflection of this:

"When people are referred to as human resources and are evaluated in the same way as money, raw materials or technology, a red mist settles over my eyes. People are not a resource, they are people; in their glory, variety and ability."
– John Harvey Jones

People are the ultimate source of any ability that any organisation has; however, and sadly rather regularly, organisational practices do not reflect this. For example:

- Organisations concentrate more on technology, products, profits etc. than they do on people.
- The importance of people is given mere "lip service" (especially common in annual reports), and nothing is effectively being done to encourage, support and develop people.
- Little (or at worst, no) recognition of the fact that everything starts with ideas from people, and that the potentially unlimited creative potential of people can be channelled.
- No real focus on creative change to solve new, ongoing and recurrent problems

In any organisation, people need to feel they are needed; if not, they may well leave and move on, or at worst, stay and become covert saboteurs.

Problems with HR as a department

It has been said that HR departments do not:

- Fully contribute or align to the business, but more to the HR profession
- Know what is going on at the "front or sharp end"
- Think strategically
- Demonstrate outcomes
- Lead organisational development
- Provide any strategic practical input

HR is said to be too concerned with aspects like payroll, basic recruitment/selection, benefits administration and union negotiations. Perhaps, therefore, a better name is, in fact the former term 'Personnel Department'?

Indeed, it is very rare that an HR person makes it into senior organisational positions such as CEO, and whilst "the HR function has the reputation of being the organisational police, the function that knows best, the one that keeps others in line, HR is actually there to help and provide the support and the ideas to help you get your job done and get the best out of the people who work for you". (**"The HR Toolkit"**, *Richard McNamara*, 2008)

So from the above comments, there is some hope on the horizon. However the main point here is that it is the individual leaders and managers who need to be the ones that drive forward best practice with people in organisations. Whilst HR people will support this, they cannot be systematically expected to be such leaders.

Individuals cannot look to subcontract leadership and management best practices to HR; it is not the job of HR to action such practices. The point is similarly made in the following case study:

Case Study: Timpson Shoe Repairs and People Management

At Timpson, the high-street shoe repair chain, the words 'human resource management', 'redundancy' and 'consultancy' are considered blasphemous.

"I don't like the grandiosity implicit in the concept of HRM, nor the metrics that so many of its practitioners hide behind,' says Gouy Hamilton-Fisher, operations director, people support. "My role is to ensure people are happy at work."

Hamilton-Fisher is impatient with HR practitioners who "get het-up about the latest fads", and who rely on textbooks rather than common sense to deal with people issues. But then Timpson has almost written its own book on management.

A family firm founded in Manchester in 1865, Timpson has had its fair share of ups and downs, including family feuds, takeovers and wrong turns. But a willingness to adapt to changing trends has made it resilient. The company is now run by chairman and chief executive John Timpson, who sold off the core shoe-shop business in 1987 to focus on shoe repair, and his son James, the managing director.

Through a combination of acquisitions and organic growth, the pair has built up a raft of related services, from key cutting, watch repair and jewellery engraving, to dry cleaning and photo developing. Sales last year topped £96 million.

While there is an almost palpable sense of culture and values about the firm, these are not formalised. Over the past 10 years, the father and son team has developed an approach they call "upside-down management". They borrowed ideas from Ricardo Semlerh's *"Maverick"* and Robert Spector and Patrick D. McCarthy's *"The Nordstrom Way"*; "Timpsonising" them and merging them with their own way of doing things, to create a management style that is both hands-on and empowers staff to come up with innovative ideas and deliver customer service in the way they think best (see below).

The Timpson Way is encapsulated in a small manual called *"How to be a Great Boss"*. Resembling the children's Mr Men books, this accessible and digestible guide is aimed at middle managers and features cartoon characters and pithy practical advice such as:

- People doing the day-to-day business know more about the company than you do, so take their advice. If they have a good idea, let them test it out.
- Don't have a special parking place.
- At times of trouble, don't cut the training budget. Your job is to help your people get better and the best way to help is to train them.
- You should praise 10 times as much as you criticise.
- Keep your door wide open. Don't stay deskbound.

"If you treat people like adults they are far more likely to make money than if you simply give them orders," says James Timpson.

Upside-down management is about outlawing rules that stand in the way of progress, says Timpson senior, who believes that "pedestrian middle managers who stifle the enthusiasm of inventive juniors are the biggest block to bright ideas".

Just as good ideas are rewarded, the 1,700-odd staff dispersed throughout the 565 branches are motivated by a raft of other measures. These includes good internal communications and regular social events, bonuses based on branch turnover and skills development, a hardship fund, internal awards such as 'shoe repairer of the year' and time off for special occasions.

In addition, the Timpsons host gourmet lunches three times a year for randomly selected employees, and have bought holiday homes for the use of staff that have been with the company for five or more years. They visit all branches at least once a year, write hundreds of letters to 'colleagues' and discourage late working. The company also invests £3 million in training every year.

The benefits feed through into staff satisfaction. Some 778 employees have been with the firm for five or more years, 362 of them for at least 10 years, and 70 per cent of areas have lists of people waiting to join the chain. This strong sense of job satisfaction, in turn, feeds through into customer service. Many of Timpson's services, including watch repairs, have been developed from ideas suggested by staff. The branches also act as help centres: customers can consult a copy of the Yellow Pages, use their toilets or phones and get change for parking meters.

As the chain has expanded, the Timpsons have inevitably had to delegate more to area managers. James Timpson therefore spends an increasing amount of time getting the right area managers and departmental heads in place. This is easier at Timpson than it might be elsewhere, given that 95 per cent of employees have grown up in the business, and 42 per cent were introduced by a colleague — so they are already aware of its philosophy. "All 25 area managers started off sweeping the floors when they were 17," he claims.

The company does recruit some departmental heads from outside — the heads of IT and finance were external appointments. But the head of health and safety started on the switchboard, while Hamilton-Fisher began his career with Timpson 26 years ago in a branch in Rotherham, running several other shops, and then a number of areas before taking on his current role in 1998.

This internal succession, which helps to "solidify the culture and values" according to Hamilton-Fisher, is only challenged when the company makes a takeover. Its acquisition of Minit (which included the Sketchley and Supasnap businesses) in 2003, which tripled the number of shops overnight, was one of the rare occasions when it was forced to make redundancies.

While all Minit shop staff and junior field management stayed, 95 per cent of the Minit Company's area and training managers left as a result of the cultural differences between the two organisations. "Minit was a very dictatorial organisation, and many of the senior managers couldn't appreciate the difference between supporting and controlling staff," says Hamilton-Fisher.

"It takes about five years to change a culture," adds James Timpson. "You start off finding out what all the stupid rules are — for example, Sketchley wouldn't pay for window cleaners, and the customer service line was an answer phone, and at Mr Minit [shoe repair business] if you wanted a stamp you had to phone head office to send you one. You slowly take the reins off, but if you don't have the right people it is hopeless."

Extracts from *Chartered Institute of Personnel and Development (CIPD)* magazine, 20 April 2006.

2: Management Vision and Strategy

Vision

A vision is that something that will often originate as a dream which describes direction, such as:

- Where you want to be
- What you want to create
- What you can commit to
- What you believe in

Visions will contain values and principles and are usually in the form of a substantial, but short statement that will encapsulate both the direction and associated guidance.

Values and principles can also come from the collective aspirations and the shared commitment of a team, for example:

"We, as a Team, committed to the following at place x on y date:
- We will use the "right" language in all our external dealings with others
- We will be "open" with each other in the team
- We will support each other, especially in front of others
- We will have the confidence to confront each other
- We will deliver quality work"

The above statement was then signed by all team members and provided an on-going record of the commitments made. It may even be visibly framed and used as a public reference point.

It certainly can be used as a checkpoint and reference point in the ongoing future workings together. It effectively provides a statement of the teams' personality.

Having clarity of values is therefore important, points well noted by Sir John Harvey Jones:

"I believe that the companies which get most out of their people are those whose values are consistent, or, at minimum, harmonious with each other. The starting point to achieve this managerial nirvana lies in ensuring that the value systems of the business are congruent with the values and aspirations of the individuals."

17

"Unless the values are lived up to at every level, unless the systems support the values, unless those who are promoted are seen to espouse and buy into the concepts, value statements are a massive switch off."
– Sir John Harvey Jones

It has already been noted earlier that money as a main value or principle is not really "a leadership thing". Indeed, this has also been noted by Peter Drucker.

"To manage a business is to balance a variety of needs and goals. To emphasise only profit, misdirects managers to the point where they may endanger the survival of the business."
– Peter Drucker

Money will however be certainly an aspect of strategy – the main question here being the degree of importance.

In addition to vision, we also find the term 'mission' being used. Mission is effectively the purpose and plan of the organisation. Missions therefore "roll down" from the vision, and are used by some organisations to take them towards the more detailed strategies and objectives.

Strategy

Strategy can perhaps be best described as a firm's theory on how to accomplish their vision by making competitive moves and business approaches. Strategy is therefore the "game plan" for the future by determining how to:
*   Position the organisation into its chosen market
*   Compete successfully
*   Achieve the required good performance

Fundamentally, strategy proactively shapes how an organisation's business will be conducted, and moulds the independent actions and decisions of managers and employees into a coordinated, organisation-wide game plan.

The following hierarchy for vision, strategy, tactics and operations shows the relationships involved. (diagram opposite)

We can also see here, that strategy uses broad objectives and converts them into policies. Tactics convert these into forecasts and plans, which operations then converts into schedules and controls.

We have also observed that one view of strategy is all about theory, as it emphasises the imperfect information and incomplete knowledge which always surrounds the implementation. However it will work in practice, when the theory is consistent with the underlying economic processes and when few other firms are unable to act on it as completely.

Meanwhile, there are many views on strategy, for example:

"The determination of the basic long-term goals and objectives of an enterprise, and the adoption of courses of action and the allocation of resources necessary for carrying out those goals."
– Chandler 1962

"A strategy is a pattern or plan that integrates an organisation's major goals, policies and action sequences into a cohesive whole."
– Quinn 1980

According to Mintzberg (1994), strategy is:
*   The formal procedure to produce an articulated result, in the form of an integrated system of decisions
*   Integrated decision-making
*   Coordinates activities
*   Future thinking
*   Controlling the future
*   Ensures that the future is taken into account
*   Rational control

"The sole purpose of strategic planning is to enable the organisation to gain as efficiently as possible, a sustainable edge over its competitors and to alter the organisation's strength relative to that of its competitors in the most efficient way."
– Ohmae *(The mind of the strategist)*

In terms of competing, Michael Porter (1996) noted that:
*   Strategy is creating fit among an organisation's activities. The success of a strategy depends on doing many things well and integrating them.
*   Competitive strategy is about being different. It means deliberately choosing a different set of activities to deliver a unique mix of value.
*   Competitive advantage means deciding to be a cost leader or a service/value leader; such characteristics are shown below:

Competitive Advantage

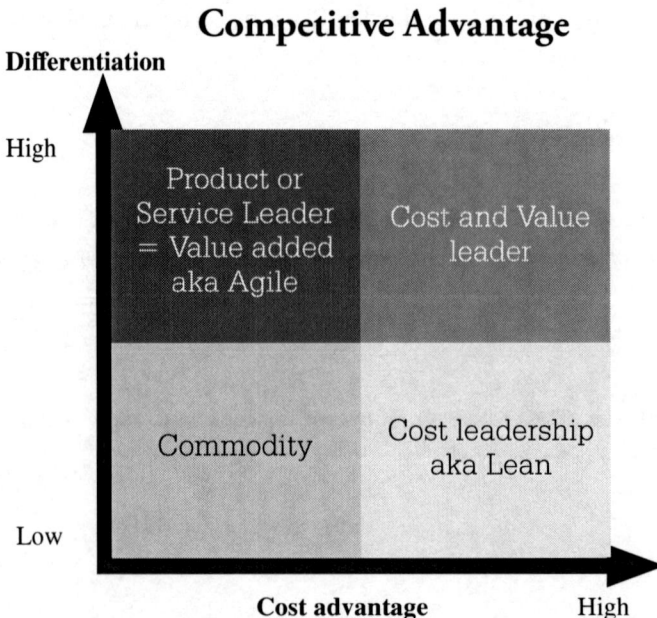

Differentiation

High	
Product or Service Leader = Value added aka Agile	Cost and Value leader
Commodity	Cost leadership aka Lean
Low	

Cost advantage　　　High

This has been observed as a choice between being a cost leader, for example, food at Aldi, or a product or service leader, for example, food at Marks and Spencer.

And just to show the tension behind such categorizations, Aldi would more than likely suggest that they are both cost and value leaders.

Meanwhile, the following shows the broad differences between these two categories:

"Do it cheaper" and being a cost leader
- Give same standard products/service at a lower price
- Standard products
- Standard offering
- Production push
- Flow and mass volume production, with high mechanisation
- Low inventory levels
- Focus on productivity and efficiency
- Stable planning
- Lowest possible costs with service a constraint
- Lead time reduction
- Minimise waste by being Lean

"Do it better" and being a product or service leader
- Give products/services that cannot be found anywhere else
- Customer designed product/services
- Value added bespoke offering
- Market pull
- Job shop production, low mechanisation
- Flexible inventory
- Focus on creativity and innovation
- Flexible planning
- Maximises innovation responses/service with cost a constraint
- Short lead times/quick responses
- Maximise service by being Agile

Porter's Five Forces Model of Competition

A key aspect here is the view of competition, and Porter has the following Five Forces view:

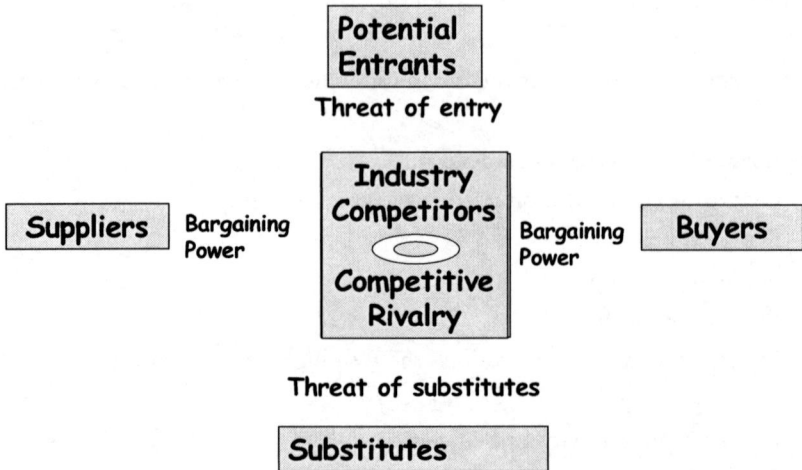

```
                    ┌─────────────┐
                    │ Potential   │
                    │ Entrants    │
                    └─────────────┘
                    Threat of entry

                    ┌─────────────┐
                    │ Industry    │
┌───────────┐       │ Competitors │       ┌──────────┐
│ Suppliers │ Bargaining         │ Bargaining │ Buyers │
└───────────┘ Power  ◯          Power       └──────────┘
                    │ Competitive │
                    │ Rivalry     │
                    └─────────────┘

                 Threat of substitutes

                 ┌─────────────┐
                 │ Substitutes │
                 └─────────────┘
```

The five threats are from substitutes, entry of new players, the intensity of existing competitors and the bargaining power of suppliers and of buyers. These can be considered as follows:

The threat of substitutes

The existence of close substitute products increases the chances of customers switching to alternatives, perhaps in response/opposition to price increases, meaning:

- Buyers have the chance to substitute
- The relative price performance of substitutes
- Buyers switching costs
- Perceived level of product differentiation

The threat of the entry of new competitors

Profitable markets that yield high returns will draw in new organisations. The results are many new entrants, which will effectively decrease profitability. Unless the entry of new organisations can be blocked by the current suppliers, the profit rate will fall towards a competitive level. Responses may be from:

- Existence of barriers to entry (patents, rights, etc.)
- Economies of product differences
- Brand equity

- Access to distribution channels
- Absolute cost advantages
- Expected retaliation by incumbents
- Government policies

The intensity of competitive rivalry

With most industries, competitive rivalry is the major factor in the competitiveness of the industry. Sometimes rivals compete aggressively and sometimes rivals compete in non-price dimensions such as innovation, marketing, etc. The following is involved:

- Number of competitors
- Rate of industry growth
- Intermittent industry overcapacity
- Exit barriers
- Diversity of competitors
- Fixed cost allocation per value added
- Level of advertising expense
- Economies of scale

The bargaining power of customers

The bargaining power and ability of customers to apply pressure is also described as the market of outputs. It also affects the customer's sensitivity to price changes and involves the following:

- Buyer to suppliers market position
- Bargaining leverage, particularly in industries with high fixed costs
- Buyer volume
- Buyer switching costs relative to suppliers switching costs
- Buyer information availability
- Ability to backward integrate
- Availability of existing substitute products
- Buyer price sensitivity
- Differential advantage (uniqueness) of industry products

The bargaining power of suppliers

This is also described as the market of inputs. Suppliers of raw materials, components, and services (such as expertise) can be a source of supplier power over the firm, for example, ink jet printer cartridges, OEM spare parts. Suppliers may refuse to work with the firm, or charge excessively high prices for unique resources and covers the following:

- Supplier switching costs relative to buyers switching costs
- Degree of differentiation of inputs
- Presence of substitute inputs
- Supplier concentration to buyer concentration ratio
- Threat of forward integration by suppliers relative to the threat of backward integration by firms
- Cost of inputs relative to selling price of the product

Many find it useful to rate the five forces on say a 1 to 5 scale as this focuses attention of the relative strengths of the forces.

The Value Disciplines

Tracey and Wiersema have the following useful view:

Operational Excellence
Best total cost

Product Leadership　　　　**Customer Intimacy**
Best product　　　　　　　*Best total solution*

They see that:
- Operational excellence is providing reliable products and services at competitive prices with minimal difficulty and inconvenience.
- Customer intimacy is segmenting and targeting precisely, then tailoring offerings to match exactly the demand of those niches. This needs combining detailed customer knowledge with operational flexibility and also taking a view of lifetime profit versus a single transaction.
- Product leadership is offering products that consistently add value and in the speed to market; thereby making rival's goods obsolete.

Four aspects of strategy

Another view can be seen in the following four different aspects for strategy to cover:

Corporate-based strategies
- Identify and strengthen key functions to support customer strategies, the secret here is the improvement in functional competence
- Improve cost effectiveness
  - cost reduction
  - greater selectivity in products, markets etc
  - share key functions

Customer-based strategies
- Identify one or more subsets of customers within the total market and concentrate efforts on meeting their needs
- How are customers segmented?
  - By product/service offered?
  - By market share/volume etc?
  - By profit?

Competitor-based strategies
- Leakage analysis
- Invest in image
- Exploit tangible advantages
- Capitalize on profit and cost structure differences
  - exploit differences in sources of profit
  - exploit differences in ratio of fixed to variable costs

Technology-based strategies
- Known for using latest equipment
- Use appropriate information communication technology
- Customer connectivity
- Capitalise on keeping up to date
  - Safety
  - Costs
  - Productivity
  - Image

Additionally, the following diagrams provide yet more views of strategy:

Strategic directions

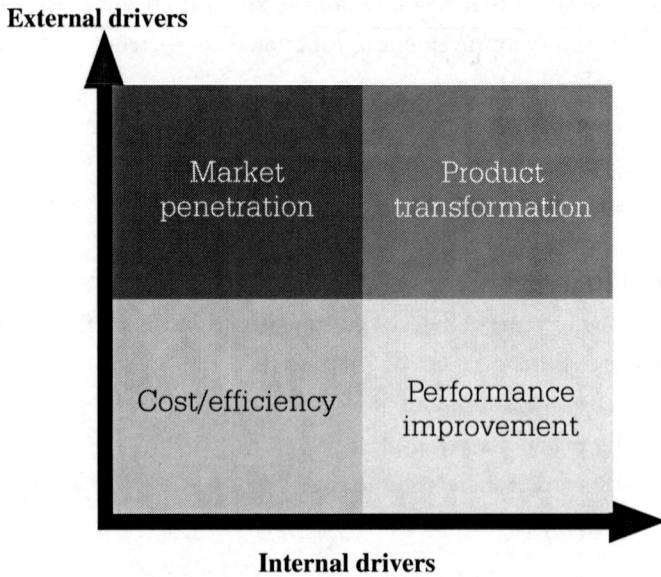

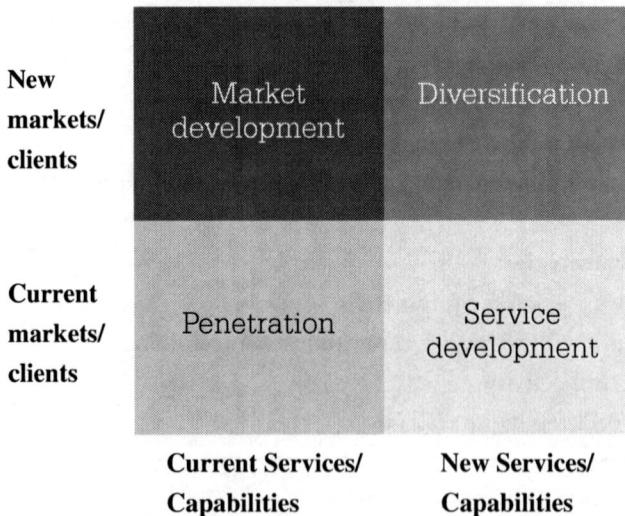

External drivers

Market penetration	Product transformation
Cost/efficiency	Performance improvement

Internal drivers

Strategic directions

	Current Services/ Capabilities	New Services/ Capabilities
New markets/ clients	Market development	Diversification
Current markets/ clients	Penetration	Service development

As the above indicate and confirm, much of strategy is about positioning the organisation in a market. The following questions will assist with this:

Checklist: Questions to ask on the Market

- Who needs my product/service?
- What is it that is inherently personal so that it can differ for each individual?
- How do my customers differ?
- How can I satisfy whoever wants my product/service?

What
- What do customers do differently with my product/service?
- What different forms can it take?
- What can I satisfy customers with from my product/service?

Where
- Where do customers need my product/service?
- How do customers differ in where they buy, receive and use it?
- How can I provide my product/service wherever customers want it?

When
- When do customers need my product/service?
- How do customers differ in when they buy, receive and use it?
- How can I provide my product/service twenty-four hours a day?
- How can I provide my product/service the instant customers want it?
- How can I provide my product/service whenever customers want it?

Why
- Why do customers need my product/service?
- How do customers differ in why they buy, receive and use it?
- Is my product a means or an end, or something in between?
- How can I add more value to help my customers completely meet their true desired end?

How
- How do customers need my product/service delivered to them?
- How do customers differ in how they buy and use it?
- What can I do to provide my product/service however my customers want it?

Strategy often fails on implementation

Making decisions on the strategy is relatively easy; it is the implementation that is the difficult aspect. This is also a reflection of the unfortunate reality of decisions being made without any regard to the impacts and how it will be implemented. The point here, of course, as with any strategy, is that it is the implementation and application that is critical; the design is the easiest part.

Merely trying to implement by the planners and strategists "waving the wand" is damaging, wrong and can be fatal. It is a pity that more strategists in organisations (and in politics) do not recognise this simple eternal truth.

Separation between the planners and the doers not only gives a poor implementation, but it may also reveal a divisive aspect and separation in organisations. Indeed one of the factors in successful Total Quality Management (TQM) implementation is the involvement of all players in decision-making; this then leads to making continuous improvements at all levels in an organisation.

There are many barriers to Strategic Development, for example:

- Vision and Strategy are not actionable
- Strategy is not linked to Tactics or to Team Goals
- Strategy is not linked to Resource Allocation
- Feedback is Tactical, not Strategic

We will discuss implementation and the management of change later in the book. Meanwhile the following shows the key issues with strategy implementations:

Checklist: Strategy Implementation
1. It is the people on the ground who make the strategy alive, so work with them
2. Have a good business case that has a sense of urgency for implementing
3. Communicate not just the strategy, but also what is/is not working,
4. Update the measurements; do not measure the old strategy
5. Culture drives the implementation, but does it fit the new strategy?
6. Ensure the processes support the new strategy
7. Reward and reinforce behaviour and actions towards the new strategy

8. Break the strategy into small components and review what was said would happen as you are doing it, and do the review:
   - every 2 weeks for the small components
   - every 12 weeks for the whole strategy

Strategy will always evolve

In most organisations there is always an ongoing need to react to:
- Shifting market conditions
- Fresh moves of competitors
- New technologies
- Evolving customer preferences
- Political and regulatory changes
- New windows of opportunity
- The crisis of the moment

Therefore, there must be ways to develop those capabilities that will help to deliver the business strategies. This will involve a complex, harmonious mix of individual and technology skills. After all, an organisation's capacity to improve existing skills and learn new ones is the most defensible competitive advantage an organisation can have; learning to do this will involve the following:

1) Clarity of the core competence
A clear core competence should provide the potential access to a wide range of markets and this should make a significant contribution to the perceived customer benefits for the organisations end product/service. It should also make it difficult for competitors to emulate.

2) A considered view of the operational excellence
Operational excellence and strategy are both essential to obtain superior performance, but an organisation can only outperform competitors if it can establish a difference and then continue to maintain it.

Managers must not become too preoccupied with improving operational effectiveness through programs such as TQM, time-based competition or benchmarking. Whilst this could give, in the short term, lower costs and higher prices with increased profitability, if managers let operational excellence supplant strategy, the results in the medium term may then be zero-sum competition, static or declining prices and pressures on cost, resulting in compromising the organisation's ability to invest in the business for the long-term.

In this regard, as earlier noted by Tracey and Wiersema, operational excellence is linked to product leadership and customer intimacy.

The essence of strategy

The essence of strategy is making a choice to perform activities that are different from rivals. However, strategic positions are often not obvious, and finding them will often require creativity and insight.

New entrants can also discover unique positions, and whilst these have been available, oftentimes the opportunity has been overlooked by the more established organisations, for example, as happened with the growth of new low cost airlines.

The following three diagrams and the checklist summarise strategy in terms of the factors shaping strategy, the levels of strategy, a model for strategy and what makes a winning strategy.

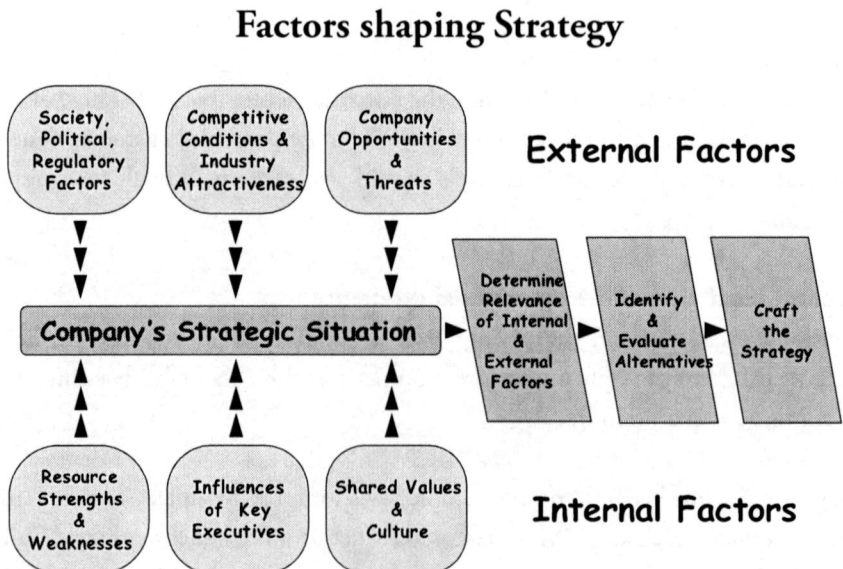

Factors shaping Strategy

Society, Political, Regulatory Factors	Competitive Conditions & Industry Attractiveness	Company Opportunities & Threats	**External Factors**

Company's Strategic Situation → Determine Relevance of Internal & External Factors → Identify & Evaluate Alternatives → Craft the Strategy

Resource Strengths & Weaknesses	Influences of Key Executives	Shared Values & Culture	**Internal Factors**

Levels of Strategy-making

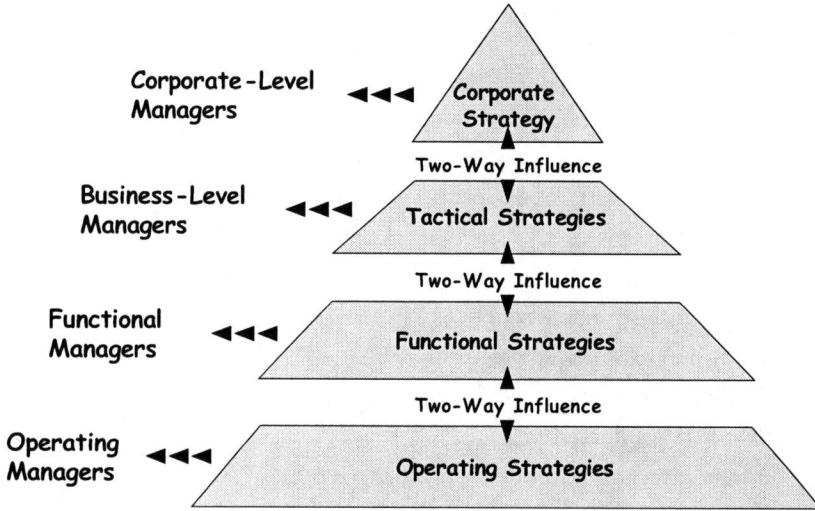

Corporate-Level Managers ◄◄◄ Corporate Strategy

Two-Way Influence

Business-Level Managers ◄◄◄ Tactical Strategies

Two-Way Influence

Functional Managers ◄◄◄ Functional Strategies

Two-Way Influence

Operating Managers ◄◄◄ Operating Strategies

Models for Strategic planning

Environmental Scan

Strengths   Weaknesses

Opportunities   Threats

Values

Mission and Vision

Strategic Issues
Strategic Priorities
Objectives, Initiatives and Evaluation

Checklist: A Winning Strategy

1. Goodness of fit test; how well is strategy matched to the situation?
2. Competitive advantage test; does strategy lead to sustainable competitive advantage?
3. Performance test; does strategy boost performance? (This assumes it has been effectively implemented)
4. What have we done to
   - Improve customer service?
   - Improve customer satisfaction?
   - Reduce costs?
   - Improve productivity?
   - Increase revenues from new products/services?
   - Be better than the competition?

(These questions can be asked at all levels in the organisation).

Organisational Culture

People working for specific organisations find that it has its own way of doing things. For example, those people who leave one organisation to join another organisation to do a similar job must soon appreciate the urgent and early need to fit into their new organisation. Whilst they will have been employed because they are technically competent, they will also now need to be culturally competent. An organisation therefore has its own culture, which we will define here as the "way we do things around here."

Blame culture

The following from Peter Drucker indicates what he sees as one unfortunate aspect of culture:

"Insecurity – not economic but psychological insecurity - permeates the entire industrial situation. It creates fear; and since it is fear of the unknown and the unpredictable, it leads to a search for scapegoats and culprits".
– Peter Drucker

Here the inherently created fear can create a blame culture. If there is a blame culture – and there are many – then changing an organisational culture will need to pass through the following stages:

Aspect	"Stormy/Blame" Culture	"Steady/Sane" Culture	"Sunny/Gain" Culture
Goals	Announced	Communicated	Agreed
Information	Status symbol and power based	Traded	Abundant
Motivation	Manipulative	Focused on staff needs	A clear goal and expected
Decisions	From above	Partly delegated	Staff make most
Mistakes	Are only made by staff	Responsibility is taken	Are allowed as learning lessons
Conflicts	Are unwelcome and "put down"	Are mastered	Are a source of new innovation
Control	From above	Partly delegated	Fully delegated
Management Style	Authoritarian/ aggressive	Cooperative	Participative/ Assertive
Authority	Requires obedience	Requires cooperation	Requires collaboration
Manager is	Absolute ruler. Feels superior	Problem solver and decision maker	Change strategist and self confident

Culture is shown both formally and informally, as the culture provides the central atmosphere in which the people operate. Some aspects will be formal and overt, some will be more informal and possibility more covert.

"Formal" culture
Organisational culture can be shown by the published vision, mission and goals, and in the rules, norms, procedures of an organisation; such formal statements provide a more hard, factual and objective view of an organisation's culture.

The formal structure of an organisation's culture may therefore be seen in the various statements made by the organisation. At least these will give an overt demonstration of the culture, for example:

1)	***Vision, Mission and Objectives statements***
•	Vision incorporates those timeless values and beliefs that are intended to give direction and move an organisation to its required future. They are an

image of what it is trying to do; they represent the future required reality. They should come from the inside of people, if they do not, the vision statement will be superficial and be merely a hollow statement of hope and desire.

- Mission incorporates the purpose, policies and power structures to achieve the vision
- Objectives or goals are the mission's strategic, tactical and operational objectives, right down to the setting of team and people's standards, targets, roles and responsibilities.

The above should be used to lead and manage the efficient running on the organisation; they will give the overall direction, guidance and checkpoints. They should therefore not be lofty, inspiring statements of vague intent, but must be practically expressed and lived out. When used this way, they must also become internalised by the people in the organisation.

2) Rules and procedures statements

Rules are very structural, as they represent pre-set standards of conduct and show the way people should behave by clarifying what is expected. Procedures in turn, are written to help people keep to the rules and to establish the methods to be used. Procedures maintain and apply the rules/standards, so that they give and show a fair and consistent approach. They will also, providing they are so written, bring clarity. Rules and procedures are therefore structurally designed into organisations.

Of course, just publishing formal statements carries no guarantees whatsoever that those things will be done in this way. Indeed, when introducing a new mission or vision statement, it seems there is all too often a corporate arrogance with introductions, displaying a one-sided view, which has made no effective attempt to get any buy-in from its people in the organisation. For example, posters on the wall and plastic pocket cards are pointless in isolation.

"Informal" culture

Culture is also, however, often more covert and informal, with values and beliefs that can remain unnamed. This is the more subjective aspect of culture. For example, contrast the difference between a charity and a private sector organisation, between an army platoon and a football team, between the civil service and a retailer, between the Royal Mail and DHL.

As well as things like formalised clothing/uniforms, office styles and the types of buildings; differences will also be found in the human "software" represented by the attitudes, values, and beliefs that operate behind the scenes and below the visible surface. Informal culture is similar to the body language in face-to-face communication; we can be subjectively and unconsciously influenced by it. Leaders and managers will ignore the informal culture at their peril; it is often not the published statements that provide an organisation's direction, it can be the informal cultures that are actually in the driving seat.

"Total" culture

In all forms of management there are the hard, objective and clearly defined ways of managing, and also those more subjective beliefs, values and soft skills. An overall and complete view of culture needs to embody both the hard and soft aspects into all of the following:

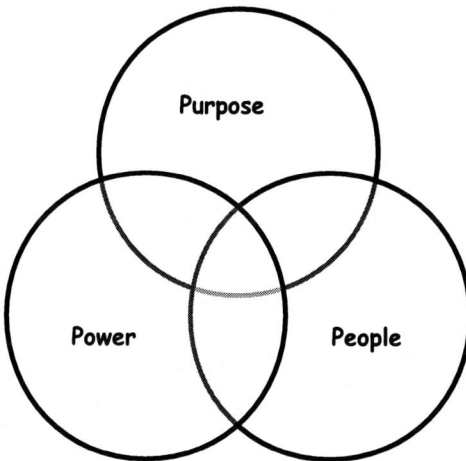

1) Purpose:

* What are the objectives, procedures and rules?
* What are the supporting structures?
* What are the supporting processes?

These explain the "why?" and the "what we do and how" of the organisation.

2) Power:
* Who has access to which resources?
* Where is the central and the decentralised authority?

This is the "where and when of decision-making" of the organisation.

3) People:
* What is the degree of support and trust?
* What is valued?
* What are the associated reward structures?

This is the "with whom?" and the "how?" of the organisation.

It may be that Purpose and Power are easier to change than People's beliefs, attitudes and behaviour. Whilst all of these three parts are interwoven, it is only these people's 'soft aspects' which will really make the difference, and ultimately represent the main differentiator between organisations.

As we have already noted, the simple truth is that it is the people who will make any of the financial differences.

The following 'test' on the culture can be undertaken, by observing and talking to the people in an organisation; it gives indications on just how the people aspects are actually working:

Friendly Culture	Unfriendly Culture
People take the initiative	People feel boxed in
Team work flourishes	Friction and a lack of appreciation between team members
People understand their contribution	People have little understanding of there role
Clear direction is found	Conflicting goals are found
Good communication exists	Mixed messages and little understanding
An even workload allowing for individual skills/abilities	Work is spread unevenly
Teams knows other team members skills/abilities	Little understanding exists on what makes the team tick
Work environment is conductive to good performance	Physical environment prevents good performance

This quick test shows the management tasks that may be needed to improve work, for example:

- Communicating regularly, for example: what do people think about their work and what do they want to do?
- Creating a shared vision, for example: so that everyone knows where they are going
- Improving the physical environment, for example: lighting
- Using ideas from the team to make improvements to work
- Using people playing to their strengths, for example: consider people's skills and aspirations and allocate work accordingly

---

Checklist: Organisation Culture Acceptance

Once a preferred culture has been identified and is fully "public", you will know that it has adopted, when people can answer yes to the following questions:

1. Is it clearly communicated?
2. Is the preferred culture linked to bottom line results?
3. Are all new people inducted into the preferred culture?
4. Do all managers understand and share the culture?
5. Is managing the culture explicit in job descriptions?
6. Do we know what cultural management skills are?
7. Do we choose managers who can manage our culture?
8. Are those managers who are deficient in our preferred culture, trained?
9. Is the culture monitored and fine-tuned like any business asset?
10. Do we continually strive to get the preferred culture in use?
11. Are we confident that the current culture serves us well?
12. Can we demonstrate how our culture impacts on the bottom line?

Leaders and managers are, ultimately, the ones who can make the difference in how the culture works. Total culture can provide the holistic perspective that can really transform and reshape organisations.

The following case study illustrates this is definitely possible to do.

Case Study: Unilever Port Sunlight: Culture Change/People Management

- Traditional history of caring for people from Methodist William Lever in late 1880s with the construction of the model village with schools, houses, and library and with no public houses selling alcohol.
- In 2000s they had lost their way. All the metrics started to fall and people were described as being "gloomy-looking".
- A change programme was started in 2005, to enable employees to believe in the site's future success and the part they play in it. Five pillars of the approach are:

1. Value: e.g. Training and development were historically the first budget to be cut, so a commitment was made that it would continue.

2. Empowerment: e.g. to encourage staff to take more responsibility, use of self managed improvement teams approach

3. Inspiration: e.g. to harness enthusiasm, the use of external "famous" speakers to say how they had achieved success and overcome adversity

4. Self-discovery: e.g. by a positive thinking 2 day training course where 45 people were selected (those who seemed able to be able to change the mood). They also were given 2 hours access to an external coach.

5. Heartbeat: e.g. sub-groups on "socials" and other topics so as to carry forward the changes

Results:
- Absenteeism fell from 8% to 3.5 % in 12 months
- Discipline and grievance procedures were reduced by more than 60%
- Factory efficiency and output reliability was increased
- Three managers however felt their future was elsewhere and resigned
- There was "more banter, smiling faces and friendly chat"

Finally some comments were:

"There is a big wide world out there and you can overcome problems if you really want to." (Employee)

"Life-changing." (Employee)

"What is exciting is that something is really happening and it's unique." (Works Director)

"The factory has improved 1000%." (TU representative)

From: **People Management**, 23 February 2006

Organisational Structure

Definition
Organisation Structure is:
"The planned design of company structure which shows the relationships and functions to be performed by each individual so that the company works effectively towards known objectives."

It therefore has a major influence on the running of and on the people of the organisation as:

"Power is rooted in the structure."

"The structure holds up and supports everything we do."

Different Structures
Structures differ, for example (see table overleaf):

Aspect	Bureaucratic or Transactional	Organic or Relational
Organisation type	Centralised	Decentralised
Procedures are	Formalised	Non-formalised
External uncertainty is	Lower	Higher
Tasks are	Repetitive	Non-repetitive
Productivity is	Higher	Lower
Flexibility is	Lower	Higher

There are many other types of structure found; from line/staff second line, organised by function, by profit and cost centres, and by programme and product groups. Additionally, there are matrix and cross-functional structures of multi skill/discipline resources, used for example in project management and to enable supply chain management. Finally some structures may be only temporary, like project teams and task forces.

Common weaknesses in structures

The following weaknesses have been identified:

- Too many levels of authority, giving perhaps slow communication and decision-making.
- Too many people to manage; creating poor communication, ignored improvements, feelings of being isolated.
- Too narrow expertise e.g. problems are solved by setting up a new department.
- One department view "rules" e.g. belief that say Finance are the "kings", whereas an alternative systems view (systems views are covered later in the book) of on organisation, is, the key cross functional processes, are, the most important.
- Top-down view e.g. belief that the organisational chart reflects the "best way" to work, yet a bottom-up view will encourage giving support and listening to the "front line".

Influence of structure

The organisation's structure has a major influence on the running of the organisation and the people within it – *"The structure holds up and supports everything we do."*

In this sense, the structure provides the stability with fixed and known rules and procedures. Within the structural framework, the operational processes of the organisation take place and, as with all processes, there is variability, dependency and interaction. These may be found within all of the following:

- Purpose or strategy, the structure is designed to achieve this purpose
- Methods and technology used
- Information and decision-making process
- Supplier and customer separation
- Scale and range of activities and resources
- Peoples' knowledge and skills, including the management style, for example, command and controlling or coaching and empowering
- Legal status, accountability and sources of finance

Any organisation will have people involved in the dynamics of interlocking contracts between people; contracts which determine what people do and how they make transactions.

Many of these contracts are not legal ones, but are informal "psychological contracts" that are often not written down, are frequently changed and are actually determined by a mix of logic and emotions.

Any structural changes made, will therefore impact on such informal contracts, not only the formal ones. The chosen structure should therefore be one that promotes the peak performance of the people, processes and product/services being delivered to customers.

Designing the structure

This s not always simple and will involve considering:

- Strategy or the purpose the structure is designed to achieve
- Legal status, accountability and sources of finance
- Methods of technology
- Processes, contracts, transactions, including the information and decision-making process
- Management style required/preferred
- Supplier and customer separation
- Scale and range of activities and resources

Finally, the following checklist and case study cover some practical design aspects on organisational structure (see checklist overleaf):

Checklist: Structure and Alignment

Research was undertaken as a basis for developing a set of actions to improve alignment, a summary of some of the action items follows:

Peers
- Support exchange programmes and job rotations across functions
- Invest in understand each other's problems and building relationships: capture the voice of other functions and be able to articulate plans in their language, not in jargon
- Develop appropriate KPIs across functions; ensure that KPIs are linked or at least coordinated and not driving conflicting behaviour
- Joint problem solving teams to tackle common issues

Individuals
- Trace and learn from the cause of lost orders; delivery time, price, specification
- Encourage open communication
- Avoid pointing blame
- Visit and "see, smell, understand customers; get under their skin"
- Create regular dialogue between sales and supplying units

Bosses
- Join sales on key customer visits to ensure you are close enough to the customer in driving the supply chain agenda and focusing efforts and service and be credible with sales when discussing service
- Align goals between functions and link those to incentives
- Encourage the use of the same language; avoiding functional jargon and promoting the use of business language (profit, customers, service etc.)
- Support appropriate forecasting tools
- Ensure that operations/supply chain is seen to take action on old issues and communicates results to other functions (don't forget to tell others what has been done.

Teams
- Collaborate on common issues not functional pet projects

- Reach consensus on priorities; do not set a functional agenda but a company wide focus that will engage peers
- Work on improving accuracy of performance information and tell peers upfront when shipments are going to be late, do not surprise peers with bad events when they happen
- Awareness training in supply chain and sales
- Improve the initiative planning process to focus on essentials peers care most for mostly (service, execution, price etc.) and articulate initiatives in those terms.

Two key areas received a lot of attention in the discussions: improving communication and training in the supply chain and operations; and improving the initiative planning process.

From: **The Challenge of Internal Misalignment** by R. I. van Hoek and A. J. Mitchell in *IJLRA*, volume 9, issue 3, September 2006

Case Study: Company Structures for Managing the Supply Chain

Points to consider:
- Restructure to a cross-functional model (CFM)
- Remember career paths
- There is no easy way to construct a CFM and it will need careful compromise on the following:

1) Organise around processes and not tasks
- Separate management from operational supervision. Management is generalised and at senior levels. Supervision is about the people actually doing the work.
- Operations may remain hierarchical and functional, reporting into (several) process-based managers.
- Operational supervisors will need training in cross-functional appreciation

2) Flatten the hierarchy
- Organise the hierarchy according to the level and type of work and

responsibility; and not the number of people. For example, warehouse operatives and courier vehicle drivers at ratios to management of 10 plus to 1 and 30 plus to 1 respectively.

3) Keep a team focus
- This encourages self management.
- Ensure there is the (normal?) clear SMART objectives, the reward mechanism is the team performance and develop multiple competencies

4) More supplier/customer contact
- Remember these are the next links in the process and are irrespective of whether they are internal and external suppliers/customers
- The customer is the only one who can give relevant feedback on how we do the job

From: **The Business Process Re-engineering Action Toolkit** *(Michael Balle, 1995)*

3: Managing Me

From our high level look at Strategy, let's now come right down to looking at ourselves. After all, it is individual people that make up organisations and it is individual people who decide and implement strategy. With people, the fundamental differentiator is found in what they say or do, this is essentially their behaviour.

Behaviour

The following gives a view of where behaviour comes from, and why it varies amongst people:

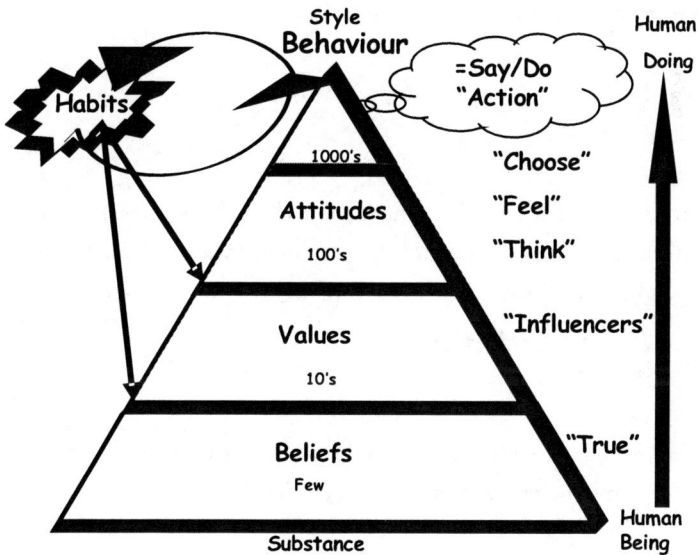

At the substance and core of behaviour are beliefs, those essential truths that humans hold. These few beliefs will drive our values; in turn values will influence our thinking/feelings and give us our attitudes.

Attitudes operate automatically as a filter through which we make decisions, and choose what we will say, or what we will do. This becomes our externally visible behavioural style.

Our behaviour is therefore a visible and external out-working of our more invisible and internal beliefs, values and attitudes. Behaviour that is automatically repeated, usually (unconsciously) becomes our habits.

Habits and beliefs

To change a habit will often involve more than a behaviour change, but will more likely require a change to the attitudes that cause the behaviour. For a deep-rooted habit, clearly the deeper under-pinning values and beliefs may also have to be changed. We can illustrate this with an example.

Driving a car is a habit that most of us do. Yet when we started out learning to drive it was not a habit; we believed we could do it and the instructor and the sight of others driving, reinforced our belief. Eventually, we passed the driving test and then we learned, again but at a different level. At some time, we learn to drive without really thinking too hard about the technical aspects, and can listen to the radio/CD, talk to passengers and hold a conversation, on (hopefully!) a hands-free phone.

Here then, is a classic illustration of taking a consciously-made belief and turning it into an unconscious habit.

A similar pattern can be also seen in operation the UK at New Year Resolution time, when the common resolutions are to lose weight or to quit smoking. At this time, the wish to lose weight is reinforced by the advertising campaigns of gyms, which endeavour to get people signed up for a year's membership; successfully it seems, as gyms are at their busiest in January.

But by February/March they have returned towards to their pre-Christmas tendencies; the majority of people revert to their former habits.

Those really committed people will however continue, and the key word here is commitment, as it is this commitment to a deeper set of values/beliefs that overcome the more superficial attitudes and behaviour. This commitment has been made consciously and will need to be continually re-in forced; then and only then, will it work upwards via attitudes and eventually become an unconscious, but a new pattern of behaviour.

With the New Year Resolutions for quitting smoking, an identical pattern follows; we only see the January advertising for anti-smoking patches and the stop smoking campaigns. The advertisements do not go into February as by then, many people have followed the similar patterns explained above and reverted back to their former habits; which here, are additionally being reinforced by the effects of the nicotine drug.

Without doubt, beliefs can be a powerful influence on behaviour.

Habits and reinforcement

All our regular habitual behaviour patterns become hard-wired in the pathways of the brain. Therefore, behaviour patterns create neural connections in the brain and eventually, with the repeated behaviour, these reinforce behaviour. The behaviour pattern is now automatic at the brain cell level, with the end result that these ways of behaving now feel natural, easy and comfortable.

Introducing a new required behaviour can now be often extremely difficult, because it means replacing the old pattern. Behaviour patterns are physically established at the brain cell level, therefore any new pattern, will seem extremely awkward; even if it makes sense and is desirable.

The brain is not like a digital computer, and there is no easy-fix 'delete' key.

The only way to replace an old behaviour pattern is to establish a new one that will prove to be more satisfying than the old "wired in" behaviour. Then with an adequate period of reinforcement, there is a chance that new connections will be made, so that this new pathway can now become the preferred wiring.

Over time, the old habitual pathway will eventually fall into disuse.

However, without reinforcement, the pathways will not establish themselves. This explains why most people will fall back on the old, comfortable patterns they are used to. The only thing therefore that can create permanent behavioural change is frequent reinforcement over the long term. This means ongoing support, feedback, guidance, praise and encouragement are required.

To summarise therefore:
*   Behaviour is "what we say or do"
*   Habits represent repeated and learned behaviour (so to change the habit you have to change the attitude that creates it. This will require supportive reinforcement)
*   Attitudes are the "way we see and think about things"
*   Beliefs/Values are "what we know to be true". Beliefs are a core and vital part of our "make up". They can and they do change lives.

"Just as athletes demonstrate continuously that is the frame of mind of the athlete, rather that sheer physical power which is the decisive factor in winning, so it with business. But the difficulty is that, while few will contest these statements, few also follow the logic of their beliefs through to a coherent and consistent philosophy which imbues their organisation from top to bottom."
– John Harvey Jones

Behaviour and Perception

A difficulty with beliefs and values and attitudes is about perception or how we see things. Where perceptions are shared. we have agreement; where they are not, disagreement.

The following sayings are all about perception:
* "Perception is 90% behind the eyes"
* "Whether you see it wrong or see it right, you are right"
* "As a person thinks, so they are"
* "Is the glass of water half full, or half empty?"
* "Perception is reality"

The following has also been usefully noted:

"In mathematics there is no difference between the 'glass is half full' and 'the glass is half empty'. But the meanings of these two statements are totally different."
– Peter Drucker

For me, this statement by Peter Drucker also clearly makes a statement that we commonly see more emotionally rather than logically. In my training work, I have held hundreds of glasses of water before course delegates and asked them what they see. I have never ever, had the perfectly logical and emotion-free response '50% water and 50% air'.

Behaviour is an inside job

People therefore differ and they will respond differently to identical stimuli. These different responses and styles are seen in the following example, where people set out to climb a mountain.

After they all set off together to reach the top, some will eventually quit en route, some will get to a place where they choose to camp and remain at, and finally, some will still continue to carry on climbing.

Quitters 20% of people?	Campers 60% of people?	Climbers 20% of people?
Abandons early	Goes half way	Gets there
"Too hard"	"Comfortable here"	"Not there yet, let's go"
Survives	Vegetates	Growth
Do just enough	Analyses	Take risks
Defends	Some progress is made	"Energiser bunny"
Blames others	Gets "too tired"	Achieves
Rejects change	Waits and see what will happen	Accepts change
Can be disruptive	Can be subversive	Embraces change
Stays in the rut	WIIFM (what's in it for me)	Looks for the next peak

This overview is interesting: why is it that some give up, whilst others "make it"? Major differences are found, and it is perhaps no surprise therefore that relationships between people also differ greatly.

What is perhaps a surprise, however, is that there seems to be little recognition of this fact? It seems that each person's/company's 'perception' remains their 'reality', to the exclusion of recognising differences and the exclusion of exploring ways to do things differently. Much learning and changing is needed!

Whilst clearly our personal 'inside job' determines our behaviour, active consideration of what this behaviour should be is critical, fundamental and foundational to being an effective leader and manager.

Managing Stress

Stress has been defined as all of the following:

- "The adverse reaction people have to excessive pressure or other types of demand placed upon them." (Health & Safety Executive)
- "The natural impact of demand on a person."

- "The body's response to pressures placed on it."
- "Combination of physical/psychological/behavioural reactions to events that threaten or challenge us."

Stress is not a medical condition in itself, but a prolonged exposure to stress can be linked to anxiety and depression, plus other physical aspects such as heart disease, back pain, headaches etc.

Stress can follow from when the body prepares for action. Here the brain senses a demand for exertion and releases hormones. These give a wave of energy, so that we can then respond to the demands being placed on us (the so called 'fight or flight' response). The hormone response is meant to be short-lived, and a genuine aid for survival, for example, so we can go the extra mile. Now however, energy is being diverted from the immune system.

The body is not built for long-term stress/continuous exertion, and when there is a long-term exertion the body needs outlets. These outlets will vary depending on the individual; some will cope, some will not. When no outlet is found, then the immune system remains suppressed, meaning it can no longer fight disease. We can then become ill.

A certain level of pressure is often desirable, as it helps to motivate and give people a 'buzz'. This is one positive aspect of pressure, and we can correctly call this positive stress or 'eustress' (which means elation, winning, achieving). Indeed the negative side of stress should not be called stress at all, but more correctly should be called 'distress'. This is the stress that has negative implications, whereas eustress is a positive form of stress, and is related to desirable events in person's life.

Both distress and eustress can be equally taxing on the body, and become cumulative in nature, however this depends on a person's way of adapting to the change that has caused the stress in the first place. Distress is the mismatch between demands placed on us and our ability to cope (real or perceived).

Stress (and bowing to common word usage, we will now use only this word instead of distress) is therefore all about the individual's ability to cope. This will always be a variable, as people will deal with pressure in different ways, and in this sense, stress is actually sometimes adopted by individuals rather than coming purely as a result of pressure.

The following diagram illustrates this:

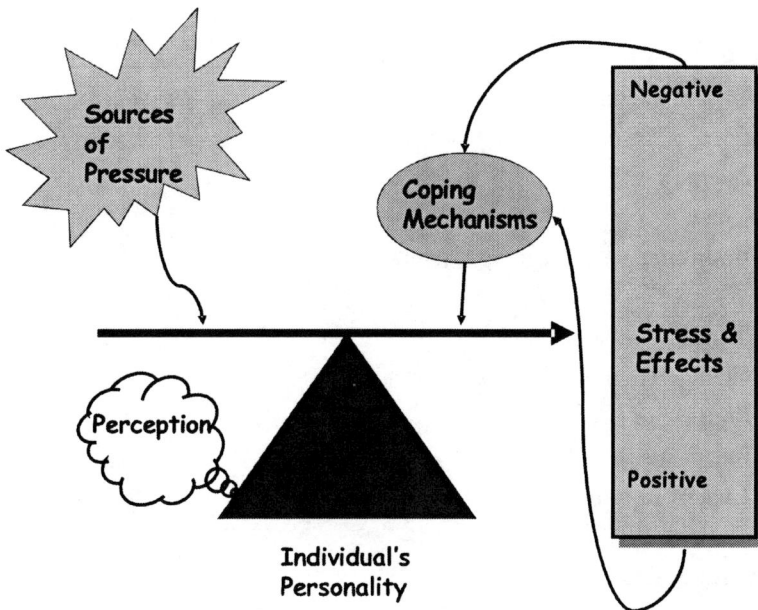

Costs of Stress

The following are UK cost estimates:

- Around 6 million people are affected each year by work-related stress
- Companies in the UK have 40% of sickness as absence, this is around 13 million work days at a cost £370 million to £700 million
- Around 1% of GNP

People at risk

The following represent a typical view of those people at risk from stress:

- Managers aged 30-45 years old; these are the middle working years, where there is often the greatest work responsibility level, coupled to demanding home life responsibilities from older/teenage children.
- Perfectionists; those who always believe everything is possible and needs to be done to "over–standard" levels
- Those who set themselves unrealistic challenges
- Those who view life as competition
- Those who do not recognise the problem is largely caused by 'me myself'; so for example, such people usually prefer to blame others for problems

Causes of Stress

These can be many causes, consider the following list:

Biological
- Lack of exercise
- Diet
- Allergies
- Genetic
- Body change, e.g. ageing, pregnancy

Socio-cultural
- Change in circumstances
- Pressure to conform
- Relationship conflicts
- Lack of support

Our subconscious mind
- Inner and repressed conflicts
- Repeated past hurtful experiences/triggers
- Lack of self-awareness

Our conscious/rational mind
- Perceptions; "perception is reality"
- Thinking; for example positive or negative?
- Achievements; for example, meeting standards
- Misinterpreting others' actions
- Not having the skills to do something

Experiential
- Too many concurrent demands
- Environmental noise/conditions/surroundings
- Unmet needs
- Threats to survival or self-esteem

Spiritual
- Violations of ethical and religious codes
- Lack of spiritual development

Stress at Work

From a management perspective, the following common causes were reported in a survey in 10 countries of 1000 managers:

- Time pressures and deadlines
- Work overload
- Inadequately trained subordinates
- Long working hours
- Attending meetings
- Work infringes on private life
- Keeping up with new technology
- Beliefs in conflict with the organisation
- Taking work home
- Lack of power and influence

The causes at work may also be from various sources such as:

- Poor job design/specifications
- Unclear objectives
- Customer complaints

Some of the problems with stress at work are that people will not admit they cannot cope, as this is seen as a sign of weakness. Also, if people do complain, then companies may ignore such complaints; perhaps because they see the real cause is in someone's personal life and is "nothing to do with us".

Stress index

The high stress factors are indeed found in our personal life, as shown below.

Life Event	Stress Index
Death of partner	100
Divorce	73
Imprisonment	53
Death of close family member	63
Personal injury or illness	53
Marriage	50

Job change	47
Retirement	45
New family member	39
Change in personal finances	38
Change in work responsibility	29
Trouble with people	29
Outstanding personal achievement	28
Change in living conditions	25
Other changes, per change event	20
Vacation	15
Major festivals/holidays	11

Following from this index, UK Research has shown the following effect on health deterioration in one year from totalling the above life event scores:

Total Score	Health deterioration
150-199	37%
200-299	51%
300/over	79% (and 21% did not)

Stress Symptoms

These can have singular or multiple causes, for example:

The physical symptoms of stress include:
- Fast breathing
- Dry mouth
- Feeling hot
- Sticky hands
- Tense muscles
- Indigestion
- Stomach pains
- Tiredness
- Headaches
- Fidgeting
- Migraine

- Ulcers
- High blood pressure

The psychological/mental symptoms of stress are feelings of being:
- Upset
- Worried
- Irritated
- Powerless
- Unable to cope
- Demotivated
- Lateness
- Low esteem
- Over careful
- Panic stricken
- Explosive

Performance and behaviour at work symptoms include:
- Lower job satisfaction
- Reduced job performance
- Work absence
- Loss of energy
- Poor decision-making
- Reduced creativity and innovation

Symptoms of stress can come therefore, from a range of causes:
Personally Physical + Personally Psychological/Mental + Performance and Behaviour at Work

Checklist: Counteractive reactions to stress
- Freeze and do nothing
- Become an ostrich
- Hit back fast
- Pass the buck
- Tough it out
- Send in my gang

Managing stress at work

To try and manage stress, we need to target the issues at the multiple levels identified above, for example;

Internal aspects

- Know that our behaviour patterns are linked to our attitudes/values/beliefs, the sum of which form our personality; therefore we must know ourselves
- When required, we must change our behaviour and habits

External aspects, such as work culture, where the positive aspects include:

- Trust
- Agreed goals
- Abundant information
- Learning through/from mistakes
- Delegation
- Participation/assertive styles
- Collaboration and support
- Clean and safe work environment

From a management point of view, the approach to managing stresses at work must be a measured one, for example:

- Where is the evidence of stress? Managers need to be initially sceptical, as stress can be become a "catch all" word
- Look for specific problems; what specifically is going on? Is it the same for everyone? Are there actually many unrelated problems?
- Assessment; can I get evidence so I can benchmark? What is the cause?
- Use specific and focussed solutions; what are we trying to change? Will the solution work here?
- Integration; how do the solutions fit into our HR policy and other initiatives?

Do other things need to change first?

- Evaluation and feedback; what is the criteria? How will we know it has worked? When will changes happen?

Some important guidelines for an organisation are shown below:

- Are the performance targets SMART (Specific, Measurable, Attainable, Realistic, Time-based)?
- Review training needs

- Check the available resources are adequate
- Monitor performance and watch for early warning signs of stress
- Check on how appraisals are conducted, for example, the core should be personnel development
  development
- Check that individuals feel involved in their work
- Review the communication methods
- Build in one to one and group sessions with teams and management
- Give regular feedback
- Ensure there is a good work environment (air, lighting, noise, decorations, ergonomics, personal space)
- Communicate any change, before it happens
- Increase your understanding about stress
- Provide opportunity for internal and/or external counselling

Managing stress as an individual

It is useful to develop an understanding of what gives stress and how you react to it. The following may be of assistance:

- Identify what you can change and what you cannot change; for the former, read on, for the latter, decide what to do (e.g. leave the situation, or accept it and change the way you view it)
- Set realistic goals
- Use a to-do list and prioritise (this is also a feature of time management)
- Recognise when pressure when is building up
- Listen to your body and review how you treat it
- Review how you spend your time and energy at work
- Review how you spend your time and energy at home
- Learn the best way you relax
- Learn to keep your emotions under control
- Learn to say no
- Review how you communicate
- Review how you deal with conflict
- Accept short-term stress instead of long-term anxiety
- Have a sense of humour

Stress Solutions

Finally, recognise that stress is unavoidable, it is unique to each person and that there is no one single 'magic-formula' answer.

It is important to recognise when there is a problem, and then look at yourself and ask 'What I can do?' After all, the solution is also largely within you, so there is always going to be an element here of needing to learn how to manage stress.

It will help to learn to create situations that will maximise 'eustress', and minimise 'distress' and finding that personal balance between:

<u>Pressure   Coping</u>

This balance can be seen in the following expressions:

- *"Stress is based on our perception that we are under threat."*
- *"Stress automatically makes us think negatively."*
- *"Stress is manifested in the mind, only by controlling the mind, can it be dissipated."*
- *"What separates good and poor managers is how they deal with stress."*

Some final thoughts

"If I treated my friends how I treat myself, would I have any friends?"

"No-one's tombstone says: I wish had spent more time at work."

"I cannot always change the world I see, but I can change the way that I see it."

The Importance of Learning

We have already noted that the ultimate organisational competence is the organisation's capacity to improve existing skills and learn new ones – learning is the most defensible competitive advantage of all.

Of course it is an individual that actually learns, therefore each individual's "learning to learn" (L2L) is critically important. The following illustrates this:

"Those who are in love with learning are in love with life."
– Charles Handy

"Learning is more important than knowledge."
– Einstein

"All experience is learning."
– Peter Vaill

"In times of change, it the learners that inherit the future."
– Stuart Emmett

Contrary to many people's thinking (and actual practice), learning to learn is not automatic. It is a skill. Yet how many of us, after having committed ourselves to learn, have never, for example, considered how we can learn better?

Many people have no idea how they learn, and they consider it all to be just plain common sense. Many others will only learn by 'accident', and unconsciously - whilst this is one way of learning, what more could actually be learned by actively considering methods for better learning?

After all, just about everything we ever do must have been learned.

What is learning?

Learning is fundamentally about thinking about and doing something new; let us consider the following definition:

"Learning is the method and process which uses your personal power, knowledge and experience to enable you to:
- *Make sense of things, by thinking*
- *Make things happen, by doing*
- *Bring about change, by moving from one position to another"*

Learning, therefore, is essentially: "I think-I do-I move" and is all about us using feedback from our actions. There is no learning without action; it is the person creating new results and new mental models.

Learning is a source of change, as when people learn, their behaviour (defined here as simply what is said and/or done) will change.

When people are at the advanced stage of wanting to learn continuously, they will actually demand learning and will seek it out in all situations.

Why Learn?

Different people will have different answers to this question.
Their answers may well include some of the following:

- To acquire knowledge.
- To gain a qualification.
- To develop skills.
- To grow and develop myself.
- To understand a subject better.
- To keep up with changes.
- To make sense of new ideas.
- Because you have been told to.
- To get a better job/employment.
- To create a future.
- To get nearer to personal goals

Whatever the reason, for learning to be successful, individuals need to 'buy into' the process. They really do have to be committed to learn. They have to want to do it. Learning is a DIY process and therefore, ultimately, it is all about individual responsibility; a strong sense of personal ownership to the process is essential.

The Learning Process

It is useful and important to our learning, to have a healthy curiosity, about the unique way we learn.

Whilst 'our way' will be unique to us, we will all go through the following stages:
- Motivation, by deciding "what is in it for me" (WIFFM)
- Obtain data and facts
- Convert this to information
- Get insight and hopefully an 'a-ha!' moment
- This will give us knowledge, we have the "know how"

- When this is used, then we develop skills and the "know how to"
- Critically, we need at each stage, to Reflect and Revise

Another view of the above stages is as follows:
- Motivation is "I Will"
- Knowledge is "I Know"
- Doing is "I Do"
- Skills is "I Can Do"
- Reflect is "I Review and Re-connect"

Learning and Motivation

Motivation is a key aspect in learning, as it effectively kick starts us. The following levels of motivation are found:

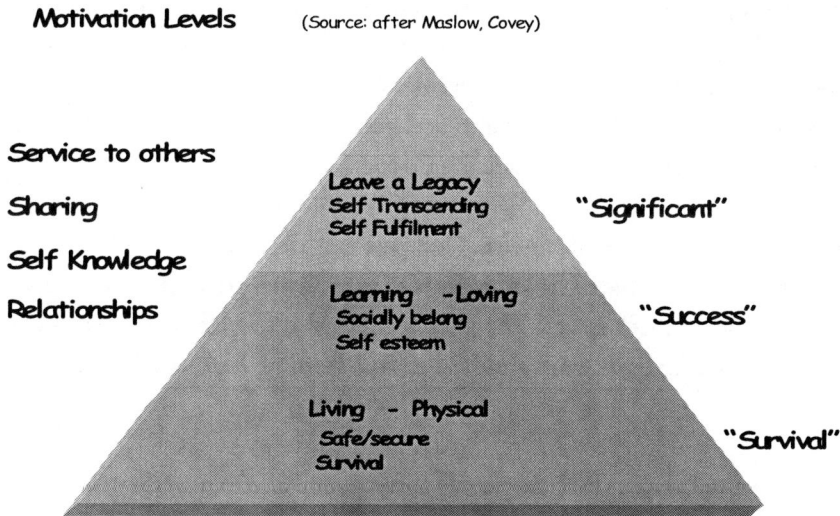

Motivation Levels (Source: after Maslow, Covey)

Service to others

Sharing

Self Knowledge

Relationships

Leave a Legacy
Self Transcending
Self Fulfilment
"Significant"

Learning - Loving
Socially belong
Self esteem
"Success"

Living - Physical
Safe/secure
Survival
"Survival"

Levels of motivation differ for different people. Some may need to learn for survival and living, others for personal success, others to fulfil themselves. (We cover motivation more fully in the Managing People section of this book)

Basic Requirements for Learning

The basic requirements for learning can be described as follows:

1) Learning, in the final analysis, is your responsibility. You need to have the sense of ownership and commitment. Learning is really, voluntary. It is your unique and personal journey.

2) Learning is a skill that develops new behaviour. Attending a training course is not in itself learning. It is only in the application and in the doing that learning happens. Learning involves new skills and new behaviour. This can involve experimenting and taking risks, and making mistakes, all of these provide learning experiences.

3) Learning requires continuous feedback. We need to hear from others to help us understand about ourselves and about what we do. Learning is harder without such feedback. Many of us for example, do not know what we need to learn. We don't know what we don't know. Also, feedback tells us and shows us how far we are on or off the track, and then we can make the necessary adjustments - and learn.

4) Learning is a process, not an outcome. With the pace of life, work, and continual change, we will need to set ourselves realistic and attainable objectives/targets to act as a spur and feedback in our ongoing achievements. These objectives need to be seen as milestones along the road of development, and not as just an end in themselves. When you are through with learning, then you are through!

5) Learning needs total involvement. Our personal development and professional development are related. The technical aspects of work issues are important, but so too are the people-management issues. The people issues also involve looking at ourselves and our relationships at both work and home. True learning looks at all aspects of our lives.

L2L is a fundamental process for how people develop, and also to how they can continue to develop. When people L2L effectively, they produce a different view of themselves; self-confidence is enhanced. They are able to deal better with change; indeed they will now embrace change opportunities.

Never confuse attending a training course with learning; you will not automatically learn anything from school, college, university or from a training course; consider the following differences between training and learning:

Teaching is	Learning is
Done to you (can therefore be Passive)	Done to self (and must therefore be Active)
Dependant on others	Can create own ways
Formal	Formal and informal
Fixed times	Discretionary time
External motivation	Internal motivation
"Proving"	"Improving" continuously
Objectives & Ends are given	Subjective, Means to ends
Outcomes driven	Process driven
Gives solutions	Solving problems

Teaching (and training) certainly can support learning, and are a means to that end; they are however very clearly not the same.

The Learning Process of a Child

As a child you learned to walk, for example, by being encouraged and supported (physically as well as mentally), with feedback and praise along the way. Also our early learning was better facilitated in a friendly atmosphere and comfortable surrounding. In summary the learning process of a child involves:

- Encouragement
- Support
- Feedback
- Friendly atmosphere
- Comfortable surrounding

The key points here are that the learning style is: holistic, exploratory, emotional and logical.

These "external to the learner" conditions are critical to the largely open learning process of a child. Unfortunately, many adults eventually become closed to learning, and in doing so they have forgotten the excellent model from children's learning.

The Learning Process as we get older

It is often said we start to get "closed down" at school. Here we meet and interact with strangers, there may be some embarrassment, our confidence may be shaken and we can develop self-doubt.

Other viewpoints, differences and experiences may run counter to our "world view". Group views tend to rule, and the learning style used will be more structured, linear, rigid and conformist. Logic and rationality now tends to rule, more than emotion.

Our earlier more individual, positive view is now faced by group views. Where such a forced and structured learning style is formalised in education, this may well close us down to learning.

We can also be closed down at home. Some home environments are not open, encouraging places, and the lessons and phrases learned here can affects us deeply in later life.

We can unconsciously struggle with these truths, as we receive fewer positive influences to support our views. Instead, we receive negative influences which can then be interpreted as criticising us; they run counter to those values and beliefs we want to have. We can start to become separated from where we want to be.

It so often becomes terminal, causing a shutdown to our learning. Our very early learning style of being holistic and exploratory is now structured, linear and rigid in its conformity to "group" and to "significant other's" views. We have been conditioned to become "single track" learners.

These group and others views can therefore separate us from and run counter to our needs for:
•   individual emotional health
•   feelings of physical safety
•   believing we are a good role model to ourselves

These needs provide us with a positive stimulus for our self-esteem and self-worth. Such emotional feelings are important to our learning as they can influence our behaviour and drive our motivation. But as our emotions are often never really understood or accounted for by others, many of these people involved in our learning processes will totally ignore our emotional needs.

This in part may be because emotions cannot be measured in the same way as writing, reading, spelling and arithmetic; whilst these will be measured and controlled at school, our emotions are so often "put down" as unnecessary or as strange behaviour.

Many learners will need therefore, to take charge of their own learning experiences, and to make them apply to "me". We will show later how to do this after we consider some theoretical aspects of learning.

Learning Theory

Understandably, this has received some attention over the years; a summary of the major learning theories follows, some of which have been around for some time.

Behaviourist theories
*   Fundamentally about Stick/Carrot reinforcement
*   Main methods used are verbal instruction from an "expert," who may also support/guide

Cognitive theories
*   Information processing and comparison to mental models to give understanding/ knowledge.
*   Main method: Facilitation on the "content" e.g. by case study, best practice

Constructivist theories
*   Personal knowledge, in context.
*   Main method: Participating/reflecting by the learner.

Social Practice theories
*   Supports all the previous three, but these must be applied in a social setting.
*   Main method: Networking, participation in communities/teams etc.

In recent times, we have discovered much more about how our brains operate. Indeed, it has been said that we have learned more about the human brain in the most recent decades, than in our total existence. So of course, those who undertook their early learning before the 1980s (and this covers most of our current leaders and managers) may not have benefited from these newer views on learning.

Indeed, we do commonly find that reflection is a very poor practiced skill. This requires us to think about what we have done and moves us into what should be done; it takes us beyond being told what to do and being told what tools we have to use.

Related to this is what we looked earlier on the role of beliefs, values, attitudes on behaviour when we used the following model:

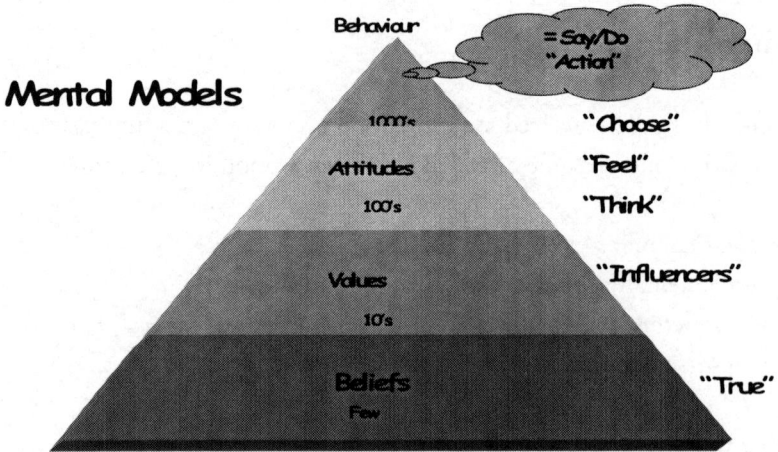

Mental Models

Behaviour = Say/Do "Action"

1000's "Choose"

Attitudes "Feel"

100's "Think"

Values "Influencers"

10's

Beliefs "True"

Few

Beliefs are a core and vital part of our "make up" and the need to keep learning is a useful belief to have. To summarise therefore:

• Behaviour is "what we say or do"
• Habits represent repeated and learned behaviour (so to change the habit you have to change the attitude that creates it).
• Attitudes are the "way we see and think about things"
• Beliefs are "what we know to be true"

Integrating Learning

The following mind map gives an overview of the approach we use in this section. We have already started discussing nurture and shall be discussing each other topic further (opposite):

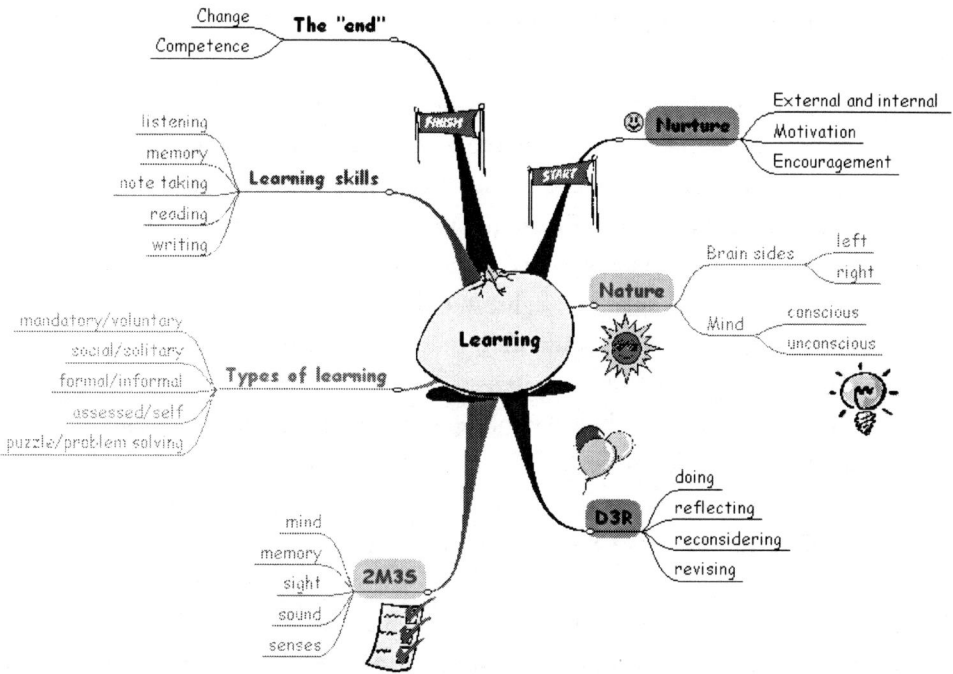

We can also see these connections in the following feedback loop model:

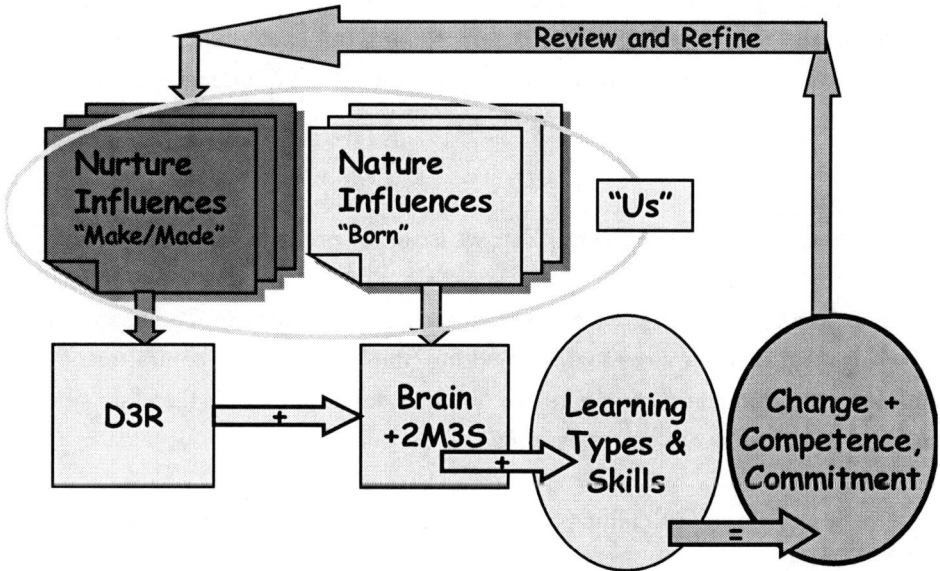

Nature or Nurture influences?

This is a perennial debate; which has the strongest influence? Are we born the way we are (our nature), or does the way we are brought up and the wider environment shape us (nurture)? In this regard, we could also see that nature "loads the gun" whilst it is our nurture that "presses the trigger." To amplify these influences further, we can see that:

- **Nature** is within us; it is what we are born with; for example, our brain, covering aspects like mind, memory, sight, sound and senses.
- **Nurture** relates to our socialisation process; for example, how we are brought up, including things like encouragement and support. It is therefore partly internal, for example, how we choose to think about something, and is also partly external, for example, the source of the encouragement (and we can of course choose to give ourselves encouragement). As we have already seen, nurture can have a direct impact on our learning styles.

Whilst there is no real evidence to support which is the stronger influence, when it comes to learning, a guess would be 33% nature and 66% nurture. This is just a 'guess-estimate' and is largely founded on the reality that we cannot, as yet, directly influence our nature or what we are born with. However, the nurture/how we are brought up and what we decide to do with ourselves can be influenced by ourselves and others. In this sense then, and to a large degree for most people, it is our choice and decision. Indeed, this choice is the important "choice aspect of humanity"; that fundamental ability that separates humans from all other living beings.

The Learning Jigsaw

It is important to appreciate the way that we naturally prefer to learn. People will only learn if they want to, they learn in different ways, they have their own preferences, as well as having different levels of competence and commitment. Competence is the knowledge and skills required to do something (the "know how"); commitment is the confidence and motivation to do it; (the "how to do"). Learning is therefore all about getting the "know how to do" something.

Learning is a cyclic and spiralling process, and the stages in this cycle are as follows:
1. Doing
2. Reflecting
3. Reconstructing
4. Revising

We must go through these D3R stages at some time in our learning; however, because of our personal preferences and personality, we may prefer some stages more than others. For example, a "task-orientated/gets things done person" will prefer more hands-on/ stage 1/doing, rather than spending time on the reflecting/stage 2.

However, we do need all stages when learning, as these are like parts of a jigsaw; all must fit together so we can benefit from the overall picture.

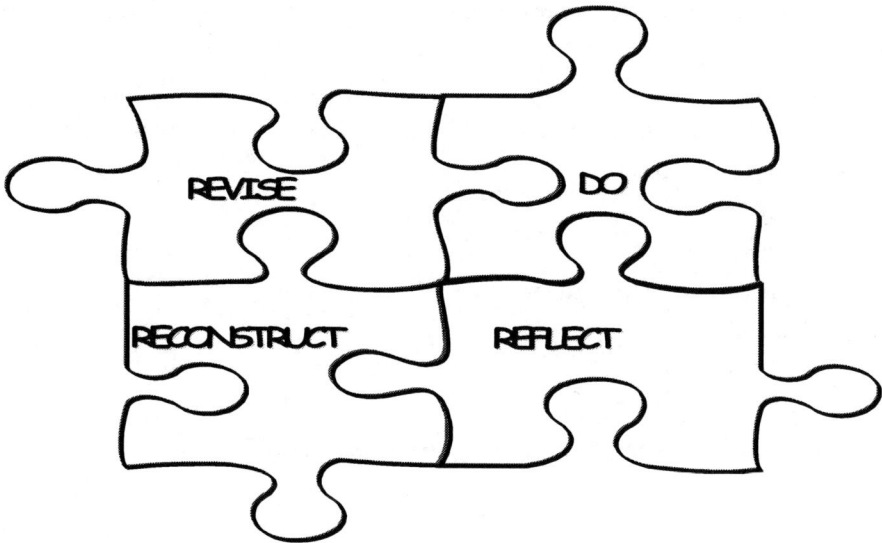

Doing

We start our learning process by gaining experience through undertaking an activity; we "do" something. This can involve the following.

- Experiencing
- Exploring
- Performing
- Trying
- Being Active
- "Hands on" learners

Key point: Get a better "Awareness" about something.

Reflecting

We then think about this experience, and attempt to understand it through analysis and conceptualisation; we "reflect" and "think".

- Getting feedback
- "Tell me" learners
- Reviewing
- Reasoning
- Evaluating
- Conceptualising

Key point: "Thinking". Most people will rush/ignore this stage; it should not be rushed, and is a critical skill that too many leaders and managers fail to acquire.

Reconsidering

Next, we make choices based on analysing the implications of alternative options; we "reconsider and reconstruct."

- Realising
- Connecting
- Implications of alternatives
- Concluding
- Reconstructing

Key point: "Understanding" and getting the "Know–how".

Revising

We decide on the next steps to take; we "revise" or "change" our behaviour.

- Refining
- Planning
- Committing
- Deciding on the next steps

Key Point: Determining "how to" and a commitment to "do".

This demonstrates that learning starts with an awareness, then with thinking, before we get the "know how to do" something. The D3R cycle is the means to do this. and requires passing through all four stages. The cycle continues, with the next new experience, and a new awareness, providing of course that we continue to be motivated to learn. Thereafter, we undergo another experience, and we "do" something again, but differently and (hopefully) better, then it is reflected upon again, reconsidered/reconstructed, and revised methods result.

All of this process can be undertaken with help and feedback from others. It is a process that is also constantly repeated. It is a learning spiral of doing – reflecting - reconsidering/reconstructing - revising – doing – reflecting – reconsidering/reconstructing – revising - doing etc.

Various ways round the spiral

There are various ways that we can pass around the learning spiral:

Single loop or adaptive learning E.g. Trial/error; learning by rote	Double loop or generative learning E.g. See/do it differently
Fixed mental model	Changed mental model
Used for skills development and in improving our existing mental models	Used for renewing and changing our perspectives and mental models
In stable and fixed situations	In turbulent and dynamic situations
"Puzzle solving" with a fixed answer	"Problem solving" with uncertain outcomes and possible "paradox"

Learning is therefore a cyclical and a never-ending spiral. It is almost automatic, but actually believing it is automatic and an unconscious process is dangerous. To learn more efficiently, people do need to think consciously about how to learn.

Learning is certainly a natural process. In contrast, having to learn about how to learn is the unnatural process. Learning how to learn (L2L) has to be a conscious process that hopefully will become a natural process!

The influence of our brain

There are many "nature" learning influences, and these largely involve our brain and the 2M3S in our earlier mind map:

* B=Brain sides: Logical left and creative right sides
* M =Mind: Conscious and unconscious
* M =Memory: Short-working-long-term
* 3S: Sight-Sound-Senses

The brain works by being stimulated through the senses. The ears (sound/hearing), eyes (sight/seeing), and body movements (sensing), all send in different signals, and it is in the way these signals are combined that a permanent impression is made on the brain.

Exposure to new material or a new experience should not be mistaken with learning about it. For example, we didn't learn to drive a car by reading or watching; to learn to drive, we needed to push ourselves to be actively involved by driving the car (or doing something); doing is essentially the only way to learn.

For example:
- When listening to lectures; take notes, draw diagrams, ask questions (especially "why?"), volunteer to participate, afterwards recite key points to yourself, review your notes with any text; above all, push yourself to be active.
- When reading; take notes, draw diagrams, read difficult material out loud, if it is instructional material, do the exercise or activity now, read and do, do and push yourself to be active.

Most of us use only a part of our brain, depending on what we're trying to achieve. For example, some situations require a clear and logical thought process; other situations may call for a more creative and open style. We may tend, unconsciously, to be more active/impulsive; we may therefore not like being reflective and thoughtful.

The main point to be appreciated here is that if we stay only on one style, then we may be missing out on the other ways. Is it not surely better to put the whole self into learning?

Left and right brain division/sides

Research has shown that our brain, in its simplest form, is in two parts: the left hemisphere and the right hemisphere. There are also front and back, as well as upper and lower quadrants. Indeed, research into brain activity continues to contribute to our understanding at a rapid pace.

The left and right separation shows we have a logical left brain and a creative right brain. The left brain will first conduct an 'analysis', will then 'act', and finally will 'feel' (for example, is the action 'correct' and 'right'?). The right brain however, works the other way, by 'feeling', then 'acting', then 'analysing'.

The following distinctions can be seen:

Logical left brain
- Prefer written, mathematical, science based approaches
- Objective, linear thinking, short-term views

- Analytical, step-by-step thinkers
- Rational, fact-based reasoning

Creative right brain
- Prefer musical, art and visual-based approaches
- Subjective, whole and parallel processing, longer-term views
- Creative, free-flowing "heart" thinkers
- Emotional feelings with synthesis that diverges

Note: The brain likes: water, oxygen, laughter, movement, challenge, change, protein and vitamins.

Logical Left brain	Creative Right brain
Written	Spoken
Mathematical	Musical
Science	Art
Objective	Subjective
Linear/parts	Holistic/Wholes
Analytical	Creative
Step by step	Free flowing
"Thinker"	"Feeler"
Convergent	Divergent
Reactive	Adaptive
Rational	Emotional
Self reliant "me"	Group orientation "we"
Hearing	Verbal/Visual
"Head" thinker	"Heart" thinker
Concrete things	Abstract emotions
Facts	Feelings
Shorter term views	Longer term view
Analyse-act-feel	**Feel-act-analyse**

You will see the brain division goes into many aspects of our total "make up" and personality. Edward De Bono, a noted thinker, has an excellent and simple view on the brain, by saying "humour is by far the most significant activity of the human brain". This is echoed in the saying that those who cannot laugh at themselves will leave the job to others. Humour is certainly a special skill and much needed personal attribute.

The brain is better designed than any machine. Its power and capacity is increased (or decreased) by the use we make of it. Think of the brain as a muscle that needs to be exercised. When exercised, not only does it maintain itself, but it also improves, develops, and increases its capacity for learning new things. Just as physical exercise will maintain and improve muscle power, learning to learn, will maintain, and improve the brainpower. This means people can extend their personal capacity and performance.

Individuals do tend to use one of the brain sides more than the other, which then means they can miss out on skills and benefits of the methods of the opposite side of the brain. To be complete, we therefore need to use both sides; this is the classic 'whole brain' thinking. Our brain is actually very similar to everyone else's; the difference comes from how we use it.

Ways of learning differ, and people will therefore react differently to different styles. As far as the brain is concerned, using it is important:
*   Absorbing = needs to use both sides
*   Retaining = needs use both sides
*   Then we are better able to:
    - Make connections.
    - Reflect wider.
    - Review all.
    - Make more connections and so on.

We can think of the brain like a coin that demonstrates its full value from using both of its sides. Thinking of the brain like this, and trying to use both sides will help to ensure that we continually benefit from new ways of thinking.

To "force" our self to use both sides of the brain, have a look at the following:

Action time – Brain Sides: Which side are you?

If you are more on the right side, then you needs to be more of a logical left. You could try the following:
*   Practice and plan a step/step approach to learning.

- Time plan each step.
- Make lists of what needs to be done.
- Order and structure your workspace.
- Set deadlines and force yourself to follow them.

If you are more on the left side, then you need to be more of a creative right. You could try the following:
- Brainstorm to create ideas.
- Make visual mind map notes to enable free flowing visual images.
- Try something new and different such as learning to play the piano.
- Break your routine by studying in a new place.
- Use all your five senses.

The real trick to developing is to force ourselves to use the style we are less comfortable with. Remember, we need to push ourselves to be active.

So in this wider sense, if you are a logical left you could:
- Try and understand your pet's feelings.
- Create your personal logo.
- Drive to "no where".
- Explore a new neighbourhood.

If you are a creative right, you could:
- Discover how a machine works.
- Be on time for appointments.
- Run a personal computer.
- Analyse a problem into its main parts.

The Mind and Memory

The mind is a part of the brain, and has active/conscious and unconscious qualities as follows:

Conscious/active mind
- Bit at a time, parts to whole
- Objective, serial function

- "Right/wrong"
- Active and controlling

Unconscious/background mind
- Big picture, whole to parts
- Subjective, parallel functions
- Errors are learning lessons
- Receptive and participatory

Processing occurs in the memory as follows:
- First into the short-term memory, therefore to hold it here, we need to ensure that we do quick repeats/reviews at least three times.
- Next into the working memory, therefore we need to deduce/think/reflect
- Finally (if necessary), into the two-part long-term memory:
  – Conscious: what we are currently experiencing from 'doing', and during 'learning'
  – Unconscious: when it becomes a habit, a skill and has been 'learned'

It can be seen here (again) why reflecting and reviewing is important (so that we can move from the short to the long term/unconscious memory).

The Influence of our Senses

Remember that how people perceive a thing is very real to them, as "perception is reality". This does not, of course, mean that one person's reality is seen in the same way by someone else, as a result of the way our brain organises and processes information. This is quite normal. However, recognising and accepting that we think differently can dramatically change the way we react and deal with other people. For example, we can be more understanding and considerate of other viewpoints. We perceive reality by seeing (sight), hearing (sound) or sensing (touch-taste-smell-physical feelings). These can all have a powerful impact on us as we take in data/facts and receive feedback as follows:

- Sound/hearing; Sounds are remembered; for example: "I hear what you're saying."
- Sight/visual; Pictures are remembered; for example; "I get the picture."
- Senses/kinaesthetic; Touch/taste/smell/"feelings" are remembered; for example: "That touches a nerve."

Consider the above in the following Chinese proverb:

"I hear and I forget, I see and I might remember, but when I do, then I understand."

It is also said that we remember:
- 20% of what we hear (Sound)
- 30% of what we see (Sight)
- 50% of what we hear and see,
- 80% of what we hear, see and do (Sight, sound, senses)

The aim therefore is to try and use all of these; at very least play to your strengths.

The following Action Time illustrates this further:

Action time – SSS (Sight, Sounds, Senses) and Memory

Think back and remember what the following means to you.

Sight/Visual
What picture, which when you see today, takes you back and gives you a pleasant memory?

Sounds/Hearing
What sound, maybe from music, which when you hear today, takes you back to a pleasant memory?

Senses/Kinaesthetic
Which of the senses (touching, tasting, smelling, physical feeling), which when repeated today, take you back to a pleasant memory?

The point here is that such triggers have acted on us, as we have locked away SSS stimuli. The taking in unconsciously of "reality" via SSS preferences is very powerful. They trigger and work on our past.

We can also decide consciously to lock away new SSS triggers, and use these for recalling and moving towards the future we desire.

It is usually the case that a group of people will have varied feelings on these SSS preferences. Research into this area is continuously being developed, but so far it would seem that each of the three preferences is approximately normally distributed across Western populations. So, in theory, in any group of people, you will find all three preferences. The "Action Time – S.S.S." will develop the understanding on this.

Action time – SSS

Most people prefer just one or two of the SSS perceptions.

Which do way do you usually speak about and do things?
Sight/visual
"That looks good"
"The way I see it"
"I get the picture"

Here, the preference is for visual images, and a tendency to remember only what is seen. You think mainly in pictures and use mental images for ideas, memory, and imagination. You get angry silently and seething. You doodle when talking or listening. You speak fast. You prefer art to music. You prefer to talk to people face-to-face. You forget names but remember faces. You believe that a picture is worth a thousand words. You learn best from books, writing things down, making mind map pictures, and watching videos.

Sound/auditory
"That sounds good"
"I am all ears"
"I hear what you're saying"

Here the preference is to listen; therefore you are easily distracted by noise, and will remember only what has been said. You think in sounds (voices or noises). You prefer lectures to reading. You get angry at an outburst of words. You forget faces but remember names. You prefer to talk to people on the phone. You speak at a medium pace. You prefer music to art. You learn best from listening to lectures, by verbally explaining to someone else and listening to audiotapes.

Senses/kinaesthetic
"That feels good"
"Hang on in there"
"That touched a raw nerve"

Here the preference is for "hands on" exercises: you remember best what has been done. You represent sounds and stimuli as feelings. You think better when moving. You find it hard to sit still. You get angry by gritting your teeth, clenching fists and then storming off. You prefer to talk to people while you are moving about. You speak at a slower pace. You prefer acting to music and art. You learn best from being "hands on", from playing games, from moving, from making things and from sorting your notes into order (continuously).

Using all our influences for effective learning

Everyone will therefore have a personal learning style. Accommodating this will result in learning that is more effective. as by finding out what our strength is, then we can "play" to that strength. But if, as an individual, we only use one style, we can close off a part of our processing power.

We usually do have a preferred style, but we also do need to be aware of all the other styles and other inputs. By doing this, we can try to widen our perception (especially when in group-learning situations).

We can also see our use of only one of these inputs as an area that we need to improve upon, an area for our personal development. Then we can consider turning it into strength by putting personal effort into those parts of learning which we don't like. To do this will take time and will take effort; things that have not been seen heard and not sensed before will now have to be looked for and opened up. Then we can maximise and increase our processing power.

Key points for using all of our influences are:
* Recognise learning is important.
* Make it a conscious process and THINK how you can learn better (then reconsider and revise and do it)
* Learn about yourself and your learning style/preferences

- Determine if your preferences may be self-limiting
- If so, do manage/improve these self limitations
- And do continue to build on your existing strengths

Making the time for learning

Time, that four letter word, is a priority; our learning time must be managed. The following "Action Time - Time" illustrates the main aspects to be considered:

Action time – Time management for learning

Ask yourself:
- What time of day are you the most alert?
- What is your daily/weekly study plan?
- What is the time allowed for breaks? (Most people remember best what is learned first and last, therefore, more breaks mean more is remembered).

It is important to set a personal timetable for learning. Often what separates out successful people from others, is how they use their time.

To create this "extra" time, we can consider doing the following:
- Get up earlier.
- Sacrifice other less important activities.
- Stop watching T.V.
- Work our learning into other activities.
- Shorten the lunch hour.
- Use train/bus/airline travelling time.
- Always have learning material with us, so we can dip into it when an unexpected opportunity is presented.
- Use a diary to plan our time.

Consciously planning and controlling the use of our time helps us to keep momentum in our learning.

However we choose to release our time for learning, we will need to set some target dates. Deadlines will focus us and force us to manage our time, for example if our learning involves assessments, then we should use these dates to work to.

The following Mind Map summarises Time Management in Learning

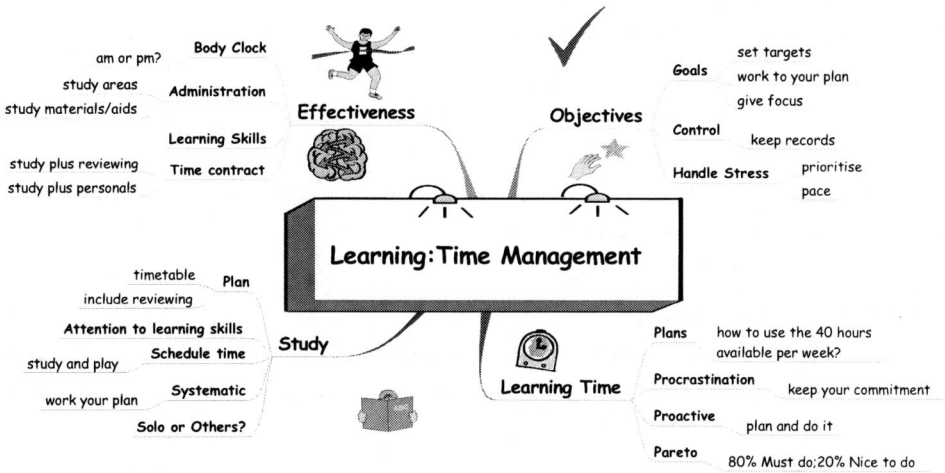

Finding the right location

Remember the importance of learning in a friendly atmosphere and comfortable surroundings. When you study, you can directly manage this, so ask yourself the following questions:

> **Action time - location**
> - Is the furniture, lighting, and temperature comfortable?
> - Will relaxing music help me relax and concentrate?
>   (silence is golden for some, for others background music helps).
> - Have I surrounded myself with 'positives'?
>   (For example, trophies, certificates, photographs etc.)
> - Have I got all the supplies I need?
>   (For example, books, pens, paper etc.)
> - Is it reasonably tidy?
>   (having a sense of order with filing etc.)
> - Does it encourage me to learn and to focus?

Sometimes a simple change of location can make a great difference. It is important therefore to discover that which works best for our learning.

Learning Skills

There are many useful techniques to help us learn:
- Listening; (Key aspects: Focus, Abbreviate, Review)

- Memory; (Key aspects: Chunk it, Review, Review, Review)
- Note taking; (Key aspects: Organised, Format (with mind maps?), Review)
- Reading; (Key aspects: Preview, Read (Questions), Read (Take notes), Read ("Got it?"), Review (Answer questions), Review)
- Writing: (Key aspects: Group ideas, Loop together by rough draft-Review, Revise, Review, Edit, Rewrite, Evaluate)

Fact files for each of these are in the Appendix and it will be seen, once again, that a common element is reflecting/reviewing.

Reflecting and reviewing

Without reflecting and reviewing, our recall deteriorates ("Use it or lose it"). Practice, try it out, reflect, talk to others, and go back to the original source of information; these are all review activities. The following diagram illustrates reviewing:

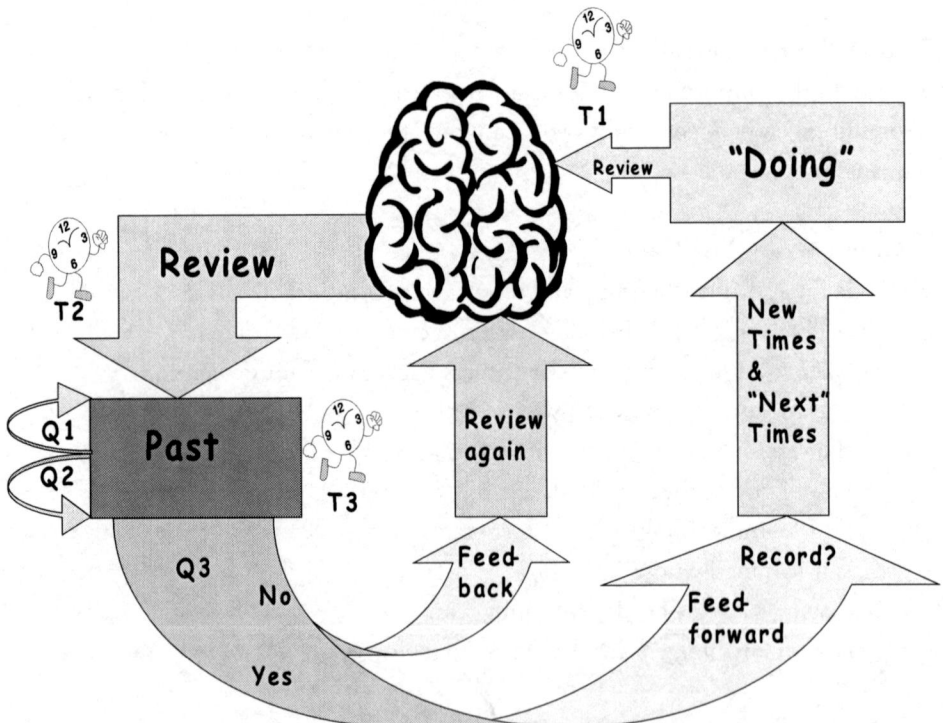

Q1: What was learnt from the "doing"/ experience?	T1: Time to leave it? – Now to one day
Q2: What was learnt about how to learn?	T2: Finding time to do it – Time management
Q3: Does it bring "new" learning and changing?	T3: Time spent on it – Seconds to one hour

Reviewing by Questioning
- What? Look back over events & gather facts objectively
- So what? Look at feelings, ideas and opinions
- Now what? Look at the future = change and development

Questioning "self"
- Do I respond by habit?
- Do I respond to feedback?
- What are my assumptions?
- How will this affect me?
- How else should I look at this?
- What else could it mean?
- How else can I use this?
- But above all; Ask…ask….ask!

Asking questions is another key skill, as noted by the following;

"The problem with Western managers is the emphasis on finding the right answer, rather than asking the right question."
– Peter Drucker

"The mark of a person is the questions they pose, not just in the statements they make."
– Reg Revans

"The problem is not to find clever people to come up with answers, but to find people who ask good questions." – Reg Revans

The End or Start of Learning?

The overall process we have looked at was the following. Please review it:

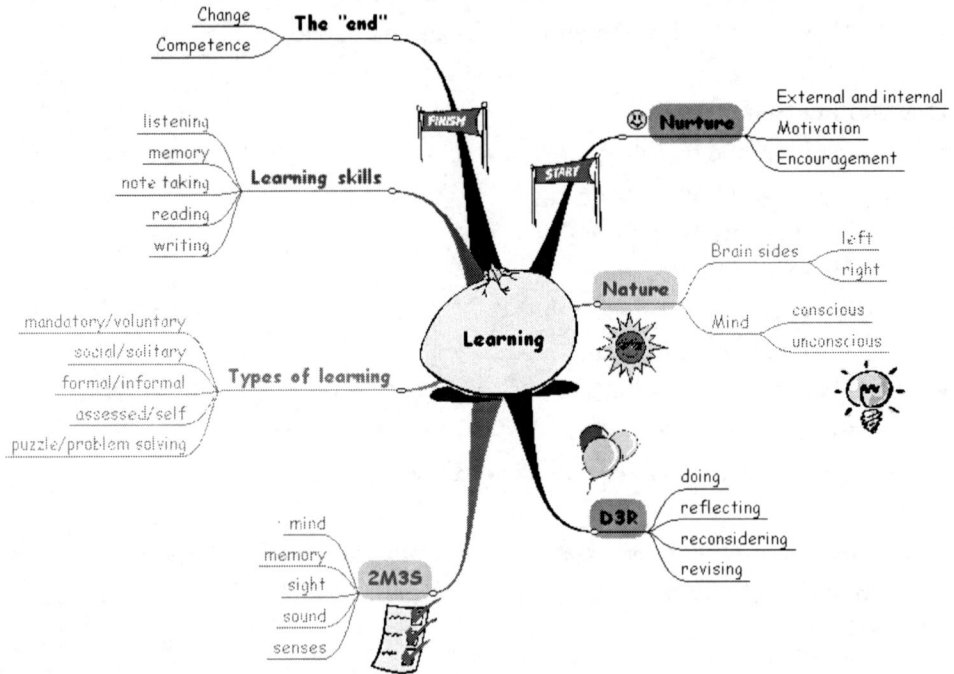

Other Learning Help

Recognise that learning is similar to physical exercise which requires us:

- To be motivated
- To repeat exercises
- Sometimes to stretch beyond what we currently do or think we're capable of

Learning is all about discovery. Having this attitude keeps us open to learning, for example:

- Don't try to decide if you like or dislike, agree or disagree. Simply look to see what it is. Explore it. Think and reflect on it. Have a go at it.
- The discoveries you will then make may be about yourself, the situation, the specific content, or the skill that you're learning.
- With this attitude of discovery, there is something to be learned in every situation.
- The more we learn, the more we understand.
- The more we understand, the more we are able to make better decisions about what to change.

- The better decisions we make, the more successful we are.
- The more successful we are, the more we want to learn.
- The learning and changing cycle can then start again.

Learning how to learn is a skill to be developed. Continuing Professional Development (CPD) will help you with this skill. CPD will certainly enhance your learning, and this conscious process is covered next in the section on Development and Learning.

You will know you have been successful with learning when you find the following:

Competence + Commitment = Change.
This involves being/gaining:
- Experience + Exercise
- Positive + Practical
- Emotions + Environment

Think + (Know how)
Do (How to)
=Move (New position)
Remember it's an ongoing "Active Creation" at this point

Please do not forget the 'Must Dos' of Learning:

Internal:
- WIIFM = my motivation
- Develop learning skills
- Use cycle: doing/thinking/understanding/determining how to.

External:
- Support & Encouragement
- Role Model
- Comfortable place

"I Must":
- "Use it or lose it": use the total brain power
- Use all of sight/sound/senses
- Review/review/review
- Be active not passive
- Be creative and do not just consume

"What we think or what we know or what we believe is, in the end of little consequence. The only consequence is what we do."
– John Ruskin

"Those unable to change themselves cannot change what goes on around them."
– Reg Revans

"There can be no learning without action."
– Reg Revans

So, finally, what will you now do about your learning?

Development and Learning

As already noted, an organisation's capacity to improve existing skills and to learn new ones is the most competitive advantage of all. Therefore, professional and personal development is hugely important, and organisations need to create opportunities for different types of experiences, thereby ensuring its people are nurtured. People development involves change (in moving people from one position to another); this means that learning is needed; as changing and learning are directly connected.

One of the difficulties with learning, however, is that many people think they already know all about it. They therefore think it is something they no longer have to do. This view is an out-dated and dangerous one to have in times of change, ongoing challenge, and new developments.

Learning is in fact, as seen earlier, not a passive activity, or an automatic process.
It may seem passive, once you have learned something, but to learn anything actually requires an active approach. Learning involves activity, it needs thinking about, and it can be hard work. We have already covered this topic fully above where we defined learning as follows:

Learning is the method and process which uses personal-power, knowledge and experience to:
- *Make sense of things (by thinking)*
- *Make things happen (by doing)*
- *Bring about change (by moving from one position to another)*

Learning is our future

We should all be learning most of the time, so that we can keep up with all changes and developments in the world and in business. The rate and speed of change is dramatic. Those who remain in the past can quickly have outdated knowledge and skills. Competence is not a constant. Development must be dynamic, not static; indeed the only thing certain about the future is that it will be different, so learning is totally fundamental to our "tomorrow."

This is not to say all change is good. But new developments do need to be examined. Often the best way may eventually be the simplest way, but only once it has been examined, thought about and applied (i.e. it has been actively learnt).

Learning needs skills

Learning involves developing skills and competencies in response to the future and to the problems we face. Learning is not just about obtaining qualifications, but is fundamentally about doing things better and doing things differently.

Individuals can no longer systematically rely on others (such as employers), to sponsor and support their learning. Leaving such an important decision to someone else is dangerous.

Self-development is your unique and personal journey. Many opportunities are available to you. It is therefore important to learn how to manage and how to lead your own development, and to cease total dependence on others to do this. As a skilled learner, you will be able to:

- Anticipate learning opportunities
- Recognise development situations
- Seek out new learning
- Take calculated risks and innovate
- Seek help and feedback
- Use interpersonal competencies
- Be critical constructively
- Filter and make connections
- Overcome barriers to learning

"Having the ability to learn, is also having the abilities to survive and to succeed."

We can and do learn anywhere and anytime. Learning activities can take place in many different situations. Learning includes informal and formal situations such as the following:

Informal (or unstructured) learning could be:
- Work experience projects
- Coaching and mentoring
- Job rotation and work shadowing
- Reading
- Attendance at professional institute meetings
- Using multi-media resources

Formal (structured) learning could be:
- Attendance at courses, conferences and seminars
- Distance learning with feedback or with some form of assessment
- Studying for a qualification
- Undertaking research
- Coaching and mentoring
- Job rotation and work shadowing

Learning does not always have to be with an outcome that is upwards and vertical, such as a promotion; it can be about broadening your skills, knowledge and/or competence at any level.

Learning can also result from making mistakes, as long as you do not keep repeating the mistake.

Learning is personal

Learning is a unique and personal process. It is not always a formal process. No two individuals have followed the same path to get them where they are today.

We also do many things without thinking about them. This is what academics would call being unconsciously competent. But when we first learned something, our learning had to become a conscious process. Think about driving a car. After we have done it for some years, we drive without thinking about all the very many complex things we do.

Do you remember when you started learning to drive?

You drove slowly; missed gear changes, used kangaroo petrol, clipped corners, got frustrated, thought you would never do it, etc. Yet, now, you drive "unconsciously" for most of the time.

Individual Development and Continuing Professional Development (CPD)

It is widely recognised that an individual must undertake, continually, personal development. This Continuing Professional Development is defined as:

"The systematic maintenance and improvement of knowledge, skills and competence throughout a professional's working life."

"The process by which a professional person maintains the quality and relevance of professional services during their working life."

CPD is an individual's commitment to ensure that their knowledge and skills are maintained at a suitable level in a changing world. CPD is therefore all about maintaining standards of competence and professionalism. It puts the emphasis on you taking responsibility for developing and directing your own career.

Many professional career development standards require that you are able to explain:
1. How wider environments affect your career
2. The relationship between your aspirations and the labour market
3. The external sources of support that are available
4. The role of outplacement and support
5. The importance of self-assessment
6. Differing and changing career needs
7. Mechanisms for evaluating career management

Always remember it is your development and nobody else's. It is all about being committed to your own growth, success and survival in a changing and developing world.

"If it is to be, then it is down to me."

Why bother with CPD?

The world is developing and evolving. For example:
• Rapid developments in technology

- New and shifting markets
- Economic pressures
- Greater emphasis on community and the environment
- A more mobile international workforce
- Preparedness for a promotion or a change of job.

All these changes place emphasis on the continuing need for an individual to be professionally competent.

Major professional institutes also have a responsibility to maintain standards and to ensure public and environmental safety. Employers, clients, and the public all require better standards, faster and at a lower cost. CPD will help you prepare for and cope with the challenges that will face you in the world of work.

The time for self-development is always "now". The pace of change has never been so fast; we have never had access to as much freely available and high quality learning as now. If we abdicate responsibility for managing our own development, then for sure we will be less valuable to those we want to work for in the future.

To be interested in your self-development will mean you move through the following levels of interest:

- Level one. I have development needs, but I am not interested in them.
- Level two. I have development needs, but I do not know what they are.
- Level three. I have development needs; I know what they are, but refuse to do anything about them, as it is not my responsibility.
- Level four. I have development needs, I know what they are, but I need a push to do anything them.
- Level five. I know about my development needs, I want to do something about them, but I do not know how to start.
- Level six. I know about my development needs, I want to do something and I am doing something.
- Level seven. I have no development needs.

How to undertake CPD

Effective learning involves combining the two halves of learning, "Knowing How" and "How to" (or, combining the two halves of knowledge and competence). As Albert Einstein has noted, "Learning is more important than knowledge." Both halves of learning are therefore needed, as knowledge can become isolated without the applied competence.

CPD will involve recording both knowledge and competence; so almost anything can count as CPD. Good and effective CPD schemes do not however mean that attendance on a training course equates to CPD points; points should not mean prizes. True CPD reflects active and applied learning, so attendance on a training course is no evidence of learning; the evidence of learning would be just how we can demostrate what we learned.

Successful CPD schemes require that you will keep written records in two areas:
1) Your record of achievements; this is a full record of the learning action taken and the respective outcomes.
2) Your development plan; this looks ahead and states your objectives, with the actions and plans to achieve these outcomes.

As learning is an individual process, such record keeping will also need to be individual-based. This is your own route map that will help you get from where you are now, to where you want to be. It will help you become an active learner.

"Learning is learnable."

Getting started

Before you complete your route map, you will find it useful to consider the following key questions. At this point, you might find it useful to review your last appraisal/ development review. However, your personal plan may be different to this work plan and may consider a wider range of aspirations.

Action time – Starting Out Qestions

Question One. Where am I now? What is my Current Position?
What is my current knowledge and competence?

Question Two. Where do I want to be, or where am I going?
What is the 'Future Situation?'
What outcome do I want at this time?
What is the target I want to aim at?
What direction am I being moved towards?

Question Three. How am I going to get there?
What is the gap between where I am now, and where I want to be?
What is the knowledge and competence required?
What actions do I need to take?
What resources do I need?
What support do I need?

Question Four. How do I know I have arrived?
Are there any intermediate steps?
What are the criteria that will tell me I have arrived?
What are the criteria that will tell me I am at the end of this current stage?

These four questions can then be looked at in greater detail by using the following:.

Step 1 – Review

To start the review process, you should review your personal and professional experience. This will enable you to identify your interests and present level of skills and knowledge. Analysis of future needs will enable you to take account of current and future job and career requirements. From this, you can draw up a profile of your personal and professional competencies, skills etc. This will help you to identify and prioritise areas for development.

Step 2 – Set your Goals

To achieve your objectives you need to set specific targets. You may have medium- or long-term goals, but it is best to concentrate on short-term goals that can be achieved in about 12 months. Many long-term goals can be broken down into a series of short-term ones. Balance your goals so that they take into account:

•   Immediate job requirements
•   Business and career aspirations
•   Personal targets
•   Family and personal considerations

Set yourself definite targets, in order of priority, that are practical, achievable and challenging. You will also need to set yourself realistic time scales with criteria to help you evaluate outcomes.

Step 3 – Development Activities

Identify the appropriate learning and development activities that will meet your needs. Think about all the available opportunities for development, as well as any preferences and constraints.

To meet your development needs and achieve your targets you can choose from a wide variety of activities, both formal and informal. We looked earlier at the formal and informal development methods and activities. The choice of activity is therefore up to you, so long as it is part of your overall CPD plan.

Although most other activities will be planned, you should also recognise and take advantage of other learning opportunities. These arise from day-to-day work experiences, unexpected challenges, and professional contacts. So, next, participate in your chosen development activity.

Step 4 – Evaluate the Outcomes

In order to assess the benefit of your CPD activities, their outcomes should be measured against the objectives that were set in Step 2. You should aim to evaluate your development in terms of new and/or improved levels of competent performance in your work, and/or new areas of knowledge acquired.

You will want to ask yourself four questions:

Have I achieved my targets?
* Fully; partially; not at all?
* If not, why not?
* If not yet achieved, do I need more time?

What improvement can I see already as a result?
* Promotion or more responsibility?
* Increased confidence?
* Better working relationships?

How else can I use the new skills and knowledge?
* Improve procedures/quality of service?

- Develop a new project?
- Coaching/mentoring of colleagues?

What am I going to do next?
- Continue with targets that need more time?
- Work towards a higher level of competence?
- Seek formal recognition/qualification?

In addition to this evaluation of your achievement against your targets, you should also reflect on the process: did the chosen method work for you? This will help you to decide which method to choose (or avoid) in future.

Having worked through these four steps, you are now well on the way to self-development. Ask yourself:
- How committed am I in progressing my CPD?
- Where am I currently limiting myself in progressing?
- What am I willing to risk so I can make outstanding progress?
- What have I recently succeeded in?
- What was special about what I did then?
- What evidence could I gather to show increased commitment to my CPD?

Finally, what next should you do? Some suggestions follow:

- Complete the following development planner.
- Getting feedback is vital to your development, so talk to those you trust about plan.
- Above all, do not be like the person who said, "I was going to read a copy of *The Power of Positive Thinking*, but then I thought 'What good would that do?'" So, commit to doing something positive about your CPD!
- Review the following characteristics of a skilled learner and ask when will you be able to identify yourself as the same?

"Unlike much of our current knowledge and skills, the capacity to learn will never become obsolete."

Finally in this first part relating to Personal Development, the following lists will help you on the journey:

Action Time: Personal Development Questions

1.   List all your personal attributes, experiences and interests to obtain an honest picture of what you are/what you want to be. Do ask a trusted friend to help with this if needed.

2.   List all the possible areas for expanding your knowledge of a topic.

3.   Compare 1 and 2

4.   Score each topic using a 1-5 scale for:
-    your interest
-    your ability
-    your potential

Pick the top three topics.

5.   Research in depth of each of the top three topics by, for example:
-    talking to someone
-    reading about them, e.g. from books, articles, magazines, and Internet searches
-    watching appropriate TV programs
-    attending training courses
-    going to exhibitions, conferences, seminars
-    going on a course
-    noting down all the contacts made
-    phoning up and talking to people, with a "can you help me?" approach

Development Plan

What do I want to achieve?
1.
2.
3.

When am I going to do this?
1.
2.
3.

How will I know it is successful?
1.
2.
3.

Target Date
1.
2.
3.

What have I done?
1.
2.
3.

What have I learned?
1.
2.
3.
......./Transfer to your Record of Achievements (see below)/..................

What do I do next?
1.
2.
3.
.........................../Transfer to your next Development plan/........................

You should always maintain a Record of Achievement. If you do not this, who else will? This record can start with keeping a copy of, for example, emails that have congratulated you; they will act as a reference with others and a personal reminder for you.

Meanwhile, a formal record may contain the following:
*   List of Qualifications/Competences, with who awarded them, and the date
*   "At Work" Experiences/Skills, with details of where this was and the dates. The experiences are what you learned, and are listed.
*   "Not at Work" Experiences/Skills, with details of where this was and the dates. This learning would come from things like courses, professional institute meetings, discussions with colleagues, reading magazines/journal/books and from relevant hobbies and interests.

Leadership and Management Styles

As individuals, people have their own style – therefore in organisations, we can find varied leadership and management styles. When leaders apply a particular style, this will automatically be evaluated as either good or poor, for example, by other people such as peers, and especially to those who fall underneath the leader. Style therefore clearly determines the outcomes that a leader and manager will either consciously (or more dangerously, unconsciously), create.

The Hersey-Blanchard situational theory, illustrated below, shows that style varies in the following three ways:
*   The amount of directive behavior from the leader.
*   The amount of supportive behavior from the leader.
*   The consequent involvement in decision-making from the follower.

Situational leadership

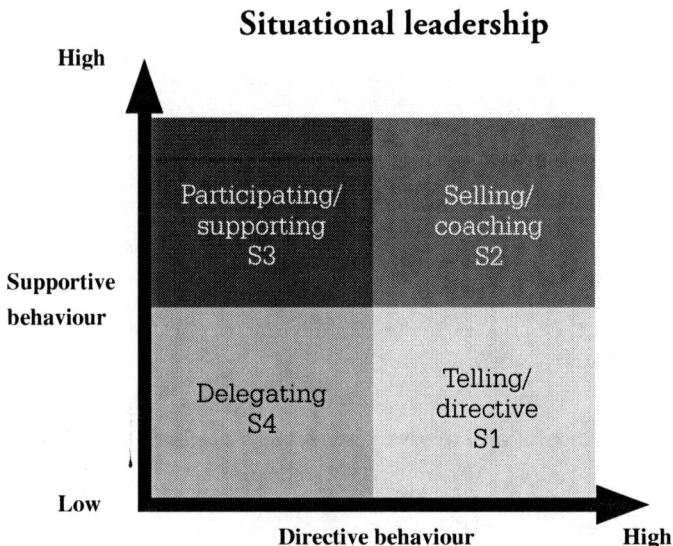

S1: Telling/Directing Leaders define the roles and tasks of the follower, who are supervised closely. Decisions are made by the leader and announced, so communication here is largely one-way.

S2: Selling/Coaching Leaders still define or tell what the roles and tasks are, but will seek ideas and suggestions from the follower, and therefore use more of a sell/suggestion of the task. Decisions will still remain the leader's prerogative, but communication is much more two-way.

S3: Participating/Supporting Leaders pass day-to-day decisions, such as task allocation and processes to the follower. The leader facilitates and takes part in decisions, but control is with the follower.

S4: Delegating Leaders are still involved in decisions and problem-solving, but control is with the follower. The follower decides when and how the leader will be involved.

Another view on styles follows, this takes an "extremes" and polarised perspective so that we can highlight and compare/contrast the differences:

1) A command and control style: the "older" and militaristic way:
- Keeps control
- People are "held onto"
- Judgemental
- "Tells"
- See though a "pinhole"
- Directive
- "Push" approach

2) A coaching style: the "newer" and empowering way:
- Lets people try
- People are given a "self release"
- Non-judgemental
- "Sells"
- Sees the wider view
- Supportive
- "Pull" approach

Another "extremes" view follows to give yet another polarised view of people's styles:

3) Autocratic and aggressive people:

- Drive and push people and are not leaders
- Have a "single", "my" viewpoint
- One-way communicator
- Demanding "do it my way, now"
- Take "fixed my way positions" and engage in a contest of wills
- Makes threats and applies pressure
- Engenders a blame and fear culture where people are fearful of trying something new, and remain within the status quo and "doing it by the book"
- People will cover up genuinely made mistakes and therefore will stifle any learning opportunity that was presented

4) Procrastinator and passive people:
- Abdicate from taking decisions
- Use group viewpoints
- Indecisive, but they believe there are being democratic
- "What do you all want to do, whenever"
- Changes positions easily and avoids any contest
- Makes offers and yields to pressure
- Engenders a lazy and stagnant culture where people eventually will increasingly become less interested and frustrated by the lack of action and direction; the good people will move on, the not so good people will stay

5) Charismatic and assertive people:
- Pulls more than pushes
- Two-way communicator
- People follow naturally, is a leader
- Makes concessions, "I think this, what do we think"
- Problem solves and explores interests
- Partnership views and reasons
- Looks for objective criteria and yields to principles not pressure
- Engenders a progressive culture where people become committed and supportive to each other; team work will flourish easily

Styles and Effects

The style used will have a dramatic effect on an organisation; fortunately, the style used is also largely a matter of making the unconscious a conscious choice. Leaders therefore have an enormous responsibility to ensure that the correct "sowing" is undertaken in setting and encouraging to others the right example, so that the eventual "reaping" will be that planned outcome of what was desired.

It seems irrefutable from the above views which two styles will be the most effective in most circumstances in most organisations. Those that noted (2) and (5) are correct! This is not to say that the other styles have no part to play. For example the directive commander (1) and the autocrat (3) maybe needed for example, when respectively dealing with procrastinators and when dealing with emergencies.

It is however an eternal sadness to find that more often than not, an inappropriate style is actually being used for most of the time. This is not only seen in organisations, but is visible at a family level, and also at macro/national/political levels.

Thought and application of the principle 'what you sow you will reap' could change this; another simple and eternal truth, and one clearly understood by Alan Leighton:

"Everyone is brought up to say that respect is something you must earn. Rubbish. It is something that you give. If you give people respect, someday you might get it back."
– Alan Leighton. Chairman Royal Mail, in **Motor Transport,** 28 November 2002.

And another gem from Peter Drucker reinforces the importance:

"Organisations do not exist for their own sake. The organisations goal is a specific contribution to individual and society. The test of its performance lies outside of itself."
– Peter Drucker

The best leadership style

It would be my proposition that the style used by each individual leader and manager should be a consciously worked out choice; making this choice and then doing it, will however present challenges to those leaders who have become fixated, perhaps unconsciously, with other styles. Changing a habit is therefore often not going to easy, a point we will discuss soon.

Meanwhile to emphasise here the importance of the coaching and assertive styles, these are therefore repeated below:

Leaders/managers will coach and empower by:
* Letting people try

- Giving people a "self release"
- Being non-judgemental
- "Sells"
- Seeing the wider view
- Supportive
- Using a "pull" approach

Leaders/managers also need to be a charismatic and assertive person who is one who:
- Pulls more than pushes
- Is a two-way communicator
- People follow naturally, as they are a leader
- Makes concessions, "I think this, what do we think"
- Problem solves and explores interests
- Uses partnership views and reasons
- Looks for objective criteria and yields to principles, not pressure
- Engenders a progressive culture where people become committed and supportive to each other; where team work will flourish easily

A "servant heart" leadership style is analogous to the coaching and assertive styles described above. This is where a leader sees their whole purpose is to serve people and not for people to serve the leader; good examples include Ghandi and more recently, Nelson Mandela.

Communication

The dictionary defines communication as "the process of conveying, imparting or exchanging information". Communicating therefore involves sharing information between people, "up/down and side/side" with the implied objective of preventing misunderstanding.

Unfortunately, much of what passes for communication is actually one way and also often, no attempt is made to check whether it has been understood (for example, as demonstrated in one FTSE 100 organisation who renamed all their notice boards to communication boards; the former description was actually the correct one). As communication is to prevent misunderstanding, then communication becomes an individual responsibility, so that we ensure there will be understanding in our communication.

However this may not occur systematically. Therefore, the following checklist of questions will help to focus on how communication should actually work in an organisation:

Checklist: Questions on how communication actually works

- Is there evidence of an interchange of ideas?
- Do employees know the reasons for the job they are being asked to do?
- Can changes be introduced without major upsets?
- Are ideas used that are put forward and if not, is it explained why?
- Are those nearest to the job consulted on matters affecting them?
- Are new employees carefully inducted?
- Do all people know what their jobs are?
- Do people show a sustained interest in their jobs?
- Is there a smooth flow of work?
- Are people seldom bypassed in the flow of information?
- Is the "grapevine" a very small one?
- Does the manager walk round at least once a day?
- Do the managers know where to go for answers to their people's questions?
- Do the managers clearly understand their responsibilities and others?
- Do the managers have good working relationships with colleagues?
- Do the managers know all your people by name?
- Can we say honestly say that communication flows well?

Communication Flows

Communication needs to flow easily between people. The following diagram illustrates this, starting with the initial tone of the communication, the general direction taken and finally, the result.

It shows the two extreme opposite types of communication: debate/confrontation that gets blocked/breaks down and dialogue/cooperation that connects/flows.

Uphill =
Hard to flow
Breaks Down

Tone	Direction	Result
Debate turning to Confrontation	Backwards and Circular. Slow progress. "Climbing"	Blocked or Ends. Delayed or Stops. "Win/lose"
Dialogue leading to Cooperation	Flows Forward. Fast progress. "Falling"	Connects. Starts/Takes off. "Win/win"

Downhill =
Flows through
Easy flowing

The tone and direction of effective communication is analogous to water flowing downhill, where gravity helps the process. It is however unnatural to flow uphill; it is an uphill struggle.

However, when people work together in flow, this give an interesting analogy; it is also a principle of teamwork (and is explored more fully in the upcoming 'Teams' section).

Communication Skills

In order for communication to be effective, it is not sufficient simply to transmit a message in some way, it must also be received and understood. For this to happen, some important communication skills are often needed such as challenging, questioning and feedback. These are amplified below.

Challenging; challenging someone involves conflict and compliance and these words can be easily misunderstood. To give clarity therefore, I have therefore explained them below with their both positive and negative sides.

- Positive conflict. This is constructive as it enables new learning through an open disagreement and discussion on ideas between people. The outcome is either a full agreement about the others position (there has been a "We" view and a "walking in each others shoes"); or, finding a new "third" position, this through taking an emotional detachment and an objective "helicopter view". All those involved believe they have gained something from the conflict process.

- Negative conflict. This is destructive as it inhibits new learning through creating personal tensions among people. The outcome is on "one" position only; "I", which sees this "own" view only. The position taken is essentially founded on an emotional subjective response. Those involved are usually divided, as whilst one may feel they have gained, the other feels they have lost something.

- Positive compliance. Open challenging encourages positive conflicts and recognises these are needed for effective learning and changing. People are now actively complying by being involved in shaping the outcome from a mutual awareness and understanding of the differences. They are allowed to change their position in the process.

- Negative compliance. This encourages blind or forced agreement which hinders effective learning and changing. It is effectively closed challenging as it discourages any open challenge and positive conflict on any differences from the "status quo" .One party remains uninvolved and keeps quiet with "unspoken disagreement". This gives a "false" agreement, which can encourage mistakes to be repeated, and little change brought to the "status quo". People will internally remain with their own position, even thought this will not be externally expressed in their "false" agreement.

Questioning

There are many types and formats of questions but the main point simply, is that how a question is asked, will help to get the right answer.

To paraphrase Peter Drucker, the problem with western managers is their emphasis on finding the right answer, rather than asking the right question.

The following are some of the types of questions that can be asked in specific circumstances.

- Directive/closed – "you need to do this"
- Informative/open – "from my experience"
- Confronting/open – "why did you get angry", and " what is it that is keeping you awake at the moment"
- Cathartic/open – "how do you feel" and "where in your life do you feel the most stuck at the moment" and "I get the impression you are concerned"

- Analytic/open – "will you go into detail" and "please make a list of the 10 things that are stopping you at the moment"
- Supportive/closed – "you did well" (very important and gives enormous benefit, to used as much as is genuinely possible)

Giving Feedback

Communications at work involves giving and receiving feedback on work related issues. It is always necessary to balance both positive and negative messages and not just to concentrate on weaknesses, but to always balance weaknesses by emphasising strengths.

"The task of management is to make people capable of joint performance, to make their strengths effective and their weaknesses irrelevant."
– Peter Drucker

It will also be necessary to choose the appropriate tone and language and to check, at the end, for understanding, for example, by asking them to repeat back the feedback given. Then, and always, end on a positive note; we all benefit from being told how we have done in a constructive and positive way.

The following checklists provide the guidelines on feedback:

Checklist: Giving Feedback

- You get more out of people if you are sensitive to their situation and treat them like adults by concentrating on their behaviour and not on personal traits/characteristics.
- Imagine how you would feel if you were on the receiving end.
- Balance both positive and negative messages.
- Don't avoid weaknesses but always balance them by emphasising strengths and directing towards the behaviour that the person can do something about.
- Choose the appropriate tone and language.
- Encourage people to take responsibility for their own development.
- Check, at the end, for understanding, for example, by asking them to repeat back the feedback given
- Then, and always, end on a positive note.

Checklist: Receiving Feedback

- Listen carefully without comment until the other person has finished speaking (avoid interrupting with explanation or defence)
- Try not to let feelings get in the way of using important information that is being offered
- If the feedback is vague, ambiguous or generalised, then ask the person to be more specific and, ask for examples if necessary, to check your understanding
- If the feedback is loaded in some way, do not immediately rise to the defensive or dissolve in dismay. Express your feelings about the statement by saying "I feel angry/upset/confused when you say that"
- Do not just swallow any criticism whole – look for consistent feedback from a number of people before you do. Take responsibility for which aspects of the feedback you will act on – it's your choice to change your behaviour.
- Choose what you will do as a result of the feedback
- Thank the person for the feedback – remember it is very difficult to give feedback

Communication and assertiveness

We talked earlier about an assertive leadership style – this also does relate to communication, as shown in the following checklist:

Checklist: Assertive Communication

The rules which follow are general and comprehensive. You will not need to follow all of them in every situation, nor will they have the same order of importance in all cases. They are, therefore, given in no significant order.

Be clear about what you want

If you don't know what you want, then you will find it difficult to communicate your wishes and needs to others. For example, do you want to improve the quality of emails that are sent to customers or do you want to encourage the staff to spend less time talking to friends? Or you may want to do both; in which case which one is more important?

Choose your time and place

Choose the most appropriate place to communicate and a time when the other person can listen. If necessary, delay the discussion (even if only for a few seconds) until you can give the matter your full attention.

Make a clear statement

It may help to rehearse your statement. Don't allow yourself to become upset or to lose track of what you want to say.

Be specific

Get straight to the point and identify clearly, and directly, what you want or what you want to convey.

Express what you feel

It sometimes helps to say that you feel anxious, happy or angry when making a statement, request or a response. But say it only once and then return to the point.

Do not be side-tracked

If the person you are talking to tries to side track, then listen to what is said and then repeat your own point. Do this again if necessary. This technique is known as the 'broken record'.

Give reasons, not excuses

It is better to give reasons rather than excuses for what you want to do, or don't want to do.

Be prepared to compromise

Think about your 'fallback position' before you start to communicate; when you have expressed your feelings, be prepared to agree an outcome which everyone can accept.

Communication and leadership consistency

Communication is only one part of an overall leadership and management style/ repertoire, and some steps to follow are to:

- Develop an awareness of your impact on others

- Try always to involve people in decision-making
- Believe that teamwork is the best approach
- Spend time mentoring coaching and developing people
- Build a positive climate in the team
- Empower and support team members rather than control them
- Develop appropriate performance reviews systems and methods
- Set challenging but achievable and measurable objectives
- Communicate one on one
- Reward success
- Agree improvements and personal development plans
- Give regular feedback
- Tackle poor performance

Methods of Communication

As we have seen, communication is data passed from one person to another person with the aim of generating information and understanding. Communication also has an impact on people, as in the process of transforming data into information, the meaning of communication is going to be found in the effect it creates with the individuals concerned.

As we use our own set of communication filters (that have been formed by our own individual life experiences), this really requires us to be curious about the reactions that our personal communication may stimulate in others. The following key factors have been reported by Albert Mehrabian, Emeritus Professor at UCLA, on the effectiveness on communication:

Key factors (in messages about feelings)	Effectiveness
Words	7%
The Voice Tone	38%
How we look (body language)	55%

This research however only dealt with messages about feelings and attitudes, for example, when people say they like or dislike something in a face-to-face communication; so if someone says they like something, but the voice tone and body language are not in congruence with the words, then the words will not be believed.

However, when communicating "plain" and objective facts, the above effectiveness percentages may not necessarily apply. Other attempts have been made to clarify the above key factors, for example when communicating objective data one-way, then:

Key factors (in messages with objective facts)	Effectiveness
Words	20%
The Voice Tone	20%
How we look (body language)	60%

With communicating issues involving interaction, opinion, emotion, discussion, agreement, negative feedback etc. the ratio has been seen as being close to Mehrabian as follows:

Key factors (in discussions etc)	Effectiveness
Words	10%
The Voice Tone	40%
How we look (body language)	50%

All of the above variances in key factors emphasise and clearly show that communication has three main attributes; words, tone of voice and body language. What is also somewhat sobering about these is to appreciate the loss of the dominant key factor of body language, when we are writing or phoning (body language being only effective when we are face-to-face with other people). What this clearly tells us is the body language is the most effective form of communication.

For those people who remain unconvinced about this, consider having only ever spoken to someone on the telephone or by email/letter and you, have never actually met the person. On the phone, we at least have the words and voice tone to help us form a view of the person we are speaking to.

With email and other forms of written communication, we only have words. Yet, when we finally meet this person that we have phoned or emailed, the view and opinion we had of them, can change when we are "face-to-face." They will be often appear and look very different from how we had imagined them. For example, terse, cold and direct words are actually, coming from a smiling friendly and warm face.

Here, it is the body language that comes from a visual contact that makes a difference in our perception.

The differences in effectiveness of communication can be seen further below, with the checklist showing the main advantages and disadvantages in communication methods:

Checklist: Communication effectiveness

Verbal Communication
Examples: meetings, one to ones, telephone, TV/radio
Advantages
- Direct, no time lags
- Immediate feedback
- Allows for discussions
- When face to face, the body language is an effective method
- Quick

Disadvantages
- Often used unplanned, acting in haste, not thought
- Forgetting vital information
- "Chinese whispers"
- Not confidential
- Poor retention, especially if information is complex

Written Communication
Examples: a note, email, reports, letters, circulars, press, books
Advantages
- Permanent record
- Convey complex information
- Identical message to many

Disadvantages
- Time and cost
- Time lag between sending and receiving
- Used to avoid face-to-face contact
- Used to negatively record those "cover your ass" (CYA) messages
- No real opportunity to test understanding

Visual Communication
Examples: fax, notices, TV, posters, histograms
Advantages
- Reinforce "verbal" communication
- Gives extra stimuli

- Simplifies words
- Illustrates

Disadvantages

- Time and cost
- Interpretation
- Design skills
- No real opportunity to test understanding

Body Language

Eye contact is the number one body language "tool" that can be used to show interest and show concern in face-to-face communication. The eyes are "the lamp of the body" that reveals, the inner self, or, as also been said, "Eyes are the windows of the soul".

They are of course many other examples of body language:

- Head movements, e.g. nodding/shaking
- Gestures "speak" a lot, e.g. smiling, finger pointing
- Posture, e.g. slouching, shrugging, leaning
- Breathing, e.g. snoring, anger
- Touching, e.g. closeness, friendly

Often, all the above methods of communication may be combined. These combinations can reveal and give varied behaviour patterns; for example:

- Passive or non-assertive behaviour = body language of little eye contact, slouching, sullen looking with few and lose ly used words, quiet voice tone, etc.
- Aggressive behaviour = body language of fixed and staring eye contact, leaning forward, finger pointing, furrowed brow with strong words, possibly swearing and loud voice tone etc.
- Receptive or assertive behaviour = body language of friendly "crinkled eyes", relaxed posture, smiling, with thoughtful and considered words, and a gentle voice tone etc.

Body language remains however the "secret" signal of communication (and also of our behaviour as this is fundamentally, what we say or do). It will go far beyond the meaning of the associated simple word use and any associated voice tones.

The following comparison also shows how body language is related to the three earlier introduced behavioural types.

Body Language	Assertive behaviour	Aggressive behaviour	Non-assertive behaviour
Posture	Upright/Straight	Leaning Forward	Shrinking Back
Head	Firm not rigid	Chin jutting out	Head down
Eyes	Direct not staring good and regular eye contact	Strongly focused staring, often piercing or glaring eye contact	Glancing away. Little eye contact
Face	Expression fits the words	Set/Firm	Smiling even when upset
Voice	Well modulated to fit content	Loud/Emphatic	Hesitant/Soft, trailing off at ends of words/sentences
Arms/Hands	Relaxed/Moving Easily	Controlled Extreme/Sharp gestures/finger pointing, jabbing	Aimless/still
Movement/ Walking	Measured pace suitable to action	Slow and heavy or fast, deliberate, hard	Slow and hesitant or fast and jerky

Effective communication therefore requires words and voice tone and body language to be in line and compatible with each other.

"I need to see the business leaders' body language and the passion they poured into their arguments".
– Jack Welsh

4: Managing People

Leaders need Followers

Leaders are needed to initiate change and to give the forward momentum and direction. But they cannot do it alone, they have to attract followers. In turn, the followers need to give willing support and find a sense a purpose for themselves when they are following. In turn, the top team of followers have then to pass on this sense of purpose to attract other followers:

"I have often believed that, although courses in leadership are necessary, courses in followership would be a useful part of the business environment."
– Sir John Harvey Jones

Leadership is not therefore a single person on a power trip; it has to become the means and prime method used by all to guide and move people forward in the desired direction. Many seem to think there can only ever be one leader in an organisation, however there must be many leaders. Whilst there needs to the one "top" person who sets the overall "heartbeat" of the organisation, the subsequent collections of leaders and followers need to follow the top leader's principles and qualities with their own people/followers. They then become the leaders of their people. Leaders therefore need to pass it on!

Leadership and Trust

Trust is fundamentally about "having to give up, to another, what you personally believe is valuable to you". It is "One for all and all for one" and it is a "willing interdependence." Trust is built when behaviour matches expectations, and involves consistency in motives and accountability for actions.

Trust becomes a self-fulfilling prophecy.

Trust is firstly built between people, one on one, and is not something that is built remotely between nebulous companies. Trust between companies will only follow on from the trust between individuals.

Fortunately trust can be won by consistently telling the truth in a way that others can verify. Trust in this way is about transparency and includes the admission of mistakes.

Building trust is a "one on one" job; this is the foundational building block for trust to develop. It therefore will involve the following:

- Doing what you say you will do
- Going beyond conventional expectations
- Undertaking open and honest communication
- Being patient
- Accepting and admitting to mistakes
- Ensuring the other party gets a fair outcome.

Trust, due to its emotional roots, can defy logic. Some people trust straight away with no real basis (this can be a good thing, as this is one of the bases for society and community). Some people will need to see repeated behaviour before they will trust. Some will need consistency in behaviour for months or years. Some, however, will never trust.

Trust does have a critical and sound logical aspect, as trust reduces uncertainty. There is no second-guessing, as what they say is true, commitments are honoured and therefore bargaining, monitoring, handling disputes are all minimised.

The following series of checklists provide some overviews on trust:

Checklist: Trust

Trust is
Confidence in own and others abilities
Experienced by working together with integrity, honesty and openness
A positive power using both the heart and the head
Learning and being flexible and willing to change
Tough and confronting without being confrontational, as expectations have to be met
Bonding, intimacy and working together face/face
Leadership is visible and driven with vision and creating mission in the right atmosphere of expectation of trust
A genuine belief system that sees it is the right thing to do as all will benefit

Trust is not
Blind faith in the unknown
Cheap, as there is high cost of failure. Sometimes failure is critical

A single "my" view
Formal rules
Easy
Keeping your distance
Invisible leadership
Used temporarily or short-term or for single benefit

Checklist: How to Build Trust

Be non-judgemental
Be open:
- Initiate self – disclosure; reveal your thinking and feelings
- Volunteer information
- Reveal your values and priorities
Be congruent and honest:
- Say what you think; state your opinion, even when different from others
- State your wants and needs
- Encourage honesty in others
- State clearly what you will and will not reveal
Be reliable:
- Do what you say you will do
- Set clear and realistic limits on both sides
- Treat commitments seriously and develop reliable processes
Be strivers for continuous improvement:
- Influence your organisation to create more mutual benefit for the relationships
- Exchange candid feedback on how well the relationship is working
And finally
- All parties must come to believe that the others will do what they have said they will do.
- All parties must find a way to be comfortable with the risk of being open and vulnerable to the others, in the secure belief that the other party will not take unfair advantage.
- All must show willingness to help the others become more successful.
- Broken agreements destroy trust and lead to bad implementations and performance.
- Continuous improvement is the fabric and product of trust in a relationship.

A final word here from Sir John Harvey Jones:

"Teams can only work together if they trust and trust requires mutuality of respect, integrity, and mutuality of regard."

Helping People to Develop

All organisations must have people working in them with appropriate levels of competence, and the following represents a view of competence development levels. It can be noted that these levels do not automatically match across to the UK NQF (National Qualification Framework) and NVQ (National Vocational Qualification) levels, as these have their own scheme.

Level of ability	Objective	Tasks	Examples of questions
1) Knowledge	What you know	Arrange, define, recognise, relate, repeat, state	"Make a list"
2) Comprehension	What you understand	Classify, describe, discuss, explain, locate, review	"Communicate the key features of"
3) Application	Applying the knowledge	Apply, choose, practice, solve, use, write	"Apply the theory of x to y"
4) Analysis	Analyse what has been done/ applied	Analyse, appraise, compare, contrast, question	"Examine in detail"
5) Synthesis	Combining knowledge and application to create and plan	Arrange, collect, design, plan, organise, prepare	"Make justified proposals"
6) Evaluation	Evaluate, recommend and make decisions	Appraise, argue, assess, judge, evaluate, attach	"Assess the feasibility of x"

As people develop, they will pass through these different levels.

As we have explored earlier, learning is not always an automatic process, and whilst an individual's personal motivation is a key aspect, people will often need help and support in their learning. This help and support process is called (by some) mentoring. However, the name used is secondary to the process involved; a process where organisations create opportunities for people to have different types of experiences and be nurtured (or mentored or supported), in their learning and development at work.

Learning development and companies

The myth exists in many organisations that the only way for anyone to learn anything is to send them on a training course. Certainly, most trainers will "plant seeds" and will work very hard to ignite the fire for continued growth and development when the learner returns to their work environment. However, there are some necessary and needed conditions for learning and development to happen in the workplace. These conditions are often all about giving support, where managers "water the planted seeds". If this does not happen, then applied learning opportunities will be missed, and the training event time/cost will be wasted.

A person being developed needs the following from their managers:

- Identification of development needs
- A development programme
- A learning culture at work which fully understands:
  - how people learn
  - how to support/coach/mentor

However, having a learning culture that practically works is a rare find in many organisations, as many simply fail to include support before and after a development programme.

The following support is needed:

1) The set-up and support before a development programme:

- Think about what work-based projects can be used to apply learning and benefit the business.
- Ask the learners to seek feedback on their current performance so that they come up with specific learning goals in this work-based area
- Let them do a pre-task
- Meet and finalise learning goals
- Stimulate interest in the programme within the organisation
- Put learners into learning sets/buddy groups
- Arrange a mentoring scheme/programme(see below)

2) The set down and support after the development programme:

- Ongoing mentoring support

- Evaluate by the success of the work based project
- Ensure specific opportunities exist with two days of the end of the programme
- Discuss learning
- Reinforce learning by letting them teach others
- Publicise the success
- Link rewards to the transfer of learning into the workplace
- Continue with successful learning sets by transforming them into improvement teams

Only when the above is successfully considered, can the crucial transfer take place into the workplace, and become effective applied learning that will work towards creating high performing organisations. Such an organisation will have the following characteristics:

- Opportunities for continuous learning
- Information sharing
- Employee participation
- Personal compensation and performance are linked
- Flat organisation structures with cross-functional working
- Supportive work environment

Learning stages

Mentoring, or supporting peoples' learning is used to help people learn and is also related to learning styles/theory, where earlier the following steps/stages were identified:

- Doing; being "active" and "practicing"
- Reflecting on what has been done, by "thinking" about it
- Reconsidering, and considering/looking at "theory" and others "best practice" or "facts"
- Revising by considering what to do differently
- And then performing the (new) practices

As explained in the earlier section on learning, effective learning conditions are as follows:

- Gaining attention, e.g. establishing 'what's in it for me' (WIIFM)
- Getting expected outcome, e.g. an achieved WIIFM
- Stimulating recall of existing knowledge/skills
- Developing new opportunities.
- Receiving feedback, e.g. praise

- Appraising own performance
- Transferability of knowledge, e.g. work applications
- Review, retention, practice

Effective supporting of learning will therefore compliment the above effective learning conditions, for example by:

- Giving attention
- Helping achievement and recall
- Providing new opportunities
- Giving feedback
- Praising performance

Learning support and behaviour change

All regular habitual behaviour patterns become hard-wired in the neural pathways of the brain. Behaviour patterns create neural connections in the brain and eventually with repeated behaviour, these reinforce the behaviour. The behaviour pattern is now automatic at the brain cell level, with the end result, that these ways of behaving now feel natural, easy and comfortable.

Introducing a new required behaviour can often be extremely difficult, because it means replacing the old pattern. As behaviour patterns have been physically established at the brain cell level, any new pattern will seem extremely awkward; even if it makes sense and is desirable.

The brain is not like a digital computer and there is no easy "delete" key.

The only way to replace an old behaviour pattern is to establish a new pattern that will prove to be more satisfying than the old behaviour. With an adequate period of reinforcement, there is a chance that new connections will be made, and this new pathway can become the preferred wiring. Over time, the old habitual pathway will eventually fall into disuse.

However, without reinforcement, the pathways will not establish themselves, and people will fall back on the old, comfortable patterns they are used to.

The only thing therefore that can create permanent behavioural change is frequent reinforcement over the long term. This means receiving support, for example by ongoing feedback, guidance, praise and encouragement. This support can be internal (DIY), and, or can be provided externally, from others, such as a learning supporter or mentor.

The Learning Supporter/Mentor

A learning supporter or a mentor is someone who is involved in:

"A one to one contact of equals, in a defined and agreed relationship; with the aim to learn and to improve personal and professional effectiveness."

This is therefore someone who:
- Helps another person through a learning experience
- Gives help which can be informal (such as seeking advice), or the help can be more formal (for example, with an organised organisation mentoring scheme)
- Gives one to one attention
- Is totally focussed on learning potential
- Is removed from organisation politics (when using an external mentor).

Checklist: What mentoring is not

Mentoring is not a place to:
- moan or whinge
- spread gossip
- be told exactly what to do
- be given specific answers to problems
- be sloppy and slapdash
- forget that learning is an active and continual process
- be managed
- ignore things that need to be changed and done differently
- expect answers to everything

There are two people involved in a mentoring relationship; the mentor/learning supporter and the learner being mentored. The learner is there for personal gain, as the following checklist shows.

Checklist: What is mentoring for the learner?

Mentoring is a place for the learner to:

- self develop
- be challenged
- recognise their strengths and weaknesses
- learn to build on their strengths
- receive feedback
- learn by example
- learn by mistakes
- talk openly
- receive wisdom and insights
- listen
- be listened to
- gain knowledge
- do things differently
- be supported
- be encouraged
- trust and discuss, for example, work issues, career development, personnel development, domestic issues

Supporting learning is well recognised as being valuable; for example, mentoring was rated highly in a 2004 survey **Motivation Matters** conducted by the Chartered Management Institute and Adecco. Here, mentoring was rated twice in the top three most effective forms of training that had been experienced by managers:

1. Informal mentoring
2. Participation in seminars
3. Formal mentoring

Checklist: Benefits of Mentoring

To an organisation
- Widening of the knowledge and skill base
- Alternative or complimenting, other learning/training
- Part of an individuals personal development programme
- Developing trust and confidentiality between the mentor and person being mentored
- Exposing the value of individuals

- Developing committed and motivated learners who contribute to the company's success
- Developing team approaches and future management
- Can develop organisation culture

To the Mentor
- Highlighting some of own learning gaps and areas for personal development
- Learning to listen and to reflect/think before acting
- Developing knowledge about other areas
- Improving leadership and communication skills
- Learning to challenge, and to balance give/take
- Increasing job satisfaction, for example, by helping others
- Passing on knowledge and skills to others, for example, by giving something "back"
- Discovering different ways of working with people

To the Learner
- Developing learning and reflective skills, the keys to personal potential
- Developing personal as well as professional knowledge
- Learning to take risks in a supportive environment
- Learning to accept criticism
- Developing autonomy and accountability
- Increasing confidence and openness to change

Learning support activities

To support learning, we need to look at the business processes activities and interpersonal skills that learners will use and are involved with, such as the following:

Business Process Activity
- Planning, for example determining what has to be done
- Recording, for example keeping minutes of meetings
- Structuring meetings, for example, review, agenda, action points
- Time management, for example looking at all activities and prioritising
- Maintaining boundaries, for example around political issues

- Scheduling, for example planning in when to do things
- Evaluating, for example after analysing
- Action planning, for example what needs to be done and when
- Facilitating, for example "oiling" the "wheels"

Interpersonal skills
- Negotiating and influencing, for example in prioritising
- Listening, actively
- Giving feedback
- Intervening, for example, being prescriptive, informative, or confronting
- Motivating and encouraging
- Coaching/Teaching
- Reflecting
- Creating positive conflict
- Challenging, honesty, openness and trusting
- Not judging, patience, tolerance and calmness
- Non-prejudicial and "value-free" from "hidden agendas, politics etc."
- Empathetic (can "walk in your shoes")
- Able to deal with different types of thinkers and learners

These activities cover those that learners may require support on. Mentoring is perhaps 80 per cent a common process, and 20 per cent unique to a particular situation, such as:
- Individuals have preferred ways of thinking and behaving.
- The mentor has technical expertise in the learners area; for example, business/ trade/profession
- The learner has some very specific needs; for example, just for ideas/sounding board only, or for personalised development only, or for challenge thinking/ objectivity only.

Much of mentoring is however, a common and structured process of learning by design, instead of, learning by chance. Mentoring as a process has to be managed, like everything, by planning, organising, co-ordinating and controlling.

Without such a clear management role, mentoring relationships may dissolve into a "cosy" relationship, without any specific outcomes.

Learner's viewpoint

We will now look at some specific aspects for individual's mentors and learners. We will firstly consider the learner's point of view.

Checklist: Learner – do I need a Mentor?

Do I need to:
- See a clear direction and feel that I am on the right path
- Get past blocking obstacles
- Stop constantly feeling that I am under pressure
- Be more self assured in handling people
- Hear a friendly and challenging supporting voice
- Get confirmation that I am at least going along the right path
- Find new ways in a fast changing world
- Find new ways to solve old problems
- Demonstrate better than I can do more than I currently do
- Get confidential advice whenever I am moving into a new area
- Have consistent help to see me through challenges and change

"Yes" answers, indicate a mentor could be of assistance

Checklist: Characteristics of a good Learner

- Willing to learn and develop
- Willing to participate
- Intelligent and able to learn quickly
- Ambitious and wants to "get on"
- Keen to succeed despite problems
- Committed to learning and personal development
- Able to make contacts
- Flexible and adaptable
- Self-aware
- Well organised
- Able to receive constructive feedback
- Want to be mentored
- Accept challenge and positive conflict
- Trust the mentor

- Prepared to be open and honest
- Prepared to make mistakes and take risks
- Active learners and committed to there own development
- Know there preferred style of learning
- Have a positive view of themselves
- Takes ownership of the learning and drives it forward
- Will do things they do not want to, so that, they will become, what they want to be

Learners must ask themselves, "do I need to":
- See a clear direction?
- Get past blocking obstacles?
- Hear a friendly and supporting voice?
- Get confirmation I am on the right path?
- Find new ways to do things?
- Have consistent help to see me through?

Learning supporter's viewpoint

We will now look at the important aspects in selecting and then choosing mentors. The following checklists show what an effective mentor is and what successful mentoring schemes are:

Checklist: An Effective Mentor

An effective mentor is:
- An open communicator
- Committed to learning
- Willing to share positive and negative experiences
- Good at giving realistic and positive feedback
- Able to help people to recognise their strengths and development needs
- Able to challenge constructively, with positive conflict
- Objective and able to stand back from day-to-day issues and focus on implications and outcomes
- "Action-orientated" and encourages actions to follow discussion
- Able to work in an unstructured programme

- Able to contribute to an open, candid atmosphere which encourages confidence and trust
- Good at asking open-ended probing questions.

Checklist: Successful Mentoring Schemes

- Participation is by willing volunteers who wish to succeed and grow.
- Recognising that individual needs and organisation needs can be both satisfied.
- Conducting an initial pilot scheme.
- Top management support is shown in action as well as by words.
- Appropriate awareness raising and marketing of the scheme to the whole organisation
- Appointing a co-ordinator to manage and "own" the programme
- Have a "no fault" opt out clause
- Making all participants aware of the potential risks and problems
- Effective knowledge of mentors, learners, line managers and any others involved, on, what it is all about
- Be clear on the learners needs and requirements
- Providing training and support for both mentors and learners
- Careful and appropriate selecting and matching and pairing of mentor/learner
- Monitoring and evaluation of the scheme linked to the defined objectives and anticipated outcomes of the scheme, involving feedback from all involved.
- Ensuring confidentiality is integral in the programme
- Allowing the appropriate time to undertake mentoring
- Setting a time limit for the mentoring programme

The Mentoring Process

There are three definable stages in the mentoring process or life cycle. The terminology may vary, but generally speaking, the stages can be defined as follows:

- Starting; the forming, initiating, orientation or courtship stage

- Core; establishing, normalising, adolescence, honeymoon, nurturing, or dependency; followed by performing, the maturing, developing independence or autonomy stage
- Ending; the mourning, termination or divorce stage

At the start, the learner is dependant on the mentor. The mentor starts out as a friendly supporter, and then moves into a more directive role, before finally the learner becomes more independent and autonomous. The ultimate aim of mentoring is to have a learner who is "self-sufficient", as shown by the following checklist:

Checklist: The Accountable and Autonomous Person

Is able to:
1) Define personal objectives and see that support/development is interdependent
2) Understand their own role and position in relation to others
3) Know how to tackle problems, interpersonal conflicts and get constructive solutions
4) Use the necessary skills/knowledge to do the job
5) Be self-confidant on their current ability and knows what they still need to learn
6) Apply knowledge/skills, seek advise/support, and is open to challenge/positive conflict and to learning and changing.

Mentoring process – starting out

This is essentially a courtship stage where bonding, rapport and trust begin to be formed. It is also similar to the forming and normalising stages in Team Building (see later). The learner is likely to be a little uncertain of what is required, so the mentor needs to give encouragement and provide a clear structure

The following will help both parties prepare for the first session, and then take the mentor through what needs to be done.

Checklist: Mentor Preparation

Why have I become a mentor?
What do I offer/what do I want?
What significant issues might arise?

What do I feel strongly about?

Which are the areas where I prefer my Learner to 'match' me; over which I am neutral about; about which I would like us to be different?

What about issues of trust and respect?

What are my own psychological/personal thinking and working styles?

How do they affect the way I interact with others?

How much time will we have?

Where will we meet?

What mutual contacts are we likely to have? How might they help?

What is my attitude towards self-development?

Who is/has been mentor to me. What did I gain?

Who else is involved in this process (e.g. senior management, learner's manager)?

Checklist: Learner Preparation

Why have I become a learner?

What do I offer/what do I want?

What significant issues might arise?

What do I feel strongly about?

Which are the areas where I prefer my mentor to 'match' me; over which I am neutral; about which I would like us to be different?

What about issues of trust and respect?

What are my own psychological/personal thinking and working styles?

How do they affect the way I interact with others?

What mentoring skills do I want my mentor to have?

How much time will we have?

Where will we meet?

What mutual contacts are we likely to have?

How might this help?

What is my attitude towards self-development?

Who is/has been mentor to me. What did I gain?

Who else is involved in this process (e.g. senior management, learner's manager)?

Agenda – First Meeting:

Start
- Pleasantries
- Agenda confirmation
- Share personal and professional information
- Establish each others learning style preferences

Core
- Discuss what both hope to get of the relationship
- Agree what is meant by confidentiality
- Set the ground rules, for example, run thorough the above checklists on preparation and establishing rapport
  In work-based mentoring when using an external mentor, the mentor can learn about the workplace context, and similarly the learner can learn about the external mentor's work context
- Discuss how the relationship will be reviewed and what to do if "problems" occur
- Discuss and agree the outcomes and what will be regarded as "success"
- Agree, at this first meeting, several dates forward for future meetings (this fosters mutual commitment to the relationship. Dates may be cancelled with appropriate notice, but a new date should be immediately arranged)

End
- Review and summarise the meeting
- Agree actions points
- Confirm the next meeting (date, time, venue, potential agenda)
- Write the meeting minutes

Mentoring process – core stage

This moves from the "honeymoon" to maturing stage, where reviewing and proposing and agreeing actions is involved.

The learner is moved from being dependent towards autonomy, with the Mentor providing support, auditing of the learners strengths and weaknesses and using listening and questioning.

This is perhaps a "delicate" stage, involving for example, the transition from dependency to independence.

Typical Agenda – Middle Stages

Start
- Pleasantries
- Agenda confirmation
- Review of last meeting

Core
- Review of targets achieved/actions taken
- Feedback and Discussion
- Action planning – targets to be achieved by next meeting and longer term

End
- Summary of session
- Agreement of details for next meeting - date, time, venue, potential agenda.

Checklist: Mid Session Reviews
- Has a clear agreement been established?
- Is the content of the agreement still relevant?
- How well are we both getting on at a personal level?
- Is the relationship a professional one?
- Are there any parallel activities taking place at the same time?
- Is there any conflicting activity processes getting in the way?
- Is a clear outcome starting to emerge for the learner?
- Are new alternatives still being generated?
- Are ideas being turned into appropriate actions?
- Is the learner now increasing in their autonomy and independence?
- What stage is the relationship currently at?

Checklist: Transition, Are We There Yet?

Is the learner:
- More fully aware of organisation politics, the culture (the way things are around there) and their own role and position in relation to others?
- More able to define personal objectives, network, and find out answers themselves?
- More able to apply knowledge/skills, seek advise/support, and remains open to challenge/positive conflict/learning and changing?
- More able to tackle problems, interpersonal conflicts and get constructive solutions/positive compliance?
- Challenging me, with positive conflict?
- More proactive and keen to take the "initiative"?
- Still eager to learn and knows what they still need to learn?

Mentoring process – end stage

This stage represents the end or a divorce, with perhaps some appropriate mourning. Whilst in the initial stages in the relationship, the learner has been more dependent, they are now more independent.

The process gone through has involved the forming aspects, going through the honeymoon period (or perhaps a storming period), developed and established the norms, before finally reaching a good maturing, and performing level. Accordingly, the steps of forming, storming, normalising, and performing now come to the final stage, which may be called a mourning stage.

This is because if the relationship has got this far, then it should have been found to be enjoyable and mutually beneficial. It is now over and a sense of loss can ensue. It is important to acknowledge any such feelings, as well as, concluding any remaining "open" business. We should now be able to see we have "arrived", as follows:

Checklist: Transition, Are We Now There?

Is the learner:
- More fully aware of organisation politics, the culture (the way things are around there) and their own role and position in relation to others?
- More able to define personal objectives, network, and find out answers themselves?
- More able to apply knowledge/skills, seek advise/support, and remains open to challenge/positive conflict/learning and changing?
- More able to tackle problems, interpersonal conflicts and get constructive solutions/positive compliance?
  Challenging me, with positive conflict?
  More proactive and keen to take the "initiative"?
  Still eager to learn and knows what they still need to learn?

Checklis: End Session/Mutual Feedback

- Is the learner really confident and autonomous?
- Did we have a good rapport for most of the time?
- Were we able to challenge each other, with positive conflict?
- Was confidentiality maintained?
- Did we keep focussed?
- Was there an appropriate balance between direction and support?
- How have we grown as a result of the relationship?
- What was specifically helpful?
- What was specifically unhelpful?
- What would we do differently next time?

Mentoring process: some problems

Finally in this section on the learning support/mentoring process, we will consider what problems may arise in the relationship. These can also show the "pitfalls" to be avoided.

Checklist: Mentoring Problems

- Mismatch of mentor/learner
- Mismatch of expectations, for example from unclear starting agreements

- Reluctant mentor/learner, for example "forced" matching and pairing, and a lack of commitment from one or both
- Lack of openness and trust, for example no challenging and positive conflict
- Relationship not valued in the organisation, for example the view that it is a "waste of time" from others
- Gender or Culture mismatch, for example creating misunderstanding
- Emotional involvement, for example "clouding" the issues
- Broken confidentiality, leading to mistrust
- Conflicting roles, for example the mentor is also the line manager
- Obstructions from/conflicts of others, for example from, colleagues, partners
- Parameters/boundaries/details not agreed in advance
- Time availability/cancelling agreed meetings, for example raising the question "are we serious about this relationship?"

Mentoring Skills

For a successful mentoring relationship, appropriate skills are needed. These include the following "rights":

Checklist: The "Rights"

The "Right" Environment
- This includes the following:
  - The atmosphere, for example one conducive to learning by being "friendly", etc.
  - The surroundings, for example comfortable, right temperature, background music, etc.
  - Good example setting, for example a role model, someone you "look up to", etc.
  - Encouragement, for example from colleagues, family, friends, etc.
  - Support, for example from a line manager, a mentor, etc.

The "Right" Resources
- These include the following:

- Having appropriate Learning Skills, for example reading, note taking, etc.
- Having an appropriate Method of Learning, for example classroom for some, distance learning preferred by others. A student studying, for example, 100 percent by distance learning would need less listening learning skills than a student attending many formal lectures.

The "Right" Individual Values and Beliefs about Learning
- Last but by no means least; these include the abilities to:
  - Know that you "can do it"
  - Give yourself support, for example, in working towards autonomy
  - Give yourself encouragement, for example, motivation.

A mentor needs skills to carry out the role. We will now concentrate on these:

Checklist: Mentor Skills Self Assessment

This is a mentor diagnostic activity. Which are true of you?

Read these statements carefully, and tick those that you need to work hardest upon.

1) I listen to the whole issue before commenting.
2) I give advice, but still expect the learner to make their own decisions.
3) I always find time to help.
4) I always question thoroughly to find the real issues.
5) I always give honest opinions.
6) I have a good range of networks and contacts that can be utilised appropriately.
7) I am not intimidating - I'm easy to approach at any time.
8) I know what I am talking about - I am good at my own job.
9) I look for the reality within which a learner works.
10) I always focus on learner needs during a mentoring session.
11) A learner who does not get the point quickly doesn't irritate me.
12) I am an optimist.
13) I am encouraging.

14) I am always well prepared in advance.

15) I am a positive role model in terms of my own achievements.

16) I can help a learner believe in their potential.

17) I am open to new ideas.

18) I know when to introduce options, which may not have been considered.

19) I can challenge assumptions skilfully.

20) I am a positive person.

21) I possess great patience.

22) I am interested in people.

23) I am an active listener.

24) I am non-judgemental.

25) I feel comfortable about having my views challenged.

26) I am enthusiastic about mentoring.

27) I am very knowledgeable about developmental issues.

28) I am tolerant.

29) I don't expect a learner to be like me.

30) I am prepared to learn with the learner.

31) I can give feedback skilfully.

32) I can allow a learner the freedom and confidence to make mistakes.

33) I see my learners as equals.

34) I have sound judgement.

35) I am able to distance myself and maintain objectivity.

36) I am keen to allow learners to make their own decisions.

37) I keep in regular contact with those I mentor.

38) I take an interest in the individual learner, I value their views and what they say.

39) I am able to probe beyond the superficial.

40) I can provide the space for a learner to express their feelings.

41) I can draw out a learners' ideas and I'm willing to use them.

42) I have a true passion for developing others, and really believes in the value of development.

43) I can avoid the temptation to direct conversation back to myself and my issues and experiences.

44) I can challenge constructively and directly to get to the important aspect.

45) I won't just tell a learner what they want to hear.

46) I never appear keen to get a mentoring meeting over with and move on to the next thing.

47) I don't talk about my own achievements too much.

48) I have a genuine desire to empower.

49) I am responsive to my learner.

50) I always look for the positive in people

Are there any learning points from this?

(Andrew. Gibbons@lineone.net on www.trainingzone.co.uk/toolkits)

There should be learning points from this for mentors – a mentor must be actively involved, continually, in their own learning!

Motivation

As a trainer and people developer since 1990, many managers have complained to me that they are unable to and just cannot "motivate" their people.

Whilst ignoring the reality that motivation at work is more about the managers having to create the right conditions and to support their people; the answer to the perennial complaint of "I cannot motivate my people" can be actually be relatively easily found and applied.

This is therefore essentially what this section is all about. It will not only help managers to create the right conditions for motivating others, but it will also give many personal guidelines for improving our own personal performance.

Definitions of Motivation

What is "motivation"?

The following gives us some definitions:

- "Motives to Act"
- "Positive Valued Rewards"
- "Goal Directed Behaviour"
- "Rewarding the behaviour you want"
- "Getting People to do things, willingly and well"
- "Getting people to do what they want to do" (Using the carrot or calculative

approach), which is the opposite to manipulation, which is "getting people to do what we want" (The stick or coercive approach)

- "It is an essential aspect of performance which requires having competent people (with knowledge and skills) and committed people (with confidence and motivation)"

Being motivated is fundamentally about moving ourselves towards a goal. But is the motivating goal source internal or external, and which of these will determine the course of action? Additionally, is there a connection between internal/intrinsic motivation (where motivation is viewed as an "inside job" and set by oneself), and the external/extrinsic motivation (where motivation is seen as something "done to you" and set by others)?

There are, therefore, the following "differences" surrounding motivation:

Intrinsic motivation
- Self-generated rewards
- Inner drive from our personal infrastructure
- For example: how much fun am I having?
- It is what satisfies me

Extrinsic motivation
- Externally-generated rewards
- Outer environmental sources taken in by our external perceptions
- For example: what do I get from you?
- It is what you give me

Some observers see that all of motivation is intrinsic, as people need to engage their own will to act; however, this can be paradoxical, as some people will also first need the extrinsic motive.

In many cases, both internal and external motivation is involved at the same time, and the specific mix will vary depending on differences in circumstances in individuals and in external sources. Motivation is, therefore, variable and, like all variables, needs special management attention. Unfortunately, as we will soon discuss, too many managers take motivation as fixed, given and automatic, or they choose to just completely ignore it.

Some thoughts on Motivation:
"Effective motivation makes a difference."

"Fire on all cylinders, it is smoother and more efficient."

"There are more chrysalises than butterflies; your job is to encourage the chrysalis to hatch and to encourage the butterfly to fly."

"It is like getting a plant to bloom."

Motivation at Work

Clearly motivation in the workplace should be an essential topic for all leaders and managers, as there is a strong link between motivation and leadership/management and performance. However, the connections and route must be clear and in accordance with each individual's perception and values; they must see it, must want it and then, they will likely move to get it.

Additionally, as management can be seen as "getting things done though people," this fits in well with our above definition of motivation of "getting people to do things, willingly and well."

Management Styles

As we have already examined, what happens in many organisations is that managers and leaders will have developed, often unconsciously, a specific style or way of doing things.

1) Commanding style
- keeps control
- people are "held onto"
- judgemental
- "tells"
- see though a "pinhole"
- directive
- "push" approach

2) Coaching style
- lets people try

- people are given a "self release"
- non-judgemental
- "sells"
- sees the wider view
- supportive
- "pull" approach

3) Autocratic and aggressive

- drives and pushes people but is not a leader
- has a "single", "my" viewpoint
- one-way communicator
- demanding "do it my way, now"
- takes "fixed my way positions"
- a contest of will
- makes threats and applies pressure

4) Procrastinator and passive

- abdicates from taking decisions
- use group viewpoints
- indecisive and believes is always democratic
- "what do you all want to do, whenever"
- changes positions easily
- avoids any contest
- makes offers and yields to pressure

5) Charismatic and assertive

- pulls more than pushes
- two-way communicator
- people follow naturally, is a leader
- makes concessions, "I think this, what do we think"
- problem solves and explores interests
- partnership views and reasons
- looks for objective criteria and yields to principles not pressure

There are major differences in the styles, and these will have impacts on motivation; for example, those using a dominating style will motivate more by what Herzberg (1968) called negative KITA (this is American-speak for a 'kick in the ass'). KITA people will attempt to push, force and "use the stick" to get people to do things. Conversely, a charismatic approach will use more a positive "carrot" approach that pulls and attracts people to do things.

Managers should ask themselves which style/behaviours are being used and which are the best to use to motivate people.

People can become trapped in the judgement of others, and also become like the company of the people they meet and deal with. A manager's style can have important ramifications for staff retention and turnover.

Motivation at work: the reality
You can usually recognise the motivation in an organisation by the following:
- The appearances of premises, e.g. tidy or untidy
- The appearance of people, e.g. appropriate clothing
- The conduct of people, e.g. the "buzz," and showing respect for others
- The workflow, e.g. unhurried, appears organised

These aspects represent the "body language" of an organisation, those secret giveaway signals that give us reality from what we perceive.

Morale at work
The general atmosphere at work will affect the people working there. Poor morale at work will exist where:
- Management shows no interest in employees
- Work objectives are not understood
- Employees are given no feedback
- Employees feel that cannot influence management
- Favouritism is shown
- Rules are not fairly and equally applied
- There is little job satisfaction
- Managers do not know their people
- There is mainly destructive criticisms
- There is poor "team sprit"
- Poor performance is not dealt with
- Poor relationships are not dealt with
- Unacceptable behaviour is not dealt with
- Unacceptable absence is not dealt with

Clearly morale at work is improved by doing the opposite of the above, plus:
- Good and effective leadership
- More supportive than directive, management styles
- Self discipline
- Good communication
- Employees involvement in decisions
- Managers who know that management is just not about technical objective hard skills, but also involves subjective emotions and applying soft skills

Do managers have any idea about motivation?
Many managers seem to have no idea at all of what motivation is, or what is involved.

Consider the following evidence from surveys:

Managers perceived motivators of their employees, in order of importance	Employees own actual reported motivators, in order of importance
1. Salary	1. Interesting work
2. Bonus	2. Involvement in decisions
3. Holidays	3. Feedback
4. Retirement	4. Training
5. Other pay/perks	5. Respect
6. Interesting work	6. Salary
7. Involvement in decisions	7. Bonus
8. Feedback	8. Holidays
9. Training	9. Retirement
10. Respect	10. Other pay/perks

The conclusion from this evidence is plain and simple; management have completely the wrong perceptions on motivation.

People differ
Of course, people do differ, and looking at the life time stage perceptions, related to the environmental external influences, reveals the following differences that show people are shaped by the "age in which they lived."
- Those born before 1942, in times of recession and depression, are influenced more by loyalty and job security

- Those "Baby Boomers" born 1942-1965, in times that were idealistic and moralistic, are influenced more by money and freedom
- Those born 1966-1979, in times of both realism and cynicism, these so called "Generation X" people, are more influenced by independence and challenge
- "Generation Y" are those born post 1980 and are said to be more worldly, seeking variety and a better work-life balance, meaning a greater willingness to move around and job-switch

Such differences not withstanding, it is important to remember that the majority of employees are good members of society, pay their taxes, educate and bring up their children well and look to work hard to obtain a good lifestyle. All of these aspirations are not lost when employees come to work, and when at work, the majority of people will look for the following:

- Challenge
- Contact with other people
- Being respected
- Enjoyment
- Successful outcomes
- Career advancement
- Meeting deadlines and seeing results
- Money and other rewards
- Being empowered.

All of these aspects are well supported by motivational theory, as we shall now examine

Motivation Theory

As motivation is central to efficient and effective management, it has received much attention from academics, researchers and commentators. The following discussion represents the main theories, and as we will see later, they can have some useful and valid applications for providing motivation at work.

Theory "X" and Theory "Y"

This theory is based on the opposites of a manager's attitude. According to its originator, Douglas McGregor, you are either an "X" or a "Y" manager.

The Theory "X" manager believes that employees will:
- Hate work and prefer to do nothing

- Dislike responsibility
- Have no ambition and no ideas
- Be unable to solve problems
- Only work for the money
- Need to be totally controlled, driven and threatened
- Need an authority figure to make the decisions and who can then be blamed when things go wrong

Therefore, the Theory "X" manager believes the only way to motivate is by:
- Telling exactly what to do/when to do it and how to do it
- Providing close supervision
- Making all the decisions personally
- Allowing no participation
- Expecting only a minimum contribution

The Theory "Y" manager believes that employees will:
- Enjoy their work and need something to do in life
- Want to make a contribution
- Willingly accept responsibility
- Make decisions and solve problems
- Make Long-term plans
- Be achievers

Therefore, the Theory "Y" manager believes the way to motivate is by:
- Giving responsibility, delegating and involvement
- Inviting and listening to suggestions
- Developing trust and showing respect
- Rewarding by non-money methods

Clearly this is a stereotype model, where the reality, may well be found between the two extremes.

Maslow's hierarchy of needs

Maslow studied McGregor's Theory "Y" manager, but felt it ignored the requirement for people to have structure and certainty, which is found in Theory "X". Maslow saw that people strive to fulfil a variety of needs, as shown overleaf.

The lower level is basic needs, and are those that are satisfied first: to keep the physical body going and to keep us safe (the physiological and safety needs); followed by the higher and more complex emotional and social needs. Finally, there are the more abstract needs that are more individual based (the personal esteem and self needs). Examples of these levels follow:

Level	Need	Name	Examples
Five	Personal	Self actualisation	Self realisation, fulfilment, achievement
Four	Social	Self esteem	Status, prestige, success, appreciation
Three	Social	Social belonging	Love, affection, belonging, friendship, acceptance
Two	Basic, physiological	Safety	Order, stability, certainty, security, protection
One	Basic, physiological	Survival	Hunger, thirst, sleep, physical

As soon as one level is met or satisfied, then as priorities change, attention may be given by some individuals to the next level above. However, some individuals may be happy staying at their current level.

For some, if they are "threatened" at the level they are currently at, then they may think about what happens to their lower levels needs. For example, when I was once made redundant, this did not bring the thought of being unable to develop self-belief, but one of how to feed the family and pay the mortgage.

It should be appreciated that Maslow's model is essentially based on Western cultures, with individualistic and more self-centred Western societal norms. In Eastern cultures, the "self" is more limited and the social and collective needs take greater precedent.

Meanwhile the essential aspects of Maslow's hierarchy of needs include:

Needs/Incentives/Motives -> Drive -> Behaviour -> To Satisfy Personal, Social and Physical needs.

Once we are satisfied at our current level, then the capacity for reward reduces. We may then attempt to move up to the next level.

If we are threatened at our current level, we may drop down a level.

Needs
These have also been covered by other commentators, as shown in the following diagram:

Motivation Levels (Source: after Maslow, Covey)

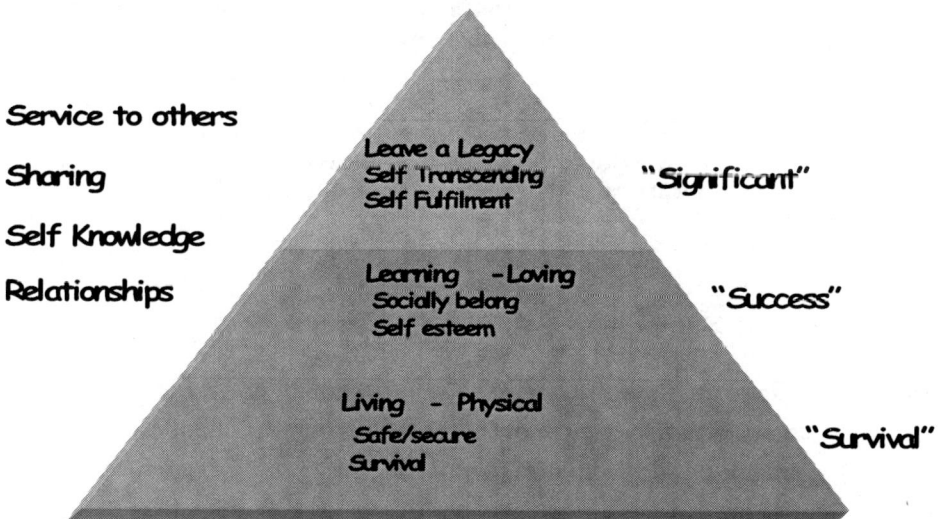

Service to others

Sharing

Self Knowledge

Relationships

Leave a Legacy
Self Transcending
Self Fulfilment
"Significant"

Learning – Loving
Socially belong
Self esteem
"Success"

Living – Physical
Safe/secure
Survival
"Survival"

Maslow's hierarchy	Covey levels	Emmett view
Higher levels		
Self-transcending (this was added by Maslow in his later work) Self-fulfilment	Spiritual "Leave a legacy"	Significant
Medium levels		
Self esteem Socially belong	Psychological "Learning & loving"	Success
Lower levels		
Security/safety Survival	Physical "Living"	Survival

Herzberg

First published as **"The Motivation to Work"** by Herzberg, Mausner and Snyderman in 1959, it is interesting to note that Herzberg's thinking was also published in the Harvard Business Review in 1968 as **"One more time: How do you motivate employees?"**

The theory covers two aspects, as follows:

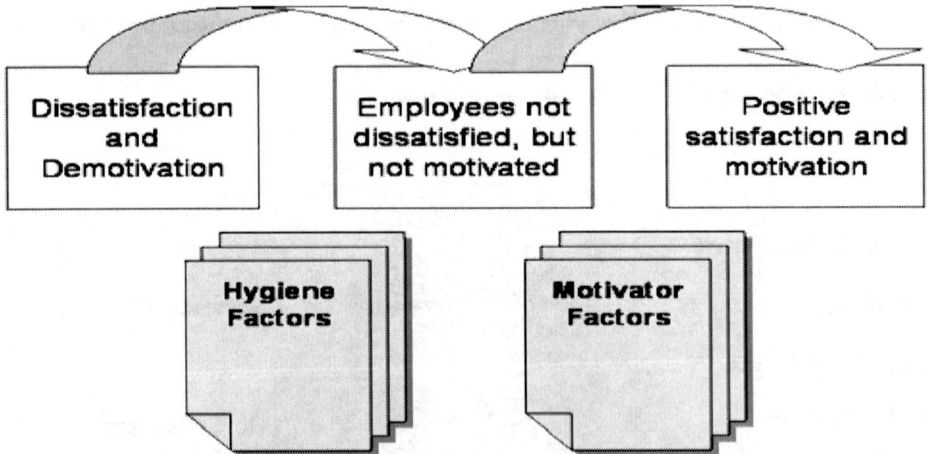

The **Hygiene factors** are those that have to be "to be cleaned up" and then be "maintained." They cause dissatisfaction for people and are as follows in order of importance:

- Organisation policy/administration
- Supervision
- Working conditions

- Personal relationships
- Salary/pay/benefits
- Job security/status

These are largely extrinsic to individuals.

They are usually a constant, independent of people's performance.

They are what people complain about, maybe, because they are bored.

If not "cleaned up" they are a continual source for "moans and groans."

The Motivating factors are those that have "to be promoted". They satisfy people and are as follows in order of importance:

- Achievement
- Recognition and being valued
- Work itself
- Responsibility
- Development/Growth

These are largely intrinsic in an individual. They are what you get through your own personal effort. Rewards need linking to performance, and these rewards could be money, but only if the relationship between the money reward and effort is a strong one. The key is to find out what it is that motivates the people you want to motivate.

Managing Motivationally

Importantly, Herzberg's theory works in practice. This knowledge comes from my personal experience as a manager up to board level, and also through feedback from those that have applied the principles. Additionally, I have also conducted a simple training exercise on Herzberg's principles with thousands of people of different nationalities and in varied cultures from Europe to Africa, and from the Middle to the Far East. The congruence in responses is amazing, with a wide recognition and agreement on just what it is that really motivates people.

Herzberg's motivating factors seem simple enough, but the "devil is in the detail." Fortunately, there are thousands of practical applications for each of these principles.

Motivation applications

Managers must appreciate that these principles must be promoted and supported. The "right" enabling culture is required to apply Herzberg's principles, so that this allows a person to motivate themselves; after all, you can take a horse to water, but you cannot make it drink.

Managers should also not forget, that the principles do already naturally exist, they are "intrinsic" and within the person. They want to get out, they just need unlocking; they are there inside, waiting to be used. Therefore, management promotion of the principles will then help to "push" people, towards being motivated.

This can be seen in those people, who when management does not create the right culture, can find "self motivation" without any management involvement. Meanwhile, some others may also find motivation, for example, with achievement from outside of the workplace, for example, a hobby – a person may be a great coach at a football club, which illustrates their leadership skills and self-motivation.

Motivation is not therefore, just about what you do for someone; it is more about what you allow them to do for themselves. What is critical here (and also why many managers complain they cannot motivate) is that management gives their people the key to unlock themselves.

"How?" I hear you ask? Examples of applying Herzberg's principles and incentives follows:

- Achievements. For example, targets, SMART objectives, interesting work, reward success, seeing results, completion of work
- Recognition. For example, create heroes, show appreciation, praise
- Work. For example, encourage participation, build pride
- Responsibility. For example, involvement, consensus management
- Development/Growth. For example, personal development, life long learning

A key aspect with Herzberg's principles and incentives is that, once they have been provided, they do not last as a motivator. Once we are satisfied; the incentive's impact is reduced needs to be changed.

It is important therefore to have the "motivation encore" ready that will go beyond the temporary effect provided by just one motivator. We shall return to this shortly, but before then, let's consider a connected aspect to having satisfied and motivated people.

The 'Dissatisfiers' (and the causes of stress)

It is my experience that when you talk with people about their perceptions of what causes them stress at work, most of the answers they give are actually Herzberg's other principle of hygiene factors. These are those factors at work that must "be cleaned up". They are sources of discontent, the creators of demotivation and the causes of dissatisfaction.

The Herzberg principles on the 'dissatisfiers' are as follows:

*   Policy/administration. For example, paperwork, rules and procedures and hearing comments like, "It is all done by the book here, but with a book that is out of touch with reality".
*   Relationships. For example, harassment, social facilities, shift patterns with comments like, "I do not have a proper work/life balance" and "I don't like my colleagues".
*   Supervision. For example, management styles with comments like, "I don't like my manager".
*   Working conditions. For example, heat, light, tidiness, safety equipment and comments like, "The working hours are too long".
*   Salary/pay/benefits. For example, "I don't earn enough money compared to others".
*   Status and Job security. For example, communication, job descriptions and comments like, "The work I do is not appreciated" and "They tell you nothing here".

Key points with the disincentives are that removing discontent does not bring motivation. It just removes the discontent and stops that particular source of "groaning and moaning." This is not to say of course that we should ignore this discontent, it needs to be removed. If it is not, then we are likely at some time to have a whiplash or bullwhip effect and a downward spiral where discontent grows into a problem = aggrieved = grievance = dissatisfaction = depression/stress = frustration = poor work = discipline procedures. This is not a good place to be, either for the individuals concerned, the manager or for the organisation. Indeed, a workforce that is dissatisfied will effectively damage both the individuals and the organisation. This is a depressing reality for many organisations, as shown below:

Reduced	Increased
Quality of work	Absenteeism
Work performance	Wasted time on breaks and private tasks

Reduced	Increased
Willingness of people	Gossip and grievances
Attention and interest	Discipline procedures
Positive organisation culture	"Playing the system"
Creativity	Negative compliance
Job satisfaction	Bureaucratic controls
Direction	Rule breaking
Team spirit	"Them and us"
Feedback	Unacceptable behaviour

Too much emphasis by organisations on removing the hygiene discontent factors only removes the source of discontent, it does not bring motivation. Money will be better spent on promoting the motivators.

Motivation and Money

It will have been seen from the above principles for satisfiers and dissatisfiers that money appears in the dissatisfiers. Whilst of course, money may be used with the motivating principles of achievement and recognition to give satisfaction, money in itself is not a motivator; money is a means to an end, not an end in itself.

This flies in the face of those managers who say that the only way to motivate someone is via the pay packet. The main problem with this, as explained earlier, is that the motivators once provided, do not last and you have to look for the encore. Additionally, managers will never have a bottomless pit of money to use when necessary, and they just cannot keep throwing money at people to motivate them.

Looking beyond financial motivation and understanding people's attitudes to money, and the things that motivate them, can only help both managers and their staff; managers need to be aware of this and not just assume that cash is the best way to drive performance.

Indeed, the 2004 UK study, **"Motivation Matters"** conducted by the Chartered Management Institute and Adecco, found that achievement (once again) and a sense of purpose at work were the two highest scorers. Performance-related rewards were not cited by many as a motivator.

Once again, proof that it is the intrinsic rewards of work, such as achievement, challenge and a sense of purpose, which really motivate.

Clearly, this is not to say that the "correct" pay rewards are not required; correct pay rewards are indeed a pre-requisite for many people at work, and are also for many people one of the necessary conditions for having to go to work.

Managers and improving motivation at work

A summary follows of the important principles for managers to use:

- "Know your people" as individuals, especially by looking for what is right about them
- Know how your people differ from each other
- Appreciate that differences in people can be interesting
- Some people will need more direction and guidance than others
- Seeing things from another's perspective can be useful
- Do not automatically censor ideas because they don't fit with your own
- Ensure you are motivated yourself
- Think about the people-related aspects in all decisions
- Think first before "jumping in." (This can prevent later embarrassment)
- List as many ideas to motivate that you can
- Spend time with your people and take time to introduce changes
- Evaluate and monitor results
- Ring the changes regularly
- Remove the sources of discontent

Implementing motivation will also require a manager to have some positive habits themselves. "If it is to be, then it is down to me" is good maxim to follow; after all, leaders must set the example for people to follow.

Some case studies follow to illustrate some of the practical aspects on applying motivation:

Case Study: Warehousing

To indicate a practical application of motivation I look at operatives in a warehouse environment, this is the context, but it is one that also has much wider application.

Warehouse Operatives are often unanimous in what they used to like and dislike about their work, for example:

They like being:

- site based
- part of a team with communication "crack" and social activity
- able to have some control on the daily work load

They dislike:

- Not having career prospects
- Low status of the job
- Remuneration

In warehousing operations, the core personnel are at the same place of work all the time and are therefore a "collective" working together work force. Face-to-face management contact is therefore possible at any time during working hours and applying motivation principles can involve the following:

Incentives are "to be promoted" to increase the sources for motivation.

- Achievements. As examples: stressing the importance of the work done and how this fits into customer/consumer requirements; increase the job status/importance.
- Recognition. As examples: appreciation of overcoming daily difficulties with changing demand patterns; tackling known internal delays ; praise and criticise fairly; what do the customers say; how the business promotes and markets itself and what the operatives can do to help on this; creating a supportive culture
- Responsibility. As examples: involvement in decisions that affect the job; involving operatives in what has been done over internal delays
- Advancement/Growth. As examples: personal development plans; moves into management; opportunities for advancement

Disincentives are "to be cleaned up" so that the sources of discontent are removed, for example:

- Policy/administration. As examples: removing unnecessary paperwork, rules and procedures; clarity in rules and procedures
- Supervision. As examples: improving management styles and communication
- Working conditions. As examples: user friendly equipment, fair work allowances, shared workloads

- Personal Relationships. As examples: tackling un-social hour shift patterns, recognising personal needs and making adjustments; tackling negative "grapevines" by creating opposite positive cultures
- Salary/pay/benefits. As examples: salaried pay with holiday and sickness benefits; demonstrated fair pay, terms and conditions
- Job security. For example, communication on developments

These examples are not meant to be extensive but are meant to illustrate what can be done by applying the simple principles identified by Herzberg. There are many different and varied applications for each principle; there really is no excuse for using single ways of motivating. Having the "encore ready" requires thinking and thoughtful management who really do want, to get the best from their people. It requires an approach that sponsors and supports and that encourages and enables. There is just no room here for a totally command and control management style.

From: **Excellence in Warehouse Management,** Emmett, 2005

Case Study: Retailing

Survey Results
- 94 per cent of staff "love" working there
- Absence is less than 2 per cent (national average is 4/5 per cent)

Management Challenge is seen as:
- To make work fun
- If people enjoy work ,then they do it better
- Be serious about staff satisfaction
- All director's spend 2 months per year on the shop floor

Staff Rewards include:
- Free holidays
- Suggestion scheme. Each suggestion received gets £25, every three months the best two, get more money.
- Give many small prizes, use good ideas and give back a proportion of the benefit.
- Training, minimum twice a year
- Five year club (the backbone of employees) get a meal "event" every year
- Ten year club get a £500 cheque

- Hardship fund, one per cent of profit
- Only ever promote from within

Comments

- "Keep coming up with new perks"
- "People always are like the organisation, they want something new and better"

Business Age, February 1999

The "final" personal motivation

The only motivation that will ever last, is one that satisfies a core internally held value/belief, for example "I will live life to the full".

Satisfying a core belief will give us an internal drive, which has an irresistible momentum that will connect to the way we think and behave.

What we choose to believe in is, after all, up to us. The only control we really have is the choices that we make.

The Motivation Model

Finally for managers, the following model will provide a summary and hopefully sponsor action.

1) Step one. Expect the best from your people

- Believe people want to do a good job
- Tell people what a good job is and the outcomes that are expected
- Involve people in mutually agreed SMART objectives to achieve these expected outcomes. (SMART = simple/specific – measurable – achievable/attainable - realistic - time bound)
- Recognise that people are different, so never assume your way is the best or the only way; expect the best, from your people.

2) Step two. Eliminate barriers to "being the best"

- Check out all the disincentives, remove/improve as appropriate
- Have non-bureaucratic rules and procedures to ensure equality and fairness

- Check out all the incentives, apply as appropriate
- Have interesting and meaningful work
- Ensure people have the appropriate resources to do the job as required
- Be prepared to be flexible and if necessary, get out of the way
- Communicate, communicate, communicate

3) Step three. Encourage people to "be the best"
- Recognise good work
- Give feedback and support
- Appraise fairly and correctly
- Lead by example and be motivated yourself
- Be accessible, stay close to people, ask and listen for feedback
- Reward with good pay, promotions, personal loyalty

And finally in this section on motivation, the following shows some simple "one-liner's" that illustrate the individual and personal aspects of motivation.

"You are what you think."
"You get what you expect."
"The impossible is what no one can do, until someone does."
"See yourself as a winner."
"Dream big dreams."
"Choose to be what you love."

Authority/delegation and empowerment

As already mentioned, for a leader or manager to be effective, they have to spread and pass on their vision through other people, the "followers". As a leader leads from the front, they cannot be everywhere at the same time, and are unable to do everything themselves. They will need to engage other people, who must have the mandate and authority to act in the leaders' name.

It can be noted that, whilst empowerment is thought by many to be a newly invented 1990s management tool, it has existed and been practiced by effective leaders for centuries; empowerment simply means to give power.

Understanding Power and Authority

Power is having the authority to act, and involves control, like that practiced by a captain in a football game. Authority, though, has varied strands:

- Coercive authority is the so-called "naked use of power" where people are forced to do things. It is generally an un-sustainable source of authority, as it causes resentment and divisions. It will bring a culture of fear and blame in the followers.
- Conferred authority is that held by someone in a position, for example as shown by a sergeant's stripes, where the visible authority held will have been given by the hierarchy above.
- Legitimate authority is that recognised by others as being genuine and acceptable, as it means something to them. They will usually have respect for authority that has been earned in this way.
- Knowledge authority comes from "knowledge is power", or when someone is recognised as an authority on a subject.
- Charismatic authority is that held by a person because of their "persona".

Whilst two of these types of authorities can be forced or given to a person (such as with coercive and conferred authority), the others have to be developed and/or earned by the individual concerned.

Accountability, authority and responsibility

These three words often get confused, when in fact they each have specific individual and related meanings.

- Accountability is having the full responsibility for actions, and is usually associated with some form of measurement, like a CEO where, "the buck stops here."
- Responsibility can be either personal/individual or corporate/collective, and represents a specific duty, obligation or a burden. Essentially therefore, it is all about having the ability or authority to do something, or to decide on one's own to do something.
- Authority represents having control, and being able to influence what happens.

Therefore, a manager can be responsible for a particular department, and has accountability to his superior; hopefully, he will also have the conferred authority and legitimate authority from that superior.

Accountability and responsibility are also used in the RACI template, a method of clarifying and documenting the person who will do something, and when it will be done. The following template is completed, and then those responsible "sign up":

The RACI Template

Task	Responsible	Accountable	Consulted	Informed

Key:

Task = what has to be done?

Responsible = who will do it and make it happen?

Accountable = who is ultimately accountable?

Consulted = who is to be consulted? E.g. experts, stakeholders etc

Informed = who is to know on progress or outcomes?

Understanding Empowerment

Empowerment gives people a sense of ownership, and works towards an assertive and coaching style of management.

Empowerment is not about "dumping" or delegating and walking away. Telling someone initially that "you are empowered so get on with it" is simply not good enough.

Empowerment represents "a whole way of life" and should not be entered into without thought and consideration, and the associated consequences of taking such an approach.

Empowerment should totally affect the whole organisation, as it can be seen as the sum of all of the individual and team empowerment, that all flows together. This will impact on Culture, Values and Job Design of the organisation as follows:

1) The Culture
- Core values with mission statements providing guidance
- Commitment, co-ordination, and commitment via shared goals, values, and traditions
- Power and decision-making devolved throughout organisation
- Mutual influence systems (participative)
- A culture of pride that will tap peoples' problem solving skills where people are seen as the greatest asset
- Individuals are trusted
- Human resource issues are a primary concern in strategic business decisions
- An open flexible system, stressing adaptability
- An external orientation, market led, close to the customer and the environment.

2) The Values
- People are an asset to be developed and a major stakeholder in the organisation
- People are unique, talented flexible resources
- People want to take pride in their work and to be productive
- People have a need for recognition, enhanced self-image, and influence on the decisions affecting their workspace
- Management empowers workers to participate in decisions and contribute to personal and organisational growth

3) Job Design
- Grouped tasks requiring multiple broad skills
- A degree of self determination
- Combined doing and thinking, everyone's ideas contribute to the organisation
- Flexible job descriptions
- Everyone is responsible for quality
- Individuals are encouraged to take decisions and to solve problems

(From: **ACAS Effective Organisations Booklet**)

Understanding Delegation
Clearly, letting all of the people go with supported delegation (or empowerment) can become very embracing in a total business and organisational setting. Delegating however, which is between individuals, is often seen as a difficult thing to do by individual leaders and managers, for example:

"They will take my job"
"How do you do it effectively?"
" Do not know what to delegate"
"It will not be done to my high standards"
" It is quicker to do it myself"
"My people are not capable"
"They are all too busy"
"I will have nothing to do"

These comments represent concerns and doubts, and impacts for the person who is delegating and also to the person who is being delegated to. Clearly however, to make progress, a leader cannot do it all themselves, and as previously noted, they must "pass it on." Indeed, it has been said that a leader should always be looking out for their replacements. Accordingly, the following is of value as a template for delegation.

Checklist: Delegating: The Five Step Process

1. Analyse the task
- What cannot you complete on your own…mark these for delegation
- Anything around in a "development stage," that can be delegated for longer-term completion?
- Will it give some challenge, or, are you "just" delegating?
- Who else needs to be informed?
- How will you give the authority and responsibility?
- Can you link delegating to coaching and development?

2. Analyse the person
- Who is a most suitable candidate?
- What is their workload?
- Do they have the resources, knowledge, and skills to do it?
- Will it dovetail into their work?
- What is in it for them (WIIFM)?
- Will it help in their development, give then greater visibility and provide a coaching opportunity?
- Stretch, but do not break people, it can be motivational, but if handled wrongly, then it is stressful and threatening!

3. Agree how to monitor
- Involve the person concerned in setting this up
- Agree goals and targets for what you want them to achieve
- Consider breaking the task down into stages
- Be clear and test understanding about what is being delegated and what is not
- Define clearly the success criteria and what the end result looks like
- Agree times to review progress

4. Set the climate for delegation
- Listen to ideas and look for fresh perspectives
- Keep communication, and your availability, open at all times
- Build in praise and feedback along the way
- Do not interfere between review periods; build trust
- Build in coaching and development, where necessary

5. Review progress
- Review on a regular basis
- Provide support and guidance
- Ask searching questions so that they "think it through"
- Do not provide all the answers
- When completed, review against the success criteria originally determined
- Review the learning and any new skill needs
- Get feedback on your role and reflect how you could improve

Teams

Teams represent a fantastic opportunity for many performance improvements, but they will not fit every circumstance. For example, they are not suited for committee/group working where there is no unified goal, or in any circumstances when an individual's specialised talent can do the job alone.

However in many cases, improving team performance brings a quantum leap forward, providing of course that the introduction of team playing is introduced and is led and managed appropriately.

Definition of a team

Teams and groups are not therefore the same, so what it is a team? The following is one definition:

"Teams are a small number of people, who have a complimentary contribution with mutual accountability and a common shared and accepted goal; this goal is the reason for the team".

The following amplifies the above definition:

"The team comes before individuals"
"Individual success is dependent on others"
"We work out problems together and individual blame is banished"
"Where the whole is more than the sum of the parts"
"Teams require individuals to connect to something bigger than them"
"Where you need to be awake, aware and in tune with others"
"United we stand but divided we fall"
"There is none of us as strong as all of us"

Teams mean success

Teams can be a great source for achieving success. Consider the following Case Study on a sports team; sports teams give many good analogies for workplace teams:

Case Study: Sports Teams

The British Lions rugby team of 1997 saw their success had come from:
- Inspired leadership
- Clear goal
- Meticulous planning
- Picking the right players
- Clear communication
- Excellent team spirit
- Committed team member
- A learning culture
- Desire and passion
- Focus on results
- Shared values
- Self and team belief

- Confidence in ability
- Pride
- Celebrate success

Teams blend together a collection of individuals, who achieve collectively far more than a group of individuals could.

When you find the word 'team' being used, it is always useful to check that it conforms to the team definition of:
- Common/shared goals
- Small number of people
- The goal is the "performance purpose"
- Complementary contributions
- Mutual accountability

Ineffective teams

As we will soon discover, teams require special skills in the blending, building and the leading of individuals. When these are not present, the following problems create an ineffective team:

- High level of moaning and complaining
- Lack of respect for the team leader
- High level of sickness/absence
- Some people in the team refusing to speak to each other
- Collaboration is avoided
- Team meetings are brief and infrequent
- People rarely say what they really feel about each other
- The quality of work suffers

Effective teams

A key principle for effective team working is for all to accept that there is a need to build and develop on individual strengths, and recognise and manage the weaknesses. Teams most definitely require a right blend of unique strengths. We do not want everyone to be the same, for example a football team does not have eleven goalkeepers. Diversity in teams therefore represents strength. This means accepting that:
- Some people are more orientated to planning, organising process and methods

- Some are more towards meeting deadlines
- Some are more directive
- Some are more creative and thoughtful
- Some are more supportive
- Some are "utility players" and flexible

Individual people all have different strengths. Recognising these differences and then blending them all together in a unique mix, is at the heart of effective team building; as has been said, "If we were all the same, then whilst we would go fast in one direction, we would leave many casualties en route."

"The task of management is to make people capable of joint performance, to make their strengths effective and their weaknesses irrelevant".
– Peter Drucker

Team Roles

Successful teams have a balanced set of team roles, and all of the following roles are needed in an effective team. In the team, each individual may have one to three team roles, and each role has its own strengths and weaknesses. Team roles have been well identified by the work of Belbin. The following eight roles were noted in his early work, with the orientations and examples, being mine.

Action skills orientation:

Shaper
- Forceful and makes things happen
- Interested in results
- Looks for a pattern, challenges, pressurises
- Has a compulsive drive
- Impulsive and dynamic
- Sometimes edgy, highly strung and impatient
- Example: Sir Alex Ferguson (Manchester United FC Manager)

Organisation Worker/implementer
- Organiser, hard-working and reliable
- Converts plans into tasks
- Tackles jobs that need doing

- Concerned with the feasible
- Sympathetic and methodical
- Can lack flexibility
- Example: John Prescott (a former Deputy PM)

Complete Finisher
- Painstaking, pedantic and conscientious
- Follows through and meets deadlines
- Impatient of slapdash
- Can be over-anxious
- Permanent sense of urgency
- Example: Bill Gates (Microsoft)

People skills orientation:

Resource Investigator
- Communicative, enthusiastic and gregarious
- Explores new opportunities
- Has masses of contacts
- Flourishes under pressure
- Relaxed and sociable
- Prone to laziness, loses interest quickly after the initial "buzz"
- Over-optimistic
- Example: Del Boy (**"Only Fools and Horses"** TV character)

Chair Person/Coordinator
- Mature and confident
- Focuses on what people do best
- Good at summing up, co-ordinating
- Talks easily but a good listener
- Self controlled and commanding
- Dominant but not domineering
- Can be bossy
- Example: Michael Parkinson (Chat show TV host)

Team Worker
- Responsive, sympathetic and understanding

- Builds on the ideas of others
- Promotes unity and harmony
- Leads from behind
- Can be indecisive
- Dislikes friction & confrontation
- Example: Terry Wogan (Radio presenter)

Thinking and Analysis skills orientation:

Plant/innovator
- Creative, produces a lot of ideas
- Imaginative and original
- Fascinated by the unorthodox
- Forthright and independent
- Problem solver
- Can be over-sensitive, impatient, poor at communicating
- Not a people manager
- Example: John Cleese (Comedian and Film Star)

Monitor/Evaluator
- Analytical, good judge of proposals, discerning
- Strategic, analyses and monitors
- Prudent and reflective
- Hard-headed and unemotional
- Spots flaws in plans and sees all options
- Can be over-critical and uninspiring
- Lacks drive
- Example: Gordon Brown (Former Prime Minister)

These 8 roles were subsequently slightly revised and the following is the latest Belbin version, from <http://www.belbin.com>

Teams Role	Contribution	Allowable Weaknesses
Plant	Creative, imaginative, unorthodox. Solves difficult problems.	Ignores incidentals. Too preoccupied to communicate effectively.
Resource investigator	Extrovert, enthusiastic, communicative. Explores opportunities. Develops contacts.	Over-optimistic. Lose s interest once initial enthusiasm has passed.
Co-ordinator	Mature, confident, a good chairperson. Clarifies goals, promotes decision-making, delegates well.	Can be seen as manipulative. Offloads personal work.
Shaper	Challenging, dynamic, thrives on pressure. The drive and courage to overcome obstacles.	Prone to provocation. Offends people's feelings.
Monitor evaluator	Sober, strategic and discerning. Sees all options. Judges accurately.	Lacks drive and ability to inspire others.
Teamworker	Co-operative, mild, perceptive and diplomatic. Listens, builds, averts friction.	Indecisive in crunch situations.
Implementer	Disciplined, reliable, conservative and efficient. Turns ideas into practical actions.	Somewhat inflexible. Slow to respond to new possibilities.
Completer Finisher	Painstaking, conscientious, anxious. Searches out errors and omissions. Delivers on time.	Inclined to worry unduly. Reluctant to delegate
Specialist	Single – minded, self – starting, dedicated. Provides knowledge and skills in rare supply.	Contributes on only a narrow front. Dwells on technicalities.

Team Culture

Culture is "the way we do things around here" and it is therefore important to test how well the team culture is working. For example, is the team climate sunny or stormy? The following aspects can be noted:

Sunny	Stormy
People take initiative	People feel boxed in
Team work flourishes	Friction and lack of appreciation between team members
People understand their contribution	People have little understanding of there role
Clear direction	Conflicting goals

Good communication	Mixed messages
Even workload allowing for individual skills/abilities	Work is spread unevenly
Team knows others skills/abilities	Little understanding of what makes the team tick
Work environment conductive to good performance	Physical environment prevents good performance

Ways to improve the culture climate are as follows:

- Communicate regularly and ask, what people think about their work and what do they want to do?
- Create a shared vision, so that everyone knows where they are going
- Improve the physical environment
- Use ideas from the team to make improvements to the work
- Use people playing to their strengths; consider people's skills and aspirations and allocate work accordingly

Understanding the Team Culture

Another view on testing and seeing how the team culture is working, is to see which of the following applies:

Aspect	Closed culture	Part open culture	Open culture
Goals	Are announced	Communicated	Agreed on
Information	A status symbol	Traded	In abundance
Motivation	Manipulative	Based on needs of individual staff	Generated together
Decisions	From above	Partly delegated	Made at the team level
Mistakes	Made by staff	Take responsibility	Are allowed
Conflicts	Unwelcome	Are mastered	Chances for innovation
Control	From above	Is partly delegated	Self control

An open culture in teams works, and to summarise, this is one where:

- Goals are clear and agreed on between team members
- Information is in abundance
- Motivation is generated within the team
- Decisions are made at the team level

- Mistakes are allowed, as learning from mistakes is seen as being valuable
- Conflicts are seen as positive and providing a chance for innovation
- Self controlled within the team

The following case study shows cultural behaviour change in a retail organisation.

Case Study: Retailer

The "Problem"
- Not customer focused
- Low quality product
- Family focus ownership of a PLC

The Plan used was:
- Establish a mission statement, e.g. on value for money, customer service, friendly environment in stores
- Establish a set of values, e.g. trust, respect, communication
- Planned the change programme, e.g., current and future cultures identified
- Worked on the top managers' behavioural style, e.g. less "tell"
- Work on the mid managers behavioural style, e.g. teams, interactions
- Worked on branch managers'/department managers' behaviour style, e.g. customer service

Other initiatives were:
- Focus groups, internal cross-functional, external on customer service
- Annual conference
- Monthly area meetings
- Weekly trading meetings

(From: **Management Skills and Development,** August 1999)

Building Teams

As already noted, teams involve a small number of people who have a common shared and accepted goal. The goal is the "performance purpose" and the team players have a complimentary contribution with mutual accountability.

Teams are not a universal "cure all" for everything. For example, they are not suitable when creativity is needed, using an individual's specialised talent, and where there is committee/group working with no unified common goal.

Effective teams will communicate and understand each other, whilst also motivating and supporting each other. The behaviours needed involve a blended mix of "togetherness" and "self". Involvement and commitment requires openness, sometimes by confrontation using honesty and truthfulness in a supporting and trusting way.

A key principle with teams is they require the right blending of unique individual strengths. These strengths and weaknesses were explained in the earlier discussed team roles. It is also very important to be able to build and develop on strengths, and to recognise and manage weaknesses. Regrettably, often the reverse is the practice, and unfortunately, some leaders/managers will concentrate more on peoples' weaknesses and leave them wondering what their strengths are. Such leaders/managers are simply getting the praise/criticise balance wrong. They also often create more serious consequences and ramifications.

"There is probably nothing worse in business than to work for a boss who doesn't want you to win".
– Jack Welsh

We will never ever build grow and develop by concentrating on weaknesses; a house cannot be built on weak foundations. We therefore need to build on strengths and not on weakness. This also involves recognising that differences and diversity amongst individual people can be strength. Some people are better at planning, some are better in organising process and methods, some are better able to meet deadlines, some to be directive, or be creative and thoughtful, or are better being supportive or to be more "utility players" and flexible. We need differences and variations in people.

"In manufacturing we try to stamp out variances; with people variance is everything."
– Jack Welch

Putting together a collection of individuals does not make a team. It requires dedicated hard work, to ensure that the right mix and blend is found. In building teams, the following stages are involved. A team coming together will need to pass through all of the following stages in order to become effective.

Stage 1 – Forming includes these feelings:

- Excitement, anticipation and optimism
- Pride in being selected for the project
- Initial, tentative attachment to the team
- Suspicion, fear and or anxiety about the job ahead

And these behaviours:

- Attempts to define the task and decide how it will be accomplished
- Attempts to determine acceptable group behaviour and how to deal with group problems
- Decisions on what information needs to be gathered
- Discussions of symptoms or problems not relevant to the task
- Difficulty in identifying relevant problems
- Complaints about the organisation and barriers to the task

Stage 2 – Storming includes these feelings

- Resistance to the task and to quality improvement approaches different from what each individual member is comfortable using
- Sharp fluctuations in attitude about the team and the projects chance of success

And these behaviours:

- Arguing among members even when they agree on the real issue Defensiveness and competition; factions choosing sides
- Questioning the wisdom of those who selected this project and appointed the other members of the team
- Establishing unrealistic goals; concern about excessive work
- A perceived pecking order; disunity, increased tension and perhaps jealousy

Stage 3 – Norming includes these feelings

- A new ability to express criticism constructively
- Acceptance of membership in the team
- Relief that it seems everything is going to work out

And these behaviours

- An attempt to achieve harmony by avoiding conflict
- More friendliness, confiding in each other and sharing of personal problems
- Discussing the team's dynamics

- A sense of team cohesion, a common spirit and goals
- Establishing and maintaining team ground rules and boundaries

Stage 4 – Performing includes these feelings
- Having insights into personal and group processes
- A better understanding of each others strengths and weakness
- Satisfaction at the team's progress

And these behaviours:
- Constructive self change
- Ability to prevent or work through group problems
- Close attachment to the team

Stage 5 – Mourning includes these feelings
- Sense of loss and sadness
- Wondering what happens next

And these behaviours:
- High and lows emotions
- Leaving the past and going forward or
- Staying "locked into" the past

There is much in these stages about how people respond and relate to each other. As explained earlier, our feelings come out of attitudes, which in turn comes from beliefs and values, and our behaviour is then visible from our actions.

As a team coming together will need to pass through the above stages before becoming effective, often their progress will be delayed or at worst, not go beyond the storming stage.

What is also important to realise here, is that each stage is a part of the process in forming effective teams, and the team will only move forward once each stage has been accepted and dealt with.

Crucially, the stages also show how individual feelings and behaviours need to change before finally reaching the performing stage.

Hopefully, then, the performing stage continues. However this may change, for example, if team members leave and new members are inducted. The whole process from forming therefore starts again.

When a team eventually disbands, the mourning stage takes place - another change process to be managed.

Effective teams

It requires continual effort to maintain effective teams, and the above stages also show that this is unlikely to happen by chance. Action is needed by leaders and managers to build effective teams; this includes the following:

- Selecting the right mix of people
- Determining the team vision and objectives
- Communicating and understanding each other
- Motivating and supporting each other
- Rewarding and rejoicing in good performance
- Reviewing team performance, jointly and regularly

Teamwork requires various skills from team members:

- Listening
- Supporting
- Trusting
- Valuing others contributions and ideas
- Giving the benefit of any doubt
- Recognising peoples uniqueness
- Accepting fully the team view
- Openness and challenge/confrontation
- Centred leadership

In turn, these skills will require team members to have behaviour that recognises the following:

- A blended "mix" and "giving up of self"
- Involvement and commitment
- Openness and confrontation
- Honesty and truthfulness

- Supporting and trusting
- Developing and mediating
- Socialising

And finally here, we should never forget that all organisations are fundamentally about people coming together into groups that must be organised into teams.

Groups of individuals will rarely be effective; unfortunately I have seen organisations which, whilst using the "team" word in job titles and procedures, are in reality merely a collection of individuals, working in groups with ineffective working practices and poor relationships, often along with blame culture attributes.

"The business enterprise is a system of the highest order; a system whose parts are human beings contributing voluntarily of their knowledge, skill and dedication to a joint venture"
– Peter Drucker

Checklist: Overall Team Review and Monitor

Objective:
- Does the team clearly understand and accept?
- Are the goals clear and agreed?

Standards:
- Does the team know what standards of performance are expected?

Size:
- Is the size correct?

Team members and roles:
- Are the right individuals together?
- Are roles clear and accepted?

Team spirit:
- What are the opportunities for teamwork in jobs?
- Do pay and bonus help or hinder team spirit?
- Are interpersonal relationships positive?

Discipline:
- Are rules reasonable?
- Are they fair and impartially enforced?

Grievances:
- Are they dealt with promptly?

- Are matters which may disrupt the team dealt with?

Consultation:

- Is it genuine?
- Are ideas and suggestions encouraged?

Briefing:

- Is it regular?
- Does it cover current progress and future?

Support:

- Do leaders and managers represent and support the team when talking to other individuals when the team is apart?

5: Managing Finance

Finance is a central aspect in business (and economies) and covers the management of money that has been generated by an organisation's business activity (where a business is an occupation for a livelihood).

Finance is connected with capital (money and profits) and capital is in turn, connected to the marketplace that involves selling and buying. Next, we have the connection to market economics that is concerned with customers, sales and the exchange of money.

Understanding Profit, Cash & Risk

There are several ways in which we could break down the activity of managing finance within an organisation. However, we find the simplest way is to break it down between the following:

- Profit; the Income less Expenditure
- Cash; Receipts less Payments
- Risk

Every decision and transaction should be considered in terms of its impact on profit, cash and risk. For example, when a firm makes a sale but gives credit to a customer, it can record a profit in the current month; however it may have to wait another month to receive payment, and there is always a chance the customer may not pay up.

Many people are, however, confused by the difference between profit and cash; the following should help:
- Profit is all about measuring what was earned in a period and the resources consumed (or costs) in that period.
- Cash (or cash flow) is the physical receipt and payment of cash.
- Profits may differ from cash flow as a profitable organisation may run out of cash and therefore fail, however, a loss-making organisation may still be able to manage its cash and survive.

Profit is a fundamental measure of performance over a period; it is a measure of our earnings, less, the cost of the resources consumed. To manage profit means understanding cost and income, where income will be based on the value delivered to customers.

Organisations may try to increase profits by cutting costs, but they should never destroy the value supplied; as Oscar Wilde said "a cynic is someone who knows the price (or cost) of everything and the value of nothing".

Therefore, to manage profit you must know (or understand) the cost of everything and the value (to the customer) of everything. So in times of cost pressures, the rule is to look at every cost saving measure and consider its impact on customers and what is important to them. You can also ask yourself if a cost "adds value" if it does not, then there may be a potential saving.

Organisations take risks, however risk should be proportional to the return. For example, we might be considering switching one of our reliable suppliers to a cheaper source, but what will be the risks of things going wrong with this alternative?

Management Accounting v Financial Accounting

Accounting is often classified as either "Financial Accounting" or "Management Accounting".

Management accounts are the internal reports and information used to manage an organisation. However, there is no legal requirement to produce these accounts but then organisations do need to ensure good governance and control, therefore most organisations do produce monthly accounts and department cost statements which are compared against a budget (which is a forecast in financial terms).

Financial accounts are the accounts produced for use outside the organisation and for shareholders. The statutory disclosure requirements do differ around the world; indeed, some forms of organisations such as sole traders and partnership, often have no requirement to produced published accounts.

In the UK from the website http://www.companieshouse.gov.uk/, for the price of a one pound, it is possible to download the accounts of any British company. Major quoted organisations will also have their accounts available on-line free of charge and here a search for the company name with the addition of "investor relations" will usually work. The regulation of financial statements is becoming harmonised around the world with the creation of International Financial Reporting Standards (IFRS). The accounting system used around the world has been in existence for over 500 years; however it has evolved in recent times and since the 1970s has been added to with ever increasingly complex rules in the form of "accounting standards". Meanwhile, the key concepts and conventions behind the accounts are however quite simple and the key concepts are:

- Accruals or Matching Concept is where the income should be matched to expenditure for a given period.
- Prudence concept does not recognise profits until goods or services have been delivered. However, losses are recognised as soon as they are known. However it can be noted that there may be some question about when a service is delivered.
- Consistency; accounting is consistent.
- Going Concern; Accounts are prepared assuming the organisation is an ongoing entity.

The key Financial Statements

These are as follows:

- Profit & Loss Account (Called the Income Statement under IFRS)
- Balance Sheet
- Cash Flow Statement

The Profit and Loss account is the primary measure of performance for most organisations (this applies to those organisations who seek to make shareholder wealth through making a profit). The profit and loss account covers a period of time, for example within the published accounts this is a year, and within the management accounts, it is typically a month. The profit and loss account is income less expenditure; where the income is the income earned in a period; this may be different from the cash received in a period.

Balance Sheet: Many people find the Balance Sheet the most confusing of the three financial statements; however it is merely a list of an organisation's assets and liabilities on a day. **Assets** consist of:

- Fixed Assets (Now termed "Non Current Assets" under IFRS)
- Current Assets

The Fixed Assets are those which give a long-term benefit and typically are land, plant, building and equipment. They can also be intangible fixed assets such as brands, patents, rights and goodwill; goodwill arises when a company acquires another organisation and pays more for the organisation than the "fair value" of the assets.

The Current Assets are short-term assets and are made up of:

- Stock (or Inventory)
- Debtors (or accounts receivable), this is money owed to the organisation, typically from customers
- Cash

The liabilities of an organisation are similarly split between short-term (Current Liabilities) and long-term (Non-current Liabilities). The main current liability is typically the trade creditors (Accounts payable); this being money owed to suppliers. The main long-term liability is long-term loans.

The total of the assets, less the liabilities is known as the Net Assets. The total of the net assets balances with the shareholders funds; in other words, shareholders ultimately own all the net assets. The shareholders funds is made up of money invested by shareholders; this is the original capital they invested when they set up the organisation, plus any retained or reinvested profits.

Managing and understanding profit

To manage profit, you must understand:

- Cost (we will look at this later)
- Value
- Margins

Value determines the price businesses can sell at. If they are selling a commodity, price will be their only differentiator, profit margins will be pushed down and competition will be about being cheapest and having the lowest cost base. Firms that cannot be the cheapest are better off competing on some basis other than price, for example, by providing some extra value that customers are prepare to pay for. This value may be in the form of:

- Availability
- Convenience
- Confidence
- Choice
- Quality

Whilst some of these attributes may be measurable, some may well be a matter of perception by the customer. For example, think about the major UK supermarkets, how do they compete, which compete purely on price, which compete on convenience, product range and premium quality?

The point here is that organisations should not attempt to manage cost, without first defining the value that they seek to provide to customers. Overall, profits may be increased by focusing on selling more products that deliver higher margins.

Managing and understanding cash

If an organisation runs out of cash and cannot meet its financial obligations, then it goes bankrupt/bust. It may go bust even if it makes a profit as profit and cash are different. The difference between profit and cash arise from accruals accounting. Income is assigned to the period it is earned, rather than when payments from customers are received; costs are assigned to the periods when the benefits from those costs arise, rather than when payments are made to suppliers.

To manage cash organisation should manage:
*   Fixed Assets; the acquisition and disposal
*   Working Capital; the cash tied up in stock (also known as inventory), the debtors (accounts receivable) and the creditors (accounts payable)
*   Funding; the cash from borrowing and owners (equity)

For most managers, operating on a "day to day" level, then managing working capital is the main area where they influence the organisations cash position. It is tempting to believe we must minimise our working capital investment, but rather than minimise working capital, we should seek to optimise it.

Managing Debtors (Accounts Receivable)

Organisations can potentially increase their cash if they reduce debtors (accounts receivable), however, giving less credit, may result in lost sales. Organisations therefore need to weigh up the costs and risks of giving credit against the benefits in terms of profit.

Organisations should have procedures to ensure no more credit is given than is justified. Credit performance should be measured; simple approaches are to measure credit in terms of average sales (debtor days) and analyse individual customers accounts by age (i.e. which customers are taking the longest to pay). If an organisation discovers customers are exceeding terms, then they should try to analyse why, before taking any action. For example, sometimes late payment can result from errors with invoicing, or from a failure to include purchase orders. Organisations should work with customers to make it easier to pay.

Managing Stock (Inventory)

We should seek to be managing inventory at just the right level; too high and we have high storage costs, cash tied up in inventory and a risk of obsolesce or deterioration; too little and we do not meet customers (internal or external) requirements. Some basic tips to reduce inventory levels follow:

- Recognize (quantify) the costs and risks of over and under stocking.
- Design to reduce stock; for example with standardization parts, components and finished products.
- Late Differentiation; make products the same and add differences at a later stage of production.
- Improve forecasting; better forecasting of demand will enable better inventory planning.
- Speed up lead times; for example, the production cycle.
- Have fixed and reliable lead times and reduce the variability/uncertainty; for example, the suppliers' delivery cycle.
- Identify and manage delay factors/bottlenecks.
- Make managers aware of over stocking; for example, by charging notional interest charges on stock to users cost centres.
- Benchmark and measure performance against other units and organisations.
- Set targets for improvement.
- Apply the 80/20 rule in stock management for example, 80% of demand comes from 20% of the lines.
- Delegate responsibility for stock control to those that can influence it.
- Maintain more accurate records.
- Improve supply chain management; for example, make it a cross-functional process and not a functional departmental silo.

Managing the supply chain and inventory are both comprehensively covered in other books in the series, for example, **Excellence in Inventory Management** (2007) and **Excellence in Supply Chain Management** (2008).

Theory of Constraints (TOC) view

Goldratt's book **The Goal** sees that business is fundamentally about:

- Money
- Sales
- And the "rates" of movement involved in these two

"Money and Sales" are connected as follows:

- Throughput: The rate at which money is generated by sales (and by the time it takes to move through the system)
- Inventory: The purchase of things that are held to maintain the throughout and the holding of finished goods. It is the money invested in things, intended to sell/awaiting sales
- Costs: The money spent, turning inventory into sales

This is illustrated below:

TOC and Money Flows

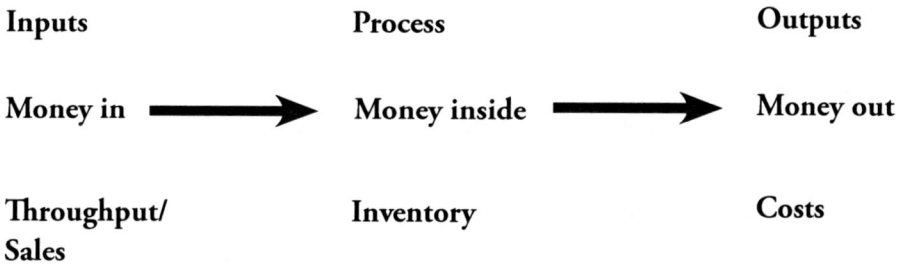

Inputs	Process	Outputs
Money in ➡️	Money inside ➡️	Money out
Throughput/ Sales	Inventory	Costs

The aim of TOC is therefore to reduce inventory, reduce operational costs/expenses and increase sales/throughout, at the same time and in balance.

However, the throughput is always going to be at the rate of the last dependency and is therefore influenced by the fluctuating rates of these other dependencies. When the chain of dependencies increases in length then we will have to:

- Increase inventory, as hold more
- Increase the operating expenses, e.g. holding/carrying costs of inventory
- Decrease the throughput e.g. movement slows

Clearly therefore TOC recognises the holistic and wider connections in which a business operates.

Understanding costs and pricing

A knowledge of costing and pricing is important for all managers, not only to help them access their own operations, but also because this gives a better view of suppliers when purchasing products and services

First a few simple costing terms need to be defined:
- Fixed costs are those paid irrespective of any activity, these are costs items for plant, machinery, premises etc.
- Variable costs, such as overtime wages, materials etc, are only incurred when there is some activity,

So for example with a car, the fixed costs are all those expenses that tick away whether the car is being used or not, for example, insurance, licence, capital loan/interest/rent/ lease or the depreciation on the capital spent. Variable cost however only kicks in when the car is moving and is being used, expenses such as fuel, maintenance, tyres, and road tolls.

To summarise therefore:
- Fixed costs do not change and do not vary directly in relation to the activity/ throughput
- Variable costs do change and do vary in relation to activity/throughput

Total Costs are the fixed and variable costs added together for a given level of activity/ throughput. From total costs, we can get Average Costs, as per the following example:

Fixed costs = £200,000 per week
Variable cost is 15 pence per unit
If produces 300,000 units per week, then
Total costs per week are £200,000 + (300,000 x 15p) = £245,000 and the Average Cost is £245,000/300,000 = 82.88 pence per unit

However, if we were to produce 400,000 per week, then the total cost is £260,000 and the Average Cost is reduced to 65 pence per unit.

The Activity Based Costing (ABC) model shows that costs do not just happen, as it is activities that use resources and it is the use of resources that give rise to costs. Resources can be identified by the 6Ms:

*   Man/ms power; e.g. labour, wages
*   Machinery
*   Materials; e.g. consumables
*   Money
*   Minutes e.g. that most precious commodity, time
*   Management information

This can be illustrated where; the resources are used by a process, which produces a product or a service, as illustrated in the following diagram:

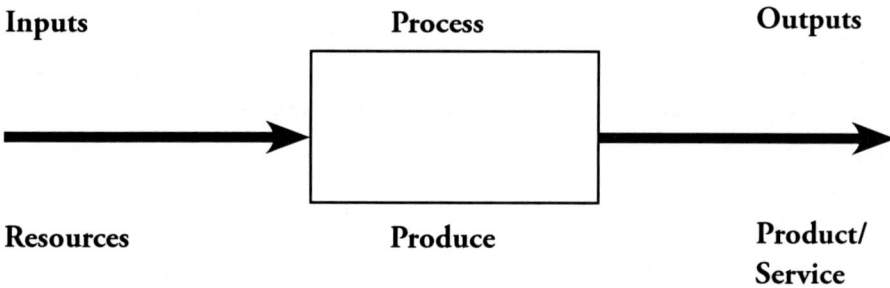

Inputs   **Process**   **Outputs**

Resources   **Produce**   **Product/**
                                                             Service

Costs however can also result from waste in the resources as waste and losses can come from:

*   Equipment downtime e.g. unexpected breakdowns, set up times and adjustments
*   Speed losses e.g. idling and stoppages, reduced speeds
*   Quality losses e.g. process defects, scrap and rework

The principles of Activity Based Costing therefore recognise that:

*   You cannot control costs without, controlling the resource
*   You cannot control costs without, managing the process
*   To control or reduce costs, you therefore need to proactively control/reduce the resources represented by those costs
    (We will return to this later when we consider Managing Performance in the next part of this book)

The traditional view of costs

This has tended to be a reactive view that looked at:

- Where costs were incurred (in what Cost centre)
- What the cost was (Account)
- When it occurred (Period)
- Who was responsible (Budget Holder)

However this view can be criticised as two important words are missing:

- Why have we spent the money?
- How are we going to reduce or get more value from it?

Budgets & Budgeting

Perhaps before considering the best way to manage or build a budget we must first decide what is the function of budgets? A budget is simply a plan expressed in financial terms.

The budget is used to:

- Plan and allocate resources.
- Monitor and control performance.
- Delegate authority and responsibility.

Budgets fail because budgetary control systems encourage managers to play games. These games include spending budgets to justify a following year's budget and setting soft targets to make managing them easier. To discourage these games we need to design the budgetary control system very carefully and remind managers of its function. Budgetary performance should be judged purely one what an individual spends but also in terms of what they achieve – performance measured in conjunction with some relevant measures, perhaps some KPIs (Key Performance Indicators).

Building a budget

When one builds a budget one must first build a plan, the following 9 steps will help:

1. Activity based

It is a fundamental quality of a good plan and budget that it is built up from activities. This means identifying what your activities will be in the budget year, then assessing what resources will be required to perform these activities. In the budget there may be assumptions about the level of activity and how much resource each activity takes;

therefore, you should be able to justify and preferably document these assumptions. Indeed, it is by reference later on to these assumptions that an explanation for variances from budget is found.

2. Prioritised activities
If there are limited resources, activities will have to be prioritised to ensure the most important activities are performed.

3. Co-ordination & Communication
Ensure the budget is co-ordinated with the other departments. Communication with these other departments will not only help co-ordination but may also reduce duplication of work.

4. Involving people & commitment
People will generally be more committed to a budget if they have some involvement in its formulation.

5. Realistic but challenging
A budget is a plan. Putting an over ambitious budget may have adverse effects if it is not achieved; however the budget may also function as a target and consequently should also present a challenge.

6. Consistency of assumptions
All budgeting assumptions should be consistent. Assumptions that affect the whole organisation should be consistent across the organisation.

7. Phasing
Try to phase the budget accurately over the year; avoid simply dividing an annual figure by twelve unless it is genuinely appropriate. For example, demand volumes are rarely constant.

8. Consistent with organisation and department objectives
Remember the budget (or plan) is part of the overall budget for a department and ultimately the organisation, it must therefore be consistent with both the department and organisation's objectives.

9. Plan ahead and allow time to complete the budget
The budget is a vital tool for managing the organisation and adequate time and resources must be devoted to it. Allocate the most time to work on the most critical figures.

Managing Budgets

The budget is our plan. Fundamental therefore to managing a budget should be comparing the performance against that plan. Managers often make an error of only focusing on the cost, but we should have measures of our performance in terms of cost and "delivery" of our plan results. A poor budget manager may under spend a budget and deliver very little against the plan in terms of results, outputs or outcomes; whereas a good budget manager may overspend a budget but have dealt with all sort of problems that were not originally in the budget.

If one overspends or underspends then there is a variance, and it is essential to understand and explain why. Analysing the variance will help the budget manger demonstrate they know what is going on and will help them to identify a remedy if a problem is identified. Many managers rely on the monthly report of income and expenditure to prompt them into action, this is a reactive approach, it is much better to seek to be proactive by identifying budget variances before they happen. As already noted, you cannot control costs without controlling the resource and you cannot control costs without managing the process.

Many organisations have a system of quarterly or monthly forecasting. Often managers confuse a forecast with the budget; however, the budget is the original plan which is normally fixed over the year, whereas the forecast may be updated throughout the year.

Checklist: Tips on Managing a Budget

- Identify and concentrate on the main income and the costs.
- Identify key factors driving the main income and costs and then, closely monitor them.
- Check monthly variance reports and explain important variances from budget, use tolerance limits to identify important variances.
- Analyse trends.
- Be aware of phasing differences between budgets and actual.
- Re-forecast expenditure. If required, take corrective action as soon as possible to meet the original budget.
- Consider comparing "Year to Date" (YTD) v Last YTD or 12 month rolling vs last year. This can help identify trends.
- Review budget with Key Performance Indicators (KPIs) as well as costs.
- Monitor other financial measures; for example, unit costs or percentages.

- Drill into details behind figures in financial reports to find answers.
- Be aware of errors and miscoding.
- Work with the finance team to ensure that "we are working as one".

Finance problems

Finance is deeply embedded within organisations, perhaps understandably so in those private profit-motivated organisations. Traditional finance controls are however not without their critics, and alternative financial views (like Activity Based Costing and the Theory of Constraints) can provide valuable options to better control finances.

Critics have noted the following on traditional financial reporting:
- Only counts physical capital and not value knowledge; for example, comparisons between say GM USA and Honda Japan
- Information is late; for example, comparing period end book closing/reporting and the need for such data to affect a balance. Often what is needed to run a business is not directly included at all in the financial accounts, for example, reliable forecasting information
- Short-term decision focus; when finance is measured monthly, then people often will only look to do better monthly; if payback for an investment is needed in within 1 year, then there is likely to be no investment
- Distorted view on cost/price/value; for example, overhead cost allocations are wrong; e.g. "A" has 60% of sales, therefore takes 60 % of overheads whereas it should be fairer allocated on the actual use of overheads by "A"
- Measures functions instead of processes; therefore individual activities are measured in isolation from the overall value/supply chain and also how overall the customer is served.

6: Managing Performance

Understanding Performance

Let's start with the diagram we used earlier:

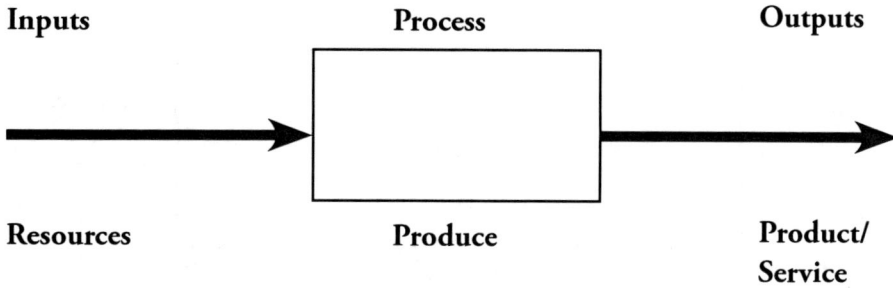

Inputs	Process	Outputs

Resources   Produce   Product/
Service

What is critical to appreciate from this diagram, is that:
- The output represents the **performance** of the product or service.
- In turn, the performance comes from what the process has produced.
- In turn, the process will have used resources; resources being what has been used by the process; for example, the usage of money, time, equipments, materials, methods of working and people (as individuals, groups and teams).

So we need therefore to have inputs of resources into a process, before, we can have a performance output.

All of the inputs of resources, the process production and the outputs of products or services are connected and interlinked. They are a process which is "a sequence of dependant events, involving time, which has a valued result for the eventual end user."

As all of these aspects are related, then therefore we cannot improve performance without considering the process and methods used, and the resources utilised in the process.

Performance and Feedback
In measuring and checking what has happened, then the output, or the performance is looked at to compare what has happened against what we expected to happen. If it does not match, then we can generate feedback to change the process, and/or the inputs, so that we can get the desired output.

The following diagram illustrates these feedback loops.

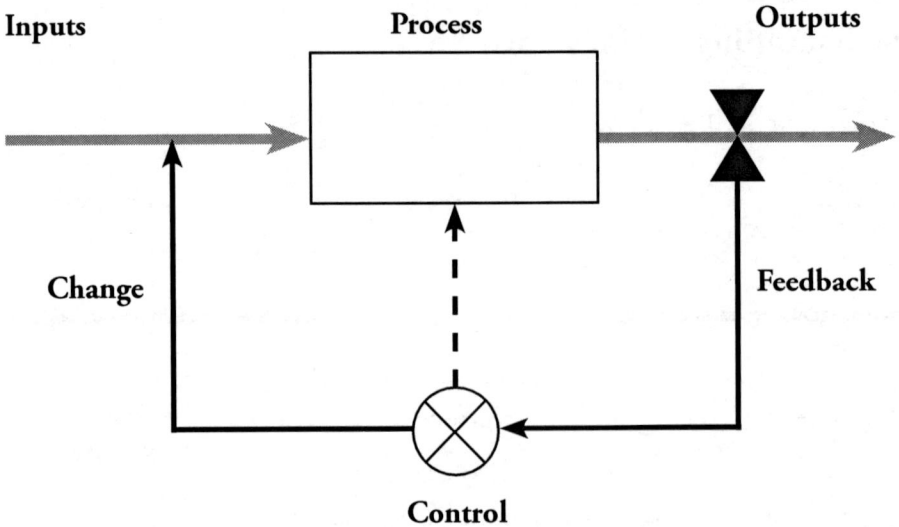

Inputs and processes can be changed by responses to feedback loops; these are at the heart of how we can improve any performance. They are also, as we will soon see, fundamental to systems thinking.

Performance measurement
The output or the performance can be measured, by looking at what we expected against what we obtained, and the input or the utilisation of resources can be measured, by seeing what was used against what available. The complete method of calculating these measurements can be seen in the following diagram:

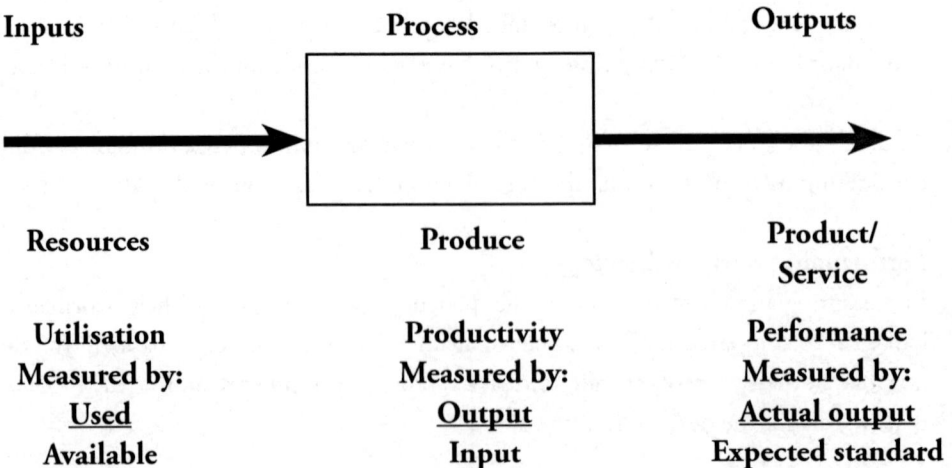

Manage on the left side

As can been seen, inputs, process and outputs are all connected. An important point with performance measurement is that the measurement is always going to be taken after the product and service has been delivered and completed; the vast majority of performance measurement will thus always be time lagged.

For example, financial budgets compare what we expected/budgeted for, against what has been actually spent. These are always going to be received some time later.

Effective performance management therefore, means recognising just what are the key inputs that affect the process and the outputs. Then, we can measure how we have best utilised the inputs for a given output. If we do this correctly, then this will automatically mean excluding random chance, so that there are no performance output surprises. As performance will always be directed towards customers (internal or external), it is critically important that we get the performance output to customers right.

Meanwhile, if the output is not the one actually required, then the process will need examining. Maybe we are doing things wrong, maybe there is a better way. Maybe we have to change the process and also the inputs; finally, we may have to change the whole system. This is real proactive performance management, and we can do this by managing on the 'left side'.

I suggest this managing on the left side is not only simple conceptually, but is also simple in practice. Unfortunately however, often, the relationship and the connection between the inputs and the output are often just not realised by managers.

For example, many organisations and managers wait for the delayed output performance measures before they will change anything; this is a classic example of reactive management. This is also not helped by the common use of the word key performance indicators (KPIs) that will only ever tell us what we have done, after we actually have done it.

Proactive performance

As the above diagrams show, there are also key utilisation indicators (KUIs) and in turn, it is the utilisation which works through to affect the performance. KUIs will therefore tell us, diagnostically, why something is not performing. A very simple operational example will highlight the use of KPIs and KUIs:

Case Study: KPIs and KUIs

A warehouse despatch department has two fork trucks and two drivers per shift who, load pallets onto road vehicles.

On one work shift, the KPI on number of pallets delivered/loaded from a warehouse was as follows:

<u>Number of pallets actually loaded per shift</u>
Number of pallets expected to be loaded per shift

This actually was, 15,000/30,000 pallets, giving 50% performance of pallets loaded per shift.

This KPI is affected by many things, for example, the process used for despatch, by the use and availability of vehicles to load to and by the information, labour and equipment etc.

Considering the key utilisation indicators for the availability of fork lift truck equipment we find:

<u>Fork truck hours used per shift</u>
Fork truck hours available per shift

This 10/20 hours giving 50% utilisation of fork lift truck hours per shift.

On the labour (drivers of fork lift trucks) the KUI for absence showed:

<u>Absent from work</u>
At work

This showed a 50% absenteeism

Comments
This shows how KUIs can explain the KPI. In this very simple operational example, we hope a manager overseeing this activity would have known at the

start of the shift, that one person was absent and would then have arranged for a replacement. Hopefully, they would not have waited for the KPI at the end of the shift to reveal the low performance.

This simple example illustrates the critical message that inputs relate to outputs and by managing the inputs; we get an early warning of performance problems and therefore can manage pro-actively. We do not need to wait for the performance measurement to tell us something needs to be changed.

The link between inputs and outputs is also a classic example of causal thinking. Potentially there can be multiple causes and this, as we will see, is an important aspect of systems thinking.

The need for proactive rather than reactive management, has also been noted by Nick Read; CEO Vodaphone UK who in The Sunday Times (1 April 2007) noted that what most managers "are doing, is not leading, but managing retrospectively what has already happened in the business".

Read continues with the following comment of how time is managed by leaders and managers:

Agenda	% Time spent Should be	% Time spent Usual
People (staff, workers)	40%	20%
Customers	40%	20%
Results	20%	60%

Performance and Processes
We have earlier defined a process as "A sequence of dependant events, involving time, which has a valued result for the eventual end user."

Processes are, so often, selected portions of larger streams of activities that are:
* Transformational (they convert inputs to outputs), and/or:
* Transactional (they exchange outputs for new inputs, thus giving feedback into the process)

This difference is especially important when considering improvements and whether we need to change the process, and/or change the inputs.

The other important aspect, when considering performance improvements to any process, is to understand the three key features of processes; dependences, variables and interfaces. It is usually these key features that will actually determine how well or not, the process performs.

Looking at each of these in turn we can see the following characteristics:

Dependences
- Receive inputs and changes them to outputs
- Are those sequential and related, "knock on effects"
- What happens "here", cause events "there", for example, consumer demand triggers many varied supply chain networks
- "A" may need to be finished before "B" can start
- Any process, is only as efficient as its most inefficient part, for example, "a chain is as strong as its weakest link"
- The most important factor to manage is therefore, the most limiting one in the process

Variables
- Variability is when the "fixed, known and expected" can become "variable, unknown and unexpected," for example, expected demand changes to be random demand
- They can causes changes from a state of "certainty" to "uncertainty"
- Each part with variability, can causes knock on effects, with sometimes, catastrophic results
- Normal statistical influences (e.g. as shown by a normal distribution curve), can often be used to measure the variablesof technical systems
- However, people's hopes and aspirations are also a variable, and are often the most important ones (see 'Motivation' in the Managing People section of this book).

Interfaces
- Are the potential friction points between processes
- Are often ignored, as our minds concentrate on "the box" and only on what happens in the box

- How we make connections at the interfaces is therefore often ignored
- However, real dependencies also exist in/at the interface; not the least of which are people relationships and how the people involved, choose to connect cognitively

What often happens, however, is that we fail to appreciate all of the input/process/output connections with their dependencies, variables and interfaces.

To use the jargon, we can then sub-optimise; this is where we only look at one part of the whole and this is usually the one making the most noise. This may be correct, but so often it is not. When it is not and we change something (the wrong thing), we then amplify the problem. This may create a catastrophic outcome.

Systems thinking

Consider systems thinking, a brave approach to ensure that we look at "wholes" or take the holistic approach. Systems thinking has a relatively recent history, with the following important milestones:

Pre-1900s: Feedback control in engineering; the above input/output diagram is an example. This introduced the feedback principle
1950s: Operational research; this started to use computing power to undertake "what if" analysis from varying the connections.
1960s: Systems dynamics; Forrester and MIT were the main movers here and the book **Limits to Growth** is a classic that shows the complexity of inputs and variables on outputs.
1970s: Soft systems; Checkland and the Open University developed the thinking into Human Activity systems
1990s: Learning organisations; Senge and the classic book **The Fifth Dimension** introduced the systems connections into organisations and also the need for a learning organisation that continually reinvents itself.

Systems, Processes and Structures

Processes do things in conjunction with structures; these are the fixed settings that include things like rules and procedures, organisational charts and formal culture. Structures have a powerful influence of how people behave and how things work in organisations.

The main characteristics of structures and processes are as follows:

Structures are mainly	Processes are mainly
Stable and fixed settings	Transient and variable interactions
Supporting and Containing; yet can also, Constrain and Limit	Building up and Making; yet can also, Break down/fragment and be Defensive
Viewed as being independent, certain and self sufficient	Involving dependencies, variables and interfaces
Bringers of stability and certainty	Forcing change to accommodate the dependencies and variabilities

The interaction of structure with processes now becomes interesting:

It is the working together of structure and process that creates a system, as shown by the following diagram:

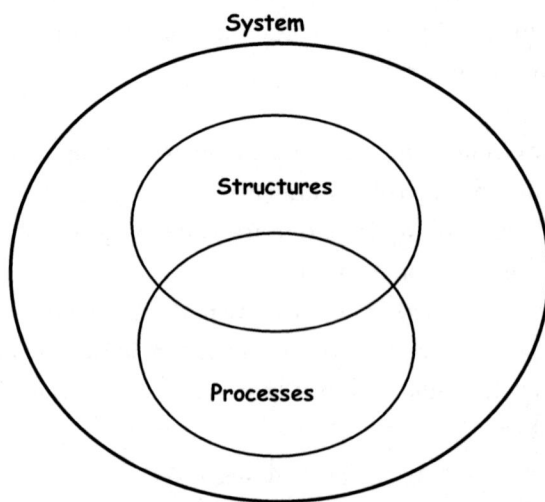

The interplay between structure and processes is critical to performance; and when making improvements, it is ultimately the behaviour of the overall system that we will have to improve. If processes and structures are both changed, then the behaviour will inevitably change.

What is a System?

Some definitions of a system follow:

"A system is a group of interacting, interrelated and interdependent parts that form a complex and unified organised whole that does something. The behaviour of the systems changes, if any of the parts, leave the system. It is the interaction of the parts, not the actions taken separately that is essential. "

"A system is a dynamic and complex whole that has information flowing between its interacting parts and its environment. Whilst the system may seek equilibrium, it can exhibit oscillation, chaos or exponential growth/decay."

We live in a complex world; we are part of this world and in turn, the world is part of us; a complex paradox indeed that is difficult to fully understand. In its own way, Systems thinking does attempt to explain this paradox, but this is not to say such explanations and understanding are easy; after all, we are dealing a paradox.

A system has a **purpose** and for optimum performance, all elements/parts must be present and must be arranged in a specific way. This arranged way will change when we require a different performance.

Additionally, systems will change in **response to feedback**. Many systems generally will attempt to maintain stability and control the system performance by making adjustments based on feedback e.g. the kettle thermostat. However, the unexpected can happen, as we will soon see.

A system is therefore an entity that maintains its existence and functions through the **interaction of its parts**. The behaviour of a system depends on how the parts are related, rather than just on the parts themselves. This requires thinking in "wholes" and not just with the "parts."

As systems are about **connections between wholes**, it does also mean writing about them has some special difficulties. We do need to break things into parts to explain them, but in so doing, we may then lose sight of the whole. We also have systems that are part of larger sub-systems and are composed of smaller systems.

The more complex the system, then the more difficulties are found due to variability, dependency and the interfaces. Systems are often complex in the detail and in the dynamics.

Hard and Soft Systems

We can identify two basic and general types of systems, hard and soft.

Hard systems are:
- Technical and engineered systems
- Generally predictable
- Quantifiable, tangible and objective; like money and products

Soft systems are:
- Organisation and human activity systems
- Complex and uncertain as they deal with behaviour, emotions, feelings, values, attitudes, politics, cultures etc
- Qualitative, intangible and subjective

To examine the hard and soft aspects further, Jack Welch has a most useful and commendable view of seeing "small, within big." (From **Jack: Straight from the Gut** – this is the autobiography of Jack Welch, the former chairman of GE USA, who has had a powerful leadership voice in the 1990/2000s).

Small, within big is personally how I have always preferred to work, where there is a small number of people who need to be closely lead and managed, but with the support from the wider and larger organisation on things like finance, research etc.

Welch in turn, sees the small and the big in an organisation as the following:

"Big" represents the hard values at the centre with:
- Technical support
- Financial support
- Managerial support

This is what Welch sees as the central and common culture.

"Small" represents the soft values at the sharp end with:
- Reality; working with the way it is and not the way we wished it was
- Quality; each person is proud of what they do
- People; creating at atmosphere where people dare to try new things

This is seen as the freedom and flexible culture.

I do like these hard and soft comparisons – it is the soft values that make the difference to organisations as they work directly on and into the people. And it is always people who do make the difference.

It is the soft values that bring "it home" at the front end, where it matters. However this soft stuff is actually the hard stuff, as it is hard to do.

Why is the soft stuff hard? Well, because management is not only about hard scientific approaches, but is, according to none other than Sir John Harvey-Jones, more about being an art:

"In my view, management is not so much a science, as an art. It is an art because management consists of enlisting the freely given support of disparate groups of people at different times to achieve, by their own free will, an agreed common purpose."
– John Harvey-Jones

In viewing this hard/soft divide, I am also very aware of some popular financially-driven management expressions such as:

"The only thing that counts is the financial bottom line."

"Achieving the financial targets are all that matters."

For some leaders and managers (and in my view, too many), these are the only ultimate truths in their organisations, and "the financials" are pursued relentlessly and without compromise.

The simple truth however, is that it is the "soft" people who will make any of the "hard" financial differences. So, by getting the effective use of people as the main inputs and driver in an organisation, the hard financials outputs must follow; assuming of course, the people choose to be consistent in achieving the financials.

Dangers of using only hard values

"Hard" value measurement alone is dangerous - using only these gives totally inappropriate standards for an organisation's total performance. This must inevitably bring failure in the medium to longer term, as the soft values are being subordinated and ignored; yet it is actually these soft values that will drive the organisation to meet its hard values.

We therefore do need both soft and hard values, and not just the hard values alone.

I fear, for example, that most of the target settings in Government bureaucracies and in the UK National Health Service are using totally inappropriate hard-value-based standards of performance. Control and regulation seems to have taken over, by using only some of the standards that are available whilst other standards are ignored.

"The whole concept of management in Britain has been debased by being seen as synonymous with control and regulation."
– John Harvey-Jones

By focussing on parts, the whole is not considered, and in looking only at the parts, then the purpose and meaning for the whole is lost. Simple really, but not at all well understood.

Control is only one aspect of management, and is concerned with planning, organising and coordination. When, however hard values and systems controls are the prime methods being used to run an organisation, then achieving these key performance indicators becomes all that matters.

Ultimately, the people in the organisation will only do what is required to be done; that which is directed by the control measurement. Most people will only do what they going to be measured on, as doing this represents their "carrot or stick" work performance rewards. (To examine rewards and motivation more fully, please see the earlier coverage in this book). Additionally, when controlling only the output actions from the people ("the human doing"), we may now find that we have lost the essential input and output of the human being.

It is clear that if an organisation is measuring the wrong things, then the work output will be wrong. People will eventually suffer as they will not be doing the right things and this in turn, can result in eventual failure and extra cost. When this is "discovered" later, and it will be later as the performance measures being used are reactive ones, then the fault with attending blame will be directed towards the people working within the organisation.

If however, meanwhile, some sub-optimal changes have been made (to show that something has been done), then it may now be some years later before it is seen not to work. Now, whilst it will be still the fault of the people, it will also now be recognised as a fault of the system. Time meanwhile has passed, and those who originated the use of hard measurements only, will not realise, or at worst will choose to forget, that they were cause of the problem in the first place.

For those who find this critique on using only hard drivers and measurements paradoxical with their management training and experiences, there is a real lesson here. A simple lesson that all leaders and managers need to ensure that the entire organisation, is actively promoting, above everything else, the soft values and the soft skills in the art of management.

And for those who still need convincing, four quotes follow from Peter Drucker:

"Organisations do not exist for their own sake. The organisations goal is a specific contribution to individual and society. The test of its performance lies outside of itself."

"The task of management is to make people capable of joint performance, to make their strengths effective and their weaknesses irrelevant."

"The business enterprise is a system of the highest order; a system whose parts are human beings contributing voluntarily of their knowledge, skill and dedication to a joint venture."

"To manage a business is to balance a variety of needs and goals. To emphasise only profit, misdirects managers to the point where they may endanger the survival of the business."

We must ensure that the right choices are made about the relative importance of hard and soft systems in the structures and processes of an organisation.

Performance and Discipline

People who are close to you will not always perform or do things as you expect. They will get things wrong sometimes. When this happens then they should be shown privately what is wrong and be dealt with one on one.

If this does not work, then there is a need to go wider and more public. If this then fails, the person can then be excluded and no longer be a part of the team.

Conducting Performance Reviews

Performance reviews are essentially a full, frank and friendly discussion about an individual's performance, undertaken by their supervising manager. They include that individual's strength and weaknesses, as well as their successes and failures; over to Peter Drucker:

"Performance is the consistent ability to produce results over prolonged periods of time and in a variety of assignments. A performance record must include mistakes. It must include failures. It must reveal a persons limitations as well as strengths."

- Performance reviews are not about reprisals, but are about the following:
- Whilst as a review they are naturally focussed on the past, there must be a focus on future performance.
- They are not to be about blame or a history lesson.
- They are not a pay review; this is a completely separate topic and must be separated out completely in time, for example six months from a performance review.
- Are more a development review, a personal development plan or a performance development plan

The aims of performance reviews are:
- Achievements in the past
- The current performance
- The future objectives
- Personal learning and development needs
- Longer term aspirations
- Identifying any under used skills/experiences

Conducting Performance Reviews – The 3-Step Approach
Preparation
- Take time to prepare
- Set aside enough time
- Keep free from interruptions
- Organise a friendly room layout for the 1/1
- Give them plenty of notice to they can prepare
- Spend time collecting relevant data
- Both parties need to prepare relevant paperwork

- Review the last sessions
- Reflect on this again and provide a checklist of points to cover

The interview

- Put them at ease
- Ask questions that encourage self analysis
- Make it two way; listen and explore
- Give helpful feedback
- Praise the good; help overcome the poorer performance
- Look ahead to see what new goals/objectives need to be set
- Get then to think about how they can develop
- Try to get them to summarise
- Record all agreements and action points
- Complete appropriate paperwork

Ongoing Reviews

- Give regular feedback as/when it is needed. The formal review should be present "no surprises" as issues are dealt with as they occur.
- Give ongoing guidance and coaching.
- Provide development and training as/when is needed. Do not systematically wait for the "yearly review".
- Remember that performance is on going activity, so therefore should the reviews. The "yearly one" being the formal one, it is "for the record" and also to make sure that nothing has been missed in the previous period.

Handling unacceptable performance

The definition of unacceptable performance at work is: "work performance that is not up to the standard expected". Too often, such problems become people problems, and personalities come into the equation. It can then become personal and with emotions involved, the outcomes will be unclear and often unintended. Sides are taken and stances are built up, that later, "in the cold light of the day", people can find difficult to withdraw from.

The action taken over unacceptable performance needs to have improvement at its root, however, sometimes, and wrongly, punishment is the first course of action. This may be because problems are associated with 'discipline' procedures, with this word creating an association with punishment. However, the root of discipline is disciplina (latin), meaning "instruction given, teaching, learning, knowledge." This is much closer to the learning of new ways and improvement.

The following indicates the substantial differences between improvement and punishment:

Punishment is:

- To cause the offender to suffer
- To inflict a penalty
- To chastise
- To give a penalty for doing wrong
- To reprimand
- To correct

Improvement is:

- To make better
- To make progress
- To grow better
- To be more prosperous
- To use for good purpose

"The task of management is to make people capable of joint performance, to make their strengths effective and their weaknesses irrelevant"
– Peter Drucker

As Peter Drucker suggests, we would do better to build on people's strengths and not on their weaknesses. We will never build firm foundations in people if we pick on their weaknesses all the time. Build on peoples' strengths and manage out the weaknesses.

People differ and as noted earlier, we do need such variations. However, as many leaders and managers try to clone themselves when dealing with other people, it becomes essential to take into account our, and other people's "style." Please consider the following two lists about our leadership and management style.

List A	List B
"I am right, I know best"	"I would like to know your opinion"
"Listen to me"	"Let me listen to your view"
Seeing obstacles and problems	Seeing solutions and opportunities
Finding fault	Giving support
Feeling frustrated when with people	Feels calm when with people
Makes others feel guilty	Makes people learn
Looks for who is wrong	Looks for what is wrong
Mistakes are to be punished	Mistakes are opportunities to learn

Perception is reality, and seeing performance problems as needing punishment will mean having more of a blame view (list A). This will not help; it will reflect in how performance problems are handled. It should always be remembered that the primary objectives on managing performance problems must always be about gaining improvement.

List B is more about gain, and such a style will show through in how performance problems are handled.

It is also important to be clear on the standards expected. These will give a clear view of the times when performance is below standard, and enable an investigation to be carried out. The following questions can be asked:
- Can the person assigned fully describe the process and the results expected?
- Does the person assigned the task acknowledge they are accountable for its completion?
- Does the person assigned the task have the knowledge and skill to carry it out?
- Has the person assigned done it before?
- Are there any consequences which discourage the task being performed?
- Are they any competing tasks to be performed at the same time?
- Does the person performing it see the task as worthwhile?
- Can the person assigned explain why it needs to be done?
- Is the working environment conducive to performing?
- Are the appropriate tools and equipment available?
- If co-operation is required from others, is it forthcoming?
- Are the right standards in place and are they understood?
- Are the standards referring to performance that the individual can control?
- Is feedback given on performance?
- Is the task adequately designed?
- Are diagnostic tools available for repetitive tasks?
- Are the expectations realistic?

It is only by getting answers to such questions that a clear view is possible so that corrective improvement action can be taken. This will require establishing if the person concerned:
- Cannot do it, or
- Will not do it.

The former is usually clear and noticeable, however, the latter may be camouflaged and not easily seen. The underlying reasons for non-performance will have to be looked into.

Reasons when someone cannot perform to standard are many, for example, insufficient training. Common factors, however, will be the lack of competence, and not having the knowledge/skills to do the job as required.

Reasons when someone will not perform to standard are also many, for example, dissatisfaction over something. But the common factors will be a lack of personal commitment, and in not having the confidence and/or the motivation to do the job as required.

We covered the solving of commitment issues earlier when we looked at motivation; meanwhile solving competence issues requires the following:
* Give the required training/tools/resources to do the job
* If they still cannot do it, check for understanding
* If they still cannot do it, maybe they are not up to it, therefore arrange a possible transfer to another, perhaps simpler job

The following model can be used:

A model approach for performance problems with people

This is not a prescriptive "works all the time in every situation" approach, but selective aspects will work and in some situations, it can be applied in full.

Step one: Establishing the Facts (Investigate)
* Recall a problem person is one whose performance or behaviour is not meeting the normal standard expected
* Performance and behaviour are essentially, what people do and, or say
* Recall that you are trying to shape and redefine performance and behaviour to the expected standard
* You need to very clear about recording performance and behaviour by using objective facts and not by using subjective feelings. The latter includes personal opinions and emotions, which may distort the facts. However the former attempts to be more objective.

Record the facts by using the Questioning Approach:
* asking what happened,
* when did it happen,
* where it happened,

- why it happened,
- how it happened,
- and who was involved?

This approach establishes objective facts, which need to be emotion free and show how things went wrong. For example, saying, "you were late" is subjective; saying, "Three of us saw you arrive at 0915 hours, you were 15 minute late" is objective. To successfully establish facts involves personal observation which must focus on facts

Step Two: Explore the Problem (Check)

Having established the facts in Step one, the problem is further explored by:

- Looking to see if there is anything significant about the deviation from "where they should be" to "where they actually are". You are looking at the deviation from the standard expected.
- Looking to see what type of issue it maybe; for example, performance, or relationship/behavioural?

Example of deviations from standards and "expectations" in rules and procedures can be:

- Timekeeping e.g. clocking in late
- Absence e.g. unauthorised absence
- Health and Safety e.g. not following the "duty of care"
- Discrimination e.g. verbally abusing others
- Deviations from standards and "expectations" could be due to significant and one off special events such as:
  - Personal circumstances e.g. "domestics"
  - Work relationships e.g. personality "clashes"
  - Job factors e.g. boredom
  - Work conditions e.g. physical noise

Step three: Establish the required action (Decide)

You have now established the Facts and have explored the Problem. You now need to investigate and Check before taking a Decision

The possible actions are as follows:

1. Do nothing

2. Get the circumstance/situation change

3. Get the person to change

We will now look at each of these three:

1) If you do nothing then the problem:

- can grow and get worse
- can show the manager is a procrastinator who never takes decisive action
- can lower the morale of others

The only time the do nothing option is valid, is, when, there has been found to be no problem.

2) If you change the circumstances, then this is valid when:

- You have looked at the "before" (those triggers of behaviour), which have caused the "after" (those deviations from the standard). These are the consequences of the behaviour
- You have investigated the observable "after"
- You have determined which "before" cause will give a different effect
- You are satisfied it is possible to do it

3) How can you get the person to change?

At a deeper psychological level, you cannot be expected to be involved. At a more superficial level of changing attitudes, then you are able to look at the following:

- Counselling, talking and listening, listening, listening
- Coaching and training
- Using the formal organisation discipline procedures

Finally, review by:

- Stepping back and looking again
- Has this happened before?
- When?
- How was it tackled before?
- Who are you dealing with?
- Do you need to approach more people?
- What do others suggest?
- What does organisation policy says?

- What does your boss think?
- What do your HR/Personnel people think?

And finally, the following "recipe" will bring you good performance results:

- Make sure your people know the standards that are required
- Communicate clearly how they are able to make these standards
- Motivate them to progress in the direction required
- Reward them and continually carry on communicating and motivating so those standards are maintained.

For a small minority of people at work, when the required standards are not being met, then as a last resort and only after trying all the aspects mentioned above, you may then have to apply the formal organisation discipline procedures. Punishment and the use of formal procedures may only be valid as a final sanction when everything else to bring about an improvement has failed, for example with formal discipline and grievance procedures.

Discipline and Grievances

Disciplines and grievances involve handling the problem behaviour or problem performance of people, where the behaviour and performance are the problem and not the person.

Seeing people as a problem can be dangerous and destructive in relationships and in managing people, therefore it is vital to separate out the person from the problem so that we can then define problem behaviour or performance as:

"Problem behaviour or performance is that which does not meet the normal standard we expect."

It needs to be clear what the expected standard is, and we will cover this in due course.

Defining Discipline
Dictionary definitions mention things such as:

- instruction
- maintaining order

- mental training
- a system of rules
- controlling behaviour

Many see discipline as punishment, this view may have originated from childhood associations and the view that discipline is all about a "wrong" which is to be "corrected". A balance therefore needs to be struck between viewing discipline as punishment or improvement, and we have defined these above.

The key aim of discipline is therefore to encourage unsatisfactory employees to improve. By keeping the focus on improvement, this means we have a view that discipline is about trying to "gain", and is not about "blame."

Punishment is therefore perhaps only valid as a final sanction when everything else has failed to work; remember that the prime objectives have to be all about gaining an improvement.

Discipline –The Key Facts
Discipline is:
- Conforming to a system of rules for conduct
- Ways and norms and expectations of behaviour
- Often accepted as necessary by the majority
- Sometimes imposed by mandatory legislation
- Visible when relationships between a company and an employee is unsatisfactory to the company
- One of the things that helps employees to keep to the standards expected
- A way to help employees improve
- What helps companies to deal fairly with those who do not keep to the standards

The Prime Objectives for Disciplining need to be about:
- Improving, correcting, preventing, re-aligning
- Conforming to Standards
- Encouraging improvement, and "doing it better"

Discipline and Misconduct offences
Offences can always be categorised as performance issues or relationship/behavioural issues, where work performance issues are about:

- Poor attendance and absence
- Poor/careless work output
- Failure to follow rules, such as Health and Safety

And work relationship issues are about:
- Refusal to obey reasonable instructions
- Disruptive behaviour

Misconduct offences will normally lead to disciplinary action, and any gross misconduct offences will normally lead to dismissal, for example on performance issues of :
- Gross negligence causing loss, damage
- Serious disregard of Health & Safety legislation
- Deliberate damage to company property, and on relationship issues as follows:
  - Theft, fraud
  - Assault, fighting
  - Conduct prejudicial to the companies reputation
  - Serious incapability due to alcohol, illegal drugs
  - Gross insubordination

Defining Grievance

Dictionary definitions mention such things as:
grounds for complaint
- a cause of grief
- uneasiness
- distress

Grievances are often below the surface; they are the moans and groans, which provide "fodder" for the grapevine. They are the Hygiene factors of the Herzburg view on motivation; they are those things that need to "cleaned up" to maintain a sense of order and include such things as:
- working conditions
- supervision
- interpersonal relationships
- company policies and how they are administrated
- money
- job security
- status

Grievances surface and become visible when the relationship between a company and the employee is unsatisfactory to the employee, and the employee is prepared to bring this, formally, to the management's attention.

The prime objectives when handling grievances need to be about:
- A means for an employee to "offload, unburden and release themselves"
- Having a consistent and equal procedure to resolve disagreements

Typical Grievances

These can really be about anything at all, and some examples follow about relationships and company aspects:

Some examples of Work Relationship issues are:
- "I am treated badly by x"
- "I cannot get on with y"
- "I am made to feel small"
- "I am not appreciated by the company"

Some examples on Company aspects are:
- On policy, "We were told to work on a Saturday and we never do that"
- On administration, "It takes three months to get back expenses"
- On work conditions, "This place is too cold and too dirty"
- On wages, "X is paid more than I am and we do the same job"
- About the canteen, "The food is poor quality, and expensive"

Keeping a positive view on handling Disciplines and Grievances

An understandable reaction from many managers who have to deal with discipline and grievance procedures is "I do not want to hurt their feelings" or, "I do not want another argument."

This however indicates a belief that is not a positive one, and having a positive view is one that sees them as encouraging people to succeed and providing guidance and direction, both for the manager and the employees. It assists here to always remember that:
- a problem is a deviation from something expected
- improvement is the better side of the improvement/punishment balance

Handling typical problems

The three root causes of discipline and grievance problems are:

*   70 per cent frustration
*   20 per cent gain (for example, stealing time, theft)
*   10 per cent, all the other reasons

When frustrations are left to fester, they can build up and become the cause behind many discipline and grievance problems. Spending time on prevention can be better than having to spend time of the cure.

As defined earlier, unacceptable performance is "Work performance that is not up to the standard expected". It is important to be clear on the standards expected, and we have already covered SMART Objectives and Standards, where:

*   Objectives are about the job and identify key outcomes
*   Standards and Targets are the measurable outcomes using for example, measures of quality, quantity, time and cost
*   Standards are achievable by all, they are the norm and are common to all
*   Targets are individually agreed with those who can exceed the standard

Before therefore considering disciplining over a performance issue, ensure that:

*   Smart objectives, standards, targets are used and are understood.
*   It is not a competence issue.
*   It is not a commitment issue.
*   Investigate fully.
*   Review with a colleague before deciding what to do.

Checklist: Handling some typical problems

Unacceptable attendance/unauthorised absence
At its extreme, this is all about stealing time from employers and the problem with absence is as follows:

*   Above 5 per cent absence is getting serious, over 10 per cent absence is serious
*   The effects absence has on colleagues, for example, having to cover extra work, poor morale
*   The effects of absence for the company, for example, extra costs

- The effects for the customer, for example, poor quality work, late deliveries, unexpected delays

Answers to consider for absence problems are:
- Start by considering the morale and motivation at work, as absence is often a good indicator on the motivation "temperature".
- Follow the company policy
- Be consistent in your approach
- Establish the facts, investigate
- Explore the problem, for example, if the absence is due to illness/injury, then make available, medical support and advice
- Consider any special circumstances
- Look for the reasons underpinning the absence
- Review the possible actions with others
- Establish what action is needed

Unacceptable Relationships/behaviour
- First-check out the possible causes for the behaviour.
  Some external causes may be cultural, lack of resources or from society norms. These may not always be discipline offences but instead require different views to be taken by a manager, for example:
    - We live in a multi cultural society requiring understanding of others values/beliefs
    - We cannot always give all the required resources
    - We live in a fast changing society
- Some Internal causes of behaviour may be personality, skills, or maturity. These may not give rise to discipline offences but instead require different views to be taken by a manager, for example:
    - Different mixes of people can be valuable
    - Selection testing/specific training is needed
    - The "world view" held by a person will vary dependant on exposure, self motivation and self awareness

A final note
In most countries, the employment of people has many legal constraints and procedures covering for example, the hiring and termination of employee contracts. For example,

UK Legal Case Law says on discipline procedures (amongst other things) that:
- Employee investigations must be "adequate"
- Employees must be told that "discipline" is taking place in accordance with the company discipline procedures
- Employees must be told in advance what the "charge" is
- Employees must be given sufficient notice of all interviews
- Employees must be given adequate opportunity to provide an explanation
- Employees must be given opportunity to be accompanied by a helper/representative
- Employees being dismissed must be given the opportunity of an appeal to a senior manager

It is not the purpose of this book to cover such legislation and HR/Personnel contacts can do this. Indeed working with HR on such issues is important; they usually have the responsibility in an organisation to ensure the legal aspects are complied with and are up-to-date – they are therefore a great source of help and advice.

7: Managing Customers

Customers and Organisations

Customers are what really drive an organisation; unfortunately some organisations seem incapable of recognising that their own performance must match the needs of their customers. Improving service is not actually a choice – an organisation's survival may well depend on it.

In capitalist market economies it is said that the market rules. The market is however made up from individual customers buying products and services; it is these individual micro choices that ultimately determine the macro economic patterns. "Let the market decide" is therefore a principle of capitalist market economies. Accordingly, giving the customer what they need becomes critically important in market-driven organisations.

Principles of customer service
Some of the most important principles of customer service are as follows:
*   Customers have needs and expectations that they look to satisfy.
*   Customer service is a source of competitive advantage. But customers may already be using a competitor's products/service, then the question is, why?
*   Customer service is always delivered by people, so how we deliver it is more important than what the product/service being delivered actually is
*   Customer service has different levels of service, so we need to experiment with different levels so we can better determine the organisations future
*   Organisations must maximise the customer service experience, so that customers will not only return, but will also tell/encourage others to buy from the organisation (repeat business is a cheaper option than having to get new business).

Using customer service this way may require a new style of management, a style that combines hard quantifiable aspects like target setting and measurement, with soft qualitative aspects of communicating and motivating.

Definitions of Customer Service
Customer service is often variably seen as an activity, as a performance measurement and as a philosophy. Accordingly, one single definition of customer service does not exist. The following five views represent some of the different definitions:

1. Customer service is seen as a need satisfier

"Customer Service is a function of how well an organisation meets the needs of its customers."
"A customer defines good customer service as how they perceive that an organisation has delighted them by exceeding to meet their needs".
"Customer service is an organisation's ability to supply their customers' wants and needs."
"Customer service is the ability of an organisation to constantly and consistently exceed the customer's needs and expectations."

2. Customer service is seen as taking care

"Customer Service is a phrase that is used to describe the process of taking care of our customers in a positive manner."

3. Customer service is seen as keeping promises

"Customer service is the ability to provide a service or product in the way that it has been promised."

4. Customer service is seen as adding value for customers

"Customer service is a process for providing competitive advantage and adding benefits in order to maximize the total value to the customer."
"Customer Service is the commitment to providing value added services to external and internal customers, including attitude knowledge, technical support and quality of service in a timely manner."

5. Customer service is seen as all of the customer contact

"Customer Service is any contact between a customer and a organisation, which causes a negative or positive perception by a customer."

Customer Service History

There have been quantum changes on customer service in recent history.

The idea that the customer was important was once not accepted by many; indeed, the customer was often seen as a "nuisance". This was in the times when many organisations were production-led, and when, if they made the products, the customers would queue up to buy. Such times of high volume, low variety production were epitomised by Henry Ford (the car manufacturer) who told customers they could have "any colour of car they wanted, as long as it was black."

Here we have organisations being able to sell what they produce easily; here the focus was really on meeting the sellers' needs!

Change came and moved the transactional power towards being market-led, where organisations must now determine what the customers' needs are, and what they want to buy. We now find competition exists in the majority of sectors. Here, high product variety and multiple choices are being offered to customers. Supplying organisations now have to try and win market share by recognising and practicing that it is now customer satisfaction and loyalty that have priority. Customer's needs now have to be better known by suppliers and, additionally, if demand can be known in advance of production, this means the organisation can then make only what they can sell.

Public and private sectors

Market changes have also been seen between the private and public sectors. The following differences between these sectors can be noted:

Feature	Public sector	Private sector
Main driver	Maintain the current due to resource constraints.	Growth.
	Political imperatives.	Commercial imperatives and customer satisfaction.
	"Survival" decisions are made by politicians and the managers "advise".	"Survival" decisions are made by managers.
	Image and politics.	Brands.
	Balance the books.	Make a profit.
Structure	Centralised and bureaucratic "by the book".	Any type of structure can be found.
Culture	Job for life/security.	Job insecurity.
	Little incentive to change.	Continual change.

	No performance linked pay.	Performance incentives often found.
Ultimate responsibility	Politicians and elected bodies. Cannot go out of business.	Shareholders or "self." Frequent close downs.
"Buying"	Tendering and long decision-making. Price sensitive.	Quicker decision-making and price discussions. Less price sensitivity and more emphasis on "value."
"Marketing"	Customer already exists and is disgruntled. Users have little choice or no choice, about using the service.	Customers have to be "sold". Competition exists and the aim is to get repeat business and retain the customer who can easily go else where.

Compiled from www.ukhrd.co.uk in March 2000 and the **Independent on Sunday** dated 11/4/93

The change from public to private sector has now come to most of the former UK public sector utility providers.

Now, with the idea that the customer has a choice, these organisations need to be more responsive to customers - they must look to become more productive and efficient.

Monopolies and Competition

The following aspects ring true for most monopoly organisations:

- Customers already exist
- Customers are often disgruntled

- Customers are called users
- Customers have no alternative provider/supplier

However, alternatives are always being searched for by customers, and consequently, it is dangerous for organisations to ignore the power of the customer. Additionally, in the UK, many former monopoly suppliers of utility services have deliberately been made subject to competitive pressures. Here, new and variable service level offerings create choice in the marketplace that is driven by competition. With competition, therefore:

- Customers have to be found and be "sold" to
- Customers can choose from competing suppliers
- Organisations aim is to get repeat business and retain the customer as the customer can easily go else where
- The customer "rules"

Quality and customer service

Quality has many parallels with customer service, as quality management represents the involvement and commitment of everyone in continuously improving work processes, to satisfy the requirements and expectations of all internal and external customers.

Quality is therefore that "something" which:

- meets customer requirements
- is fit for purpose
- delights the customer
- is of value to the customer (value being quality plus price)

The role of the customer is again seen in the following ten basic principles of Quality Management:

- agreed customer requirements
- understand and improve customer/supplier chains
- do the right things
- do things right first time
- measure for success
- continuous improvement is the goal
- management must lead
- training is essential
- communicate more effectively
- recognise successful involvement

Total Quality Management (TQM) is also an approach towards larger scale organisation change and improves existing process and functions. TQM needs strong direction and leading from the top. It also needs commitment and involvement from all. TQM is therefore about:

- Customer setting the standards
- Reducing total cost
- Continuous improvement
- Strategic change is lead by managers
- Doing all of the right things that add value
- Everyone is involved
- Avoiding waste and eliminating errors

TQM is not about:

- Meeting only our own standards
- Compromising quality
- Control
- Quality experts being the only ones who check what is done
- Luxury

The importance of customer service

We have already established that customer service is fundamentally about satisfying customer needs and we will now explore this further. Getting this right will enable an organisation to view whether it has a competitive advantage with its customers (who may also be internal).

However, whether serving internal or external customers, customer service needs to be a total offering. Products and services have different aspects and the relative importance of each will be discussed in this section.

Customer needs

This solution to a need is also more important than the product or the service features. So what are these needs? For example, why do we buy food? Is it for the packaging, the brand, the touch, the feel, the status? All of these may be involved, but fundamentally we buy food to eat, so that we can survive. Survival is the ultimate need for buying food.

Any organisation therefore will need to know what its customer's expectations are, for example the:

- Attributes of products
- Expectations from services
- Price sensitivity

Then, after considering how these expectations may change over time, an organisation will need to answer how they actually meet the customer's expectations.

Competitive advantage

In the customer-focused marketplace, organisations need a competitive advantage. They must be better than the competition and they can do this by "doing it better" and/or "doing it cheaper."

Consider the following table on cost leadership ("doing it cheaper") and service differentiation ("doing it better").

Cost Leadership	Service Differentiation
Standard products produced cheaply	Customer designed products
Production push	Market pull
Flow and mass volume production, with high mechanisation	Job shop production with low mechanisation
Low inventory	Flexible and varied inventory
Focus on productivity	Focus on creativity
Stable planning	Flexible planning
Centralisation	Decentralisation
Standardisation	Bespoke and "one-off's"

As "Supply chains now compete, not individual companies" (after: Prof. Martin Christopher), then organisations will need to:
- Segment customers (we shall look at this soon)
- Have good relationships with customers and suppliers and connect "cognitively" (for example, to have visibility of demand, to release "hidden" supplier innovation) – again we return to this later.
- Use technology that can "enable" and "connect the data"
- Recognise there is global competition, meaning a growth of alliances

Internal Customers

Customers are internal and external. Whilst many have no problem with understanding about the external customer, many have a poor understanding with low service applications when it comes to dealing with internal customers. An internal customer may be any of the following:

- Board of directors e.g. as sponsors of a project
- Manager (s)
- Employees
- Users e.g. other departments who may be local or global

Additionally, they may be a supplier in one transaction, but a customer in another transaction.

We can view many internal supplier/customer relationships, for example in the office, the passing on of paperwork to the next person; in manufacturing, the passing of a sub-assembly to another for completion into a finished product.

If each supplier would view the next connection in line as a customer and treat them accordingly, then relationships would change for the better. Additionally, and overall, the ultimate end service to the final customer would be "perfect."

Total customer service

Top leadership must have the commitment to serving customers, with customer-focussed procedures in place. We shall look the setting of service standards and marketing shortly, all of which will need active management support and individual roles involving the knowledge, skills and desire to be totally customer focussed. In this regard, the following checklist will help:

Customer focus checklist

- Are customer requirements communicated to service employees?
- How are changing requirements of customers captured?
- Do people have an appropriate timeframe to respond to customer needs?
- Do people anticipate customer expectations?
- Is customer retention a priority?
- Do we encourage the satisfaction of internal customers?
- Do we pay particular attention to personal service?
- Are customers encouraged to complain?
- Are customer complaints measured?

- Is delivery performance measured?
- Is the customer satisfaction level measured?
- Are major/loyal customers rewarded?
- Is the quality of relationship with customers measured?

Based on: Adebanjo and Kehoe (2001). **An evaluation of factors influencing teamwork and customer focus Managing Service Quality.** Vol. 11 No. 1 pp49-56

What is important to accept in providing total customer service, is that the customer is: the business:
- the most important person we have contact with
- what we depend on
- who pays our wages
- the purpose of what we do
- part of our business
- a human being with feelings and emotions
- not one to win arguments with
- someone who can build our business and give us a competitive advantage

Therefore we must:
- know who they are
- know what they need
- anticipate their changing needs
- develop a long-term relationship

All customers are driven by needs, and when a need is not met, then this becomes a problem that causes a customer to look for solutions , perhaps elsewhere. Therefore, any feature of a product or service that solves their problem will be perceived as a benefit. In turn, any feature that does not solve the customer's problem will be seen as a waste.

From the customer's perspective, any money, time and effort spent in finding a solution and satisfaction of a need, is seen as a cost. Customers look for solutions that give them value. They will buy, if they believe the benefits (or the value) exceed the cost of the product or service.

Finally, individual managers in organisations can appreciate that if customer service works well, then for them personally this will mean:

- Job satisfaction
- Job achievement
- More friendly contacts
- Reduced complaints
- Less fire fighting

Products and Services

There are some important differences to consider here. A list of some absolute differences between products and services follows, where we can see that products are those things bought and owned, that will satisfy a want or need.

Product characteristics are as follows:

- Goods are tangible.
- They can be specified in quantifiable terms such as dimensions, weight, colour, conformance to a standard of workmanship and the required reliability standard.
- There is usually a time gap between production and consumption.
- Has features; those characteristics beyond the product's basic functioning
- The performance is the designed output levels that may have been engineered into the product to give a specific level of reliability for given operating conditions.
- Has an expected operating life.
- Reliability; the probability that a product will not malfunction or fail within a specified period of time.
- Reparability; the ease of fixing a product that malfunctions or fails.
- Style; how well the product looks and feels to the buyer

Services are also bought to satisfy needs and can be defined as:

- "The performance or act from one to another that does not result in ownership".
- Services are an intangible exchange that may or may not be connected to a physical product; they are perishable and cannot be stored.
- Compared to products, the performance of services may be often highly variable and unreliable – whilst products can be engineered and certified/tested to give a standard and known reliable performance, services will nearly always rely on the performance of people to give the value/satisfaction.

Services have the following characteristics:
- Are intangible:
  - cannot really be seen, tested, touched, felt etc.
  - have to be experienced/bought
- Are produced and consumed at the same time
- May have a variable performance
- Are perishable and cannot be stored
- Often the success in delivery of services appears to be due more to qualitative factors such as the human interactions between the user and provider; rather than the terms of the supply contract

Services can however, also be directly involved with products as follows:
- Installing; the work done to make a product or service operational in its planned location
- Training; ensuring the customer's employees can use products properly and efficiently
- Consulting; data, information systems and advising services that the seller offers
- Repairing; describes the quality of repair service available to buyers of the organisations product.
- Delivering; how well the product and supportive service has been delivered/received/used

Product life cycle

Products have a life cycle, as shown by the following diagram:

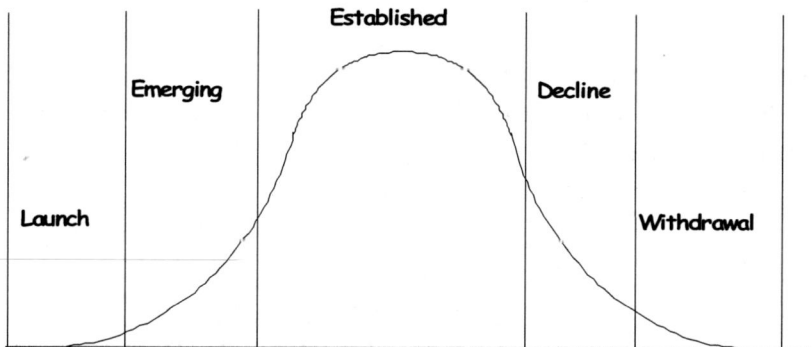

The following stages show the connections of customer service to both the product life cycle and to the organisations functions:

Launch/introduction
- Product design and development is critical involving customer need assessment
- Many design changes
- Short production runs with high production costs
- High stock levels
- High levels of product promotion

Emerging/growth
- Forecasting demand is critical
- Reliability of product and processes
- Competitive improvements and options
- Capacity issues
- Distribution and availability is important

Established/maturity
- Standardisation
- Minor product changes
- Optimum capacity and stock levels
- Stable processes
- Longer production runs
- Product improvements and cost cutting

Decline
- Little product differentiation
- Cost cutting
- Overcapacity in the industry
- Line item pruning
- Reduce capacity

Withdrawal

The Market and the Boston Matrix

This provides a view of how market share and growth of products and services are related (diagram opposite):

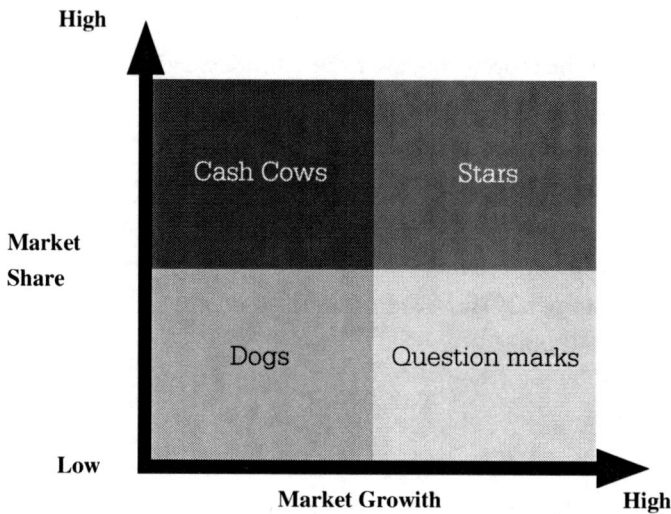

Cash cows: these have a high market share with low costs and therefore can be "milked", for example, most branded products.

Stars: have a high market share in growing market, but the costs are still high - likely to be future "cash cows".

Question marks: have a low market share in growing market and are at an early stage of development. High costs are involved and a decision on payback potential, research, investigation and evaluation still needs to be made.

Dogs: are those that have a low market share in low growth markets and are likely to be draining the organisation of cash and using up too much management time. They may be a previous cash cow that is at the end of its product life cycle or, maybe a question mark or star that has not made it.

Customers and Marketing

"Marketing is so basic that it cannot be considered a separate function. It is the whole business seen from the point of view of its final result, that is, from the customer's point of view. Business success is not determined by the producer but by the customer."
– Peter Drucker

Marketing is the process of defining, developing and delivering value to carefully chosen customers, where value is defined by customer needs, perceptions, expectations and use systems. In turn, value is developed around the firms distinctive competences and is delivered by managing expectations and building long-term relationships.

The Marketing Mix

This mix represents all of the aspects that are to be considered:

Product/service supplied looks at the following:

- Features (Physical, service, psychological)
- What does it "look like"?
- What will be delivered?
- Description, including benefits
- Value to the customer/WIIFM (what's in it for me)?
- Customisation/tailoring?

Place will examine things like:

- Distribution channels; how to get products to the marketplace e.g. direct, via wholesalers, via retailers etc.
- Market positioning and competition in the marketplace
- Inventory levels; where and what format to hold?
- Physical distribution management or logistics; the moving of products to the marketplace
- Internet marketing and e-shopping

Physical facilities involve the following;

- Premises
- Impacts and impressions given to visitor/users
- Stationery/PR materials and presentations/appearance

Price considers:

- Cost plus process, or
- Market nature/market based prices?
- Competition pricing
- Customer perceptions and expectations

Promotion looks at the following:

- Communications
- Two way/Understanding
- Moving through stages of customers being unaware-aware-comprehension-conviction-action
- Using negotiation/persuasion

People considers:
*   Image, such as how they look and "come over"
*   Skills and experiences, here they way people are managed must reflect the giving of good service to customers
*   Attitudes and behaviour shown towards customers

Working through the "Ps" will show the basis of customer's needs and the resulting customer segmentation required.

Customer segmentation

The marketing mix has to be applied according to needs, as customers are not all the same. This will also involve segmenting customers, or putting them into categories.

The following questions can be asked:

How should we segment, for example:
*   Profitability derived from customer
*   Demand/unit sales/volume derived from customer
*   Payment history/credit rating
*   Customer growth/future potential
*   Customer loyalty
*   Customer needs (this has to be a highly recommended method for segmentation)

For each segment:
*   Is it viable?
*   How does it differ from other segments?
*   Is it profitable?
*   Who is the decision maker
*   How do they decide?

Such segmentation can use names as follows:
*   Standard products/services
*   Segmented standard
*   Customised standard
*   Tailored customised
*   Pure customised product/services

Segmentation may also mean, for example:

- Small orders are delivered within two days with a high price
- Large orders are price competitive with agreed lead times that are guaranteed

This segmentation can be applied to service levels, as not every customer will require the same level of service. This principle is accepted and applied, as we find with first or second class postage stamps; first class, business class or economy class air travel etc.

In inventory management, the principle is also well founded, where varied levels of stock holding can be found. These stock holdings relate to the eventual fulfilment of customer orders, for example:

- A customers get 95 % service in terms of availability from the stocking of products
- B customers get 90 % service
- C customers get 85% service

This varied service level also relates to the cost of providing the service, in this case, the amount of stock to be held and therefore the cost. The following pattern is the typical relationship for random demand.

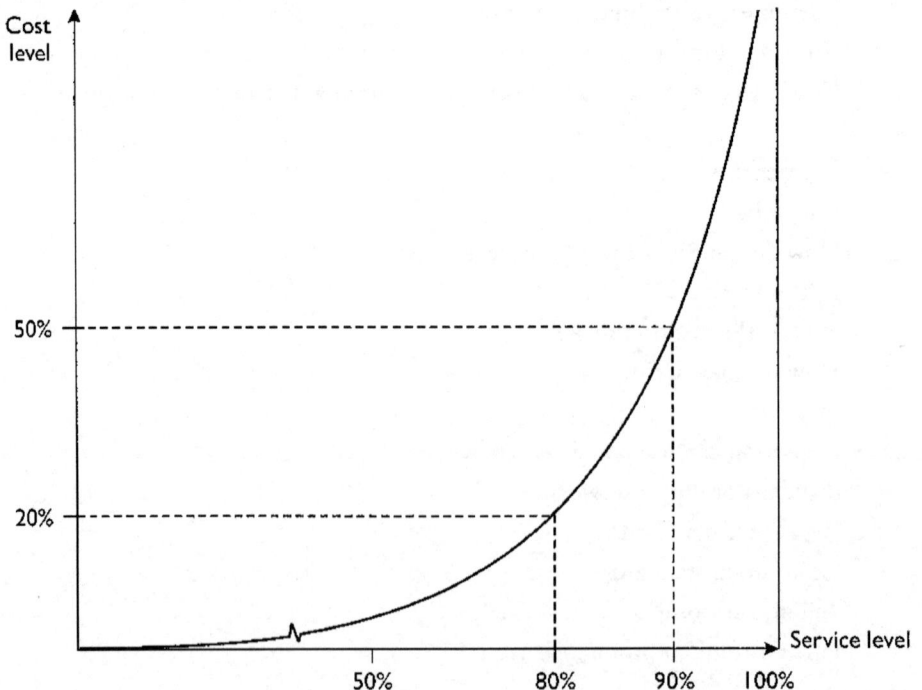

It can be seen that the relationship between cost and service is not linear, but exponential. In this example, the higher levels of service require a proportionately higher level of cost. This will nearly always apply when a cost/service trade off or balance is being looked for between just two variables. However, it can be possible to increase service and reduce costs, both at the same time. (More on Inventory Management is found in **Excellence in Inventory Management**).

Organisations need to review, for example:
*   What do we/can we, offer, in terms of product features and service performance.
*   What benefits will our offer have; for example, lower total costs, risk
    avoidance, increased service, higher quality, marketplace advantage,
    added value etc.
*   How does our offer, match the customer's requirements and expectations?

In this regard, we should always appreciate that customer expectations are often set by the other suppliers of the product/service. Therefore, we may be competing with more responsive competition. Customer expectations are therefore continually evolving, changing and growing. This is one of the principles of the market.

Market Changes
Market changes are continuous, and consequently organisations must also continually examine their markets. The following gives guidelines on doing this:
*   Who needs my product/service?
*   Why do customers need my product/service?
*   What about it is unique so that it can differ for each individual?
*   How do my customers differ?
*   How do customers differ in when they buy, receive and use it?
*   What do customers do differently with my product/service?
*   What different forms can it take?
*   How do customers differ in where they buy, receive and use it?
*   How can I satisfy whatever customers want from my product/service?
*   Where do customers need my product/service?
*   How can I provide my product/service wherever customers want it?
*   How do customers differ in why they buy, receive and use it?
*   How do customers need my product/service delivered to them?
*   How do customers differ in how they use it?

Organisations therefore need to ensure that they communicate with customers effectively in response to changing needs.

Effective customer communication

Communication has been defined as:

"Sharing information between people."

"Exchange of ideas that require a reaction."

"The objective of communication is to prevent misunderstanding."

"The sending and receiving of verbal and non verbal messages."

It takes two to communicate, it is a two-way process. Communication is an active, not a passive process, with sharing and exchanging that signifies active involvement between people. As NLP practitioners have noted, "The meaning of communication is in its effect".

Communication should ideally always be clear, direct, short and simple as possible, and if important enough, should be done in person by using more than one communication method, with reinforcement and repetition.

Delivering Customer Service

It is important to have good relationships when dealing with customer service. Relationships are always at least two-sided, for example, between a supplier and a customer. How relationships work in practice can vary, please therefore consider the following questionnaire:

Score: 1 to 10 as follows: 1 = totally agree with list A, 5 = neither, 10=totally agree with list B

	List A	List B	Score
Customers are called	Users	Partners	
Approach with customers	"Attack/Defend"	Collaborative and problem solving.	
Dependency	Independent	Inter-dependence	
Expected Outcome	Win/lose. Self survival	Win/win. Mutual survival	

Score: From 4 to 40 =_____
4 to 19: List A favoured: Combative approach
20 totally neutral
21-40: List B favoured: Collaborative approach

This relationship area has been more fully covered in **The Relationship Driven Supply Chain** from which the following extract is taken.

Transactional relationships	Collaboration relationships
Contacts with suppliers	
Short term	Long term
Multi sourcing	Single sourcing
Distant and Contractual relationships	Close and collaborative relationships
Little commitment beyond the contract	Involvement and "shared destiny"
Information exchanged is orders	Information is shared including forward strategy
Trust is not needed	Trust is essential
Style is competitive, win/lose, power base is combative with command/control behaviour	Style is collaborative, win/win, power base is non existent with honest, open and truthful (HOT) behaviour
Price/Risk	
Price orientation	Total cost of ownership
Price dominates	Shared destiny dominates
One way	Two way exchanges
Customer demands sensitive data	Exchanges of sensitive data
Customer keeps all cost savings	Mutual efforts to reduce costs, times and waste
All risk with supplier, the buyer risks little	Shared risk and benefits
"What is in it for me"	"What is in it for us"
Short term	Long term

Negotiations	
Strong use of ploys in negotiations	Mutual gains "rule" discussions
Power based	Equality based
Win/lose	Win/win
"One off" deals	"For ever" together
Walk in and out of, change is easy	Difficult to break, change is difficult
Easy to set up	Difficult to set up
Adversarial and maybe inefficient for one party	Challenging to implement and continue with
"Partnershaft"	Partnership
Inter Personal Relationships	
No personal relationships	Strong personal relationship
Separated/arms length	Close/alliance
Low contact/closed	Shared vision/open
Predatory power based	Proactive and more people based
Hierarchical/superior subordinate	Equality
Blame culture	Problem solving "gain" culture
Alienated employees	Motivated employees
Trust	
Trust is based on what the contract says (contractual trust)	Trust is based on goodwill, commitment and co-operation
Little ongoing trust	Continual trust plus risk/benefits sharing
Power based "spin"	Pragmatic "tough" trust

Controls	
Strong on tactical/departmental controls	Strong on marketing strategy and supply chain alignment
High formal controls	Self controlled
Rigid contracts	Flexible contracts
Technical performance and the specifications "rule"	Work beyond just "one" technical view
Resource and capacity capabilities	Mutual Long-term capabilities
Measure by non compliance	Both measure and agree remedial action

The change from transactional methods to collaborative approaches goes beyond the technical issues, and fully embraces the soft skills.

The view and belief here from sponsors of collaborative approaches, is that if all players would work well together, that a lot more would get done more efficiently and more effectively. The evidence for this from basic relationship principles is overwhelming.

The UK Audit Commission has used use the term 'partnership' to describe a joint working arrangement between suppliers and customers where the partners:
- are otherwise independent bodies;
- agree to achieve a common goal;
- create a new organisational structure or process to achieve this goal, separate from their own organisations;
- plan and implement a jointly agreed programme
- share relevant information
- pool risks and rewards

(From: **The Audit Commission: A Fruitful Partnership: effective partnership working**)

In respect to supplier/customer collaboration, the following summary is relevant:
Deciding to go into partnership
- Does this organisation have clear and sound reasons for being involved in partnerships?

- Are changes in behaviour or in decision-making processes needed to avoid setting up partnerships with only limited chances of success?

Operating efficiently and effectively

- Do partners share the same main objectives for the partnership?
- Do the partners know where the boundaries between the activities of the partnership and of their own organisations lie?
- What actions are taken to build and maintain trust between partners?

Reviewing success

- Does each partner have a shared understanding of the outcomes that it expects to achieve, both in the short and longer term?
- What means have been identified for measuring the partnership's progress towards expected outcomes and the health of the partnership itself?
- Has the partnership identified its own performance indicators and set jointly agreed targets for these?
- Are the costs of the partnership known, including indirect and opportunity costs?
- Are these costs actively monitored and weighed against the benefits that the partnership delivers?

Customer touch points

An order from a customer has the following six processes involved.

1. Sales
2. Order processing
3. Sourcing and Stock holding
4. Delivery
5. Invoicing
6. Payment

What is important to appreciate is that all of these steps represent touch points with customers.

Customers deal with many different people in an organisation and each customer contact is a touch point. Each touch point provides an opportunity to:

- exceed customer expectations
- provide excellent service to customers
- create the right customers perceptions

- show how efficient you are
- lead to conflicts, angry and unhappy customers

What must never be forgotten is that customers are always buying experiences, and that everything done for customers is part of that experience and part of how to differentiate and make a difference.

> **Making a Difference**
> Someone was walking along the beach with a friend.
> Millions of crabs had been washed ashore from a wild storm the night before.
> One of them picked up a crab and threw it into the sea.
> The other person said, "That won't make any difference", to which came the reply, "It will to that crab".
> **Lesson:** Small things can make a difference to someone

It is always people who deliver customer service; therefore, all of these touch points that must be properly managed.

Determining Good Customer Service

We all have a view of good service. Consider for example, what happened when you walked into a restaurant:

- How were you greeted?
- How promptly were you attended to?
- How do you think you were regarded by the person serving you?
- How did you feel about this?
- Did the service meet your expectations?
- Has that experience affected your future dealings?

Additionally, we all can name three companies that have a good reputation, and we all have a view on what it is that gives an organisation a good name; our answers representing our perception of good service.

The following questions should be asked:
Self-analysis

- As a customer, what would you say about your organisation?
- How do you encourage customer loyalty?

- How do you handle complaints?
- How often do you respond to the same problems?
- How many customers have you lost in the last three years?
- Why did these happen?
- What are the strengths and weaknesses of your customer service?
- How do you know your customer service is good?

Do we as an organisation:
- Do what has been promised?
- Respond quickly?
- Have positive employee attitudes?
- Proactively communicate?
- Include all of the extras?
- Look good?

Are we:
- Reliable?
- Knowledgeable?
- Honest and open?
- Attentive to detail?
- Nice people to deal with?

Answers to these questions will help us to focus on our customer service offering. Ultimately, our offering will need to satisfy what customers expect from us.

Customer Satisfiers

All customers will expect as a minimum, the following:
- Reliability
- Responsiveness
- Accessibility
- Accuracy

Providing customers with the above will prevent them from being dissatisfied. However these will not, by themselves, provide satisfaction – to provide customer satisfaction, the following is required:
- Fully meet their expectations (and prevent dissatisfaction)
- Responsiveness

- Courtesy
- Empathy
- Provided exceptional quality
- Good people relationships
- Delivery of value
- Handled well any complaints
- Obtained the repeat business

Customer Perception

One of the obvious difficulties in meeting customer's expectations is that "Perception is Reality." Therefore, we are entering into variability and subjectivity. Everything done for customers is the customer's perception, and how they perceive it is real to them. Your reality is therefore, this perception of your performance by the customer. Accordingly, perceptions do really matter, as customers can react differently to the same levels of service being offered.

Many are uncomfortable with this and see it as an unsolvable problem. However attitudes and feelings will all affect the way any service delivery is going to be perceived. This will require flexibility from management, such as giving discretion to staff to deal with customers, and not only relying on standard and fixed, procedural manuals and guidelines.

Customers are individuals, and organisational procedures must support this. Service is all about delivering: not only what it is like doing business with your organisation, but also with you personally. Feelings and attitudes are important.

The importance of attitudes

We have referred many times to the importance of attitudes, and that these are underpinned by our beliefs and values, which work through into how we behave.
We will therefore tend to judge from our perspective alone, and will not always fully consider the other parties.

Good customer-focussed people will have a deep belief that customer service is important, they will value and lead by example. This belief will work through into their attitudes and be shown and reflected by what they say and do. Good customer-focussed people will:

- pull more than push
- be a two-way communicator
- make concessions, "I think this, but what do you think"
- problem solve and explore interests
- hold views and reasons that partnership works and is the best approach

Customer complaints

Common complaints from customers are found when:

- Their expectations are not met
- Inflexible service has been delivered
- Mistakes have been made
- Communications are poor
- Delays have been made in delivery
- Dealing with unprofessional people

There are of course, some benefits in receiving complaints, as they give an opportunity to reverse perceptions and ultimately to delight the customer.

When handling complaints, it is therefore important not to:

- Be defensive
- Pass on the customer to someone else
- Leave them waiting for a reply
- Make it a drama

If complaints are not handled correctly, not only can this affect you personally (stress, anger etc.), but you can lose a customer, which creates bad PR. Plus the customer will, for sure, tell others; we know this will happen, because we do this ourselves when we receive poor service.

When, however, complaints are handled well, then everyone wins. The customer knows that they matter and feel satisfied, and it has highlighted problems that you can overcome and solve.

Dissatisfied customers; some reported facts:

- A typical business hears from only 4% of its dissatisfied customers

A survey on customers who "walked" found:

- 5% were influenced by friends

- 9% were lured by competitors
- 14% were dissatisfied with the product
- 68% quit because of an attitude of indifference toward them by the owner, manager or some other employee
- A typical dissatisfied customer will tell 8 to 10 people about their problem
- 70% of complaining customers will do business with you again, if you resolve the complaint in their favour
- If you resolve a complaint on the spot, 95% will do business with you again
- The average business spends 6 times more to attract new customers, than it does to keep old ones

Handling verbal complaints

When dealing with these, the guidelines are as follows:
- Listen without prejudice. Done well, this alone, can resolve the compliant
- Repeat back
- Apologise
- Acknowledge their feelings
- Explain what will be done
- Thank them

Good listeners are the best communicators who listen sympathetically. If necessary, apologise (this is not an admission of guilt) for the fact that they have experienced a problem. Take responsibility to solve the problem and say what you will do. Obtain the customer's agreement to this action, and then do ensure that you follow up.

Problem customers

You will always hear people say about certain customers, "They always complain, they are a problem". Yes, they may regularly complain, but why do they complain? After all it costs them time and effort to do so.

Usually, the person saying "they always complain" is the one who is actually causing the problem. Those who see people as a problem can reflect this destructive attitude when they deal with people; they are unable to separate out the person from the problem.

It is important therefore to see problems as a way towards succeeding, and a way to find remedial action that prevents further problems. It may help, therefore, to see problem customers as simply those who have not had their needs met.

However, does this mean that the customer is always right? Frustrated customers will sometimes "embellish", so it is important to ask for specifics. Sometimes they can be abusive, so here check your organisation policy and be assertive. Finally, however, there will be some, despite all efforts, that you cannot help and you are happy to lose. This should represent a very small minority.

Always remember that a problem is a deviation from something that was expected, and that improvement is the better side of the "blame/gain" balance.

Perception is reality, so how we see things is important. Consider the following lists

List A	List B
"I am right, I know best"	"I would like to know your opinion"
"Listen to me"	"Let me listen to your view"
Seeing obstacles and problems	Seeing solutions and opportunities
Finding fault	Giving support
Feeling frustrated when with people.	Feels calm when with people
Makes others feel guilty.	Makes people learn
Looks for who is wrong.	Looks for what is wrong
Mistakes are to be punished.	Mistakes are opportunities to learn

List A is all about blame, List B is more about gain. As perception is reality, then seeing complaints as problems will involve you taking more of a blame view.

Service Performance
Service performance should always be traceable back to organisation goals and objectives, so for example, if a competitive advantage is the speed of delivery, then it is important for the organisation to measure how quickly things get done.

As service is an output to customers, then the measurements of service should always reflect the needs of the customer; for example, what is "success" for them? To develop the measurements, the following steps can be followed:

1. Identify who is the customer
2. Determine the customer needs/requirements
3. What process output does the customer receive
4. Determine effective measurements or key performance indicators (KPIS), see below, that link together 2 and 3
5. Understand the key goals of your organisation
6. How do the KPIs in 4 above, relate to the key goals of the organisation and fit into the other process of which they are a part?

The purpose of setting measurable objectives is to give guidance on the existing performance, and to "flag up" any needed improvements. We can view the connections here as follows:

Measurement used = Current performance + Competitive comparison =
Improvement needed = Target performance required.

Key Performance Indicators (KPIs)

These are standards, targets, or outcomes that enable us to determine when a process has been done a job in accordance with expectations. They also provide a benchmark for a comparison with what actually happened (the actual outcome), against what should have happened (the outcome expected).

KPIs can be grouped into the six QCTDSM categories: quality, costs, time, delivery, safety and morale/motivation and the QCTDSM factors that can be used for measurement are as follows:

Quality
* Are products or services delivered to an agreed specification?
* Do you analyse rejects?
* What is the quality of communication and paperwork like?
* What is the quality of relationships with suppliers/customers?
* % orders with complaints against no complaint orders
* % of customers who give repeat business

Examples of Measures:
* Functionality

- Service
- Defects
- Returns
- Rework
- Complaints
- Re-work
- Warranties
- Complaints

Cost (s)

- Are costs kept within agreed limits?
- Are there cost reduction programmes in place?
- Is cost examined related to value and service?
- Do we purchase using total acquisition cost of acquisition and total cost of ownership analysis

Examples of Measures:

- Stock value
- Activities such as labour
- Over time
- Expenses
- Downtime

Time

- Are time standards available for example processing of orders (e.g. if the order is received before 17:00 hours, then despatched by 19:00 hours)
- Response times to requests,(e.g. response times; phone response in two rings, emails response in 24 hours, letters in 48 hours)

Examples of measures:

- All of the Lead times by:
    - Minutes/Hour/Shift, or
    - Day/week/month/period

Delivery/Speed

- Are goods or services delivered at the right time to right place in the right quantity and right condition?
- Goods delivered (e.g. if the order is received before 17:00 hours on day one, then delivered by 12:00 hours on day two)

- Are products packaged correctly?
- Queuing (e.g. not left queuing for more than 3 minutes)

Examples of Measures:
- On time, in full (O.T.I.F)
- Reliability
- Output
- Accuracy of delivery to location
- Tracking steps whilst in transit
- Emergency response

Safety
- What is the accident record?
- How is the legal requirements effectively carried out?

Examples of Measures:
- Accidents
- Suggestions

Morale/motivation
- Are people there, because they want to be or have to be?
- What is the "temperature" of the people interactions?

Examples of Measures:
- Absences
- Lateness
- Staff Turnover rate
- Suggestions
- Job satisfaction
- Promotions
- Training days
- Skill levels
- Appraisal ratings
- Contacts managers/staff

Watch however, for the danger of measuring and then ignoring other things that matter, for example:
- answering a phone at the second ring, but ignoring the customer that is standing in front of you
- replying to an email in 24 hours, saying you will respond the next day, but you do not respond

- despatching on time, but the order is short and not in full (or complete)

Service level agreements (SLAs)

These can be defined as the following:

"A contract that defines the relationship between a supplier and a customer."
"A negotiated agreement designed to create a common understanding about service."

SLAs therefore set objective targets that prioritise customer's needs and wants, by defining what is acceptable, for both customer and supplier. SLAs will therefore attempt to clarify the following:

- What is expected by the customer?
- What the supplier will supply/deliver?
- How often will it be supplied?
- To what quality standards will it be supplied?
- At what price?
- What are the customer's obligations?
- What is the recourse for both parties if things go wrong?

Typical clauses in SLAs are as follows:

- Service description
- Service levels
- Duration
- Reporting levels
- Level monitoring
- Performance standards
- Review meetings/frequency
- Dispute resolution
- Termination

Is the Customer satisfied?

The only way to ever find out an answer to this question is to ask customers how satisfied they are with your service. The following methods are available to do this:

- Face-to-face or by telephone surveys; using open questions to get expansive answers or closed "tell me" questions to get specific answers
- Questionnaire surveys by post or electronic/web based. These typically use Yes/No response or a rating on a 1-5 point scale

- Focus group surveys; these involve selecting a group of people who have awareness of your product/service and seeking their opinions
- "Mystery shopper;" the "invisible" visitor that experiences your service and is specifically looking to see how you perform. Perhaps also they may even test how complaints, they make, are handled by your people
- Free phone help/support line
- Planned, but seemed to be random, visits/calls on customers

Specimen questions that can be asked to customers, especially in surveys, are as follows:
- How often do we do things right the first time?
- How often do we do things right on time?
- How quickly do we respond to your requests for service?
- How accessible are we when you need to contact us?
- How helpful and polite are we?
- How well do we speak your language?
- How hard do you think we work at keeping you a satisfied client?
- How well do we deliver what we promise?
- How much confidence do you have in our products/services?
- How well do we understand and try to meet your special needs and requests?
- Overall, how would you rate the appearance of our facilities, products and people?
- Overall, how would you rate the quality of our service compared to our competitors?
- How willing would you be to recommend us?
- How willing would you be to buy from us again?

One danger of course, with involving customers in completing questionnaires, is that they have others things to do than answer your questions. Additionally, any responses may be hurried and only give lose indications.

However, customer surveys can give vital information on core customer needs, for example; reliable, predictable response times are rated higher than price, acceptability that immediate response can be premium priced etc.

Another example on after sales service in **The Mckinsey Quarterly** 2003 number 4 reports that when customers are segmented into what they need, then they tend to fall into three categories:

- "Risk avoiders" want to avoid non-supply and are not bothered about anything else
- "Basic needs customers" want a standard level of service
- "Hand holders" want a high reliable service and will pay for the privilege

The Customer Service-focussed organisation

To be a customer service focussed organisation, you will need to know:

- Who your customers are
- What they expect and need from you
- How well you are meeting these expectations
- How to provide customer care and follow up
- What benefits customers have obtained from your service
- What needs to be done to make improvements
- What are the barriers to making these improvements
- How you can remove these barriers
- How you will know what you are delivering, is exactly what the customer is expecting from you

The following view of a customer service focussed and non customer focussed organisations shows what is important:

Customer service focus	Non customer focus
Profit comes from customer satisfaction	Profit comes first, then customer satisfaction
Prevents problems	Detects problems
People "rule"	Numbers "rule"
High training spend	Low training spend
Explicit standards	Vague standards
Complaints seen as a chance to learn	Complaints are a nuisance
Run by people working with other people using systems, if appropriate	Runs by systems and procedures and then people

The customer service focussed organisation will have the following five key attributes:

- Reliability: Dependable, accurate performance consistently, in all of the details
- Ownership: Front line ownership, so that those who receive complaints are also able to sort them out; (it is not unusual for only 5% of complaints are resolved at the first point of contact, thus creating delays with dissatisfied customers)

- Responsiveness: Clear evidence of "willingness to help"; for example, answer letters within 2 days, answer the phone in 5 seconds, answer emails in 24 hours
- Attitudes: Courtesy, friendly, empathy and caring by employees for the customers' "unique" requirements
- Appearance: Clean and tidy facilities, equipment, people etc.

The following case study gives a practical application of customer service:

Case Study: Service Disney Style

Disney World enjoys a 40% repeat business ratio, with a high emphasis on making the Disney experience pleasurable, knowing that a high proportion of their guest will return.

The Service theme is "We create happiness by providing the finest in family entertainment".

The Disney System includes a broad philosophy that addresses the following issues:
- Promotion from within
- Treating visitors as "Guests"
- Treating staff as "Cast Members"
- Treating what the guest see as "On-Stage"
- Treating behind-the-scene activities as "Back-Stage"

The Disney people view quality service as "Putting yourself in the mind of the guest", with an overall emphasis on "Attention to detail, and always exceeding the guests' expectations".

All guests are treated as VIPs (Very Individual People).

Measurable criteria, in the following order:
- Safety; this is of paramount importance, and is built into everything that happens in Disney World as a primary consideration.
- Courtesy; there is a concentration on providing courteous service to the guests, and a general display of cheerful good manners. These include greetings in a host of languages.

- Show; there is a "theme" which imparts an implied message in every activity, from eating lunch to taking rides or visiting the attractions.
- Efficiency; is never carried out at the expense of the above criteria. For example, the gates of the Magic Kingdom are closed in peak season, once 50 000 guests are inside. This ensures the safety and enjoyment of all.
- Setting; relates to the physical environment, such as cleanliness and other objects within the environment. All systems and procedures that affect the environment take into account the fact that guests are continually taking pictures. Therefore lawns need to be manicured; streets kept clean, etc., since photographs invariably highlight the conditions that the guest has experienced. Each cast member takes responsibility for cleanliness in the space that they occupy. Litter is everybody's problem.
- Delivery; the Disney theme is generally to combine "thinking" with "doing". The Disney system goes beyond thinking creative imagination, to the actual implementation of strategies and tactics which are designed to carry out the concepts initially visualised on the drawing board.

It is interesting to note that the Disney management convey the message to all cast members that they do not have "problem guests"; they merely have "disillusioned guests". To this end, various strategies are in place to respond to disillusioned guests. For example, if a disillusioned guest had a bad experience with Captain Hook, Peter Pan would respond to the guest offering solutions.

Benefits of good customer service

As has been seen, the road to improving customer service may not be easy; however the benefits can be huge and immense. The following benefits will all make contributions to the survival, wellbeing and the profitability of any organisation:

- Reliable service is a marketable product with a price difference
- Market changes, and many are always coming to most organisations, can be better handled and managed
- Continuous improvement becomes a part of the culture, with innovative and responsive staff; there is a new enthusiasm and support amongst people
- A positive view of your organisation from shareholders, the community and potential employees, with competitors who "fear" your organisation

Customers see the organisation as:
- responsive and listening
- collaborative and sharing
- understanding what is critical to their own success
- "good people to deal with"

8: Managing and Improving Systems

"The same problems keep happening and no matter what we do, the system beats us."

The system referred to in this quotation, is not an ICT hardware/software system, but are human activity systems such as society and organisations. Such systems have both structure and process and will be:

- Dynamic and non linear with many interfaces
- Interlinked and interdependent with many dependencies
- Unpredictable and uncertain with consistent variability.

We introduced systems thinking earlier in the Managing Performance section. The aim here is that we must ensure that when managing, that we must not compartmentalise all of the individual parts. Putting things into boxes, will most likely mean that we will lose the overall systems meaning, therefore we must see and think about the whole of the structure and the processes, the total organisational culture, the purpose of what the system is supposed to do and the associated power and people aspects.

Problem solving

In a traditional problem solving approach however, we analyse by breaking down into parts and look at each part separately. This is essentially a reductionist approach that may give sub-optimal solutions. For example, we may fix only one part, but we still have recurring problems and these may have now been made worse. Why? Well, in changing one part only, we now have the overall system working in a different way; all of the other ignored parts are now reacting differently with the one part we have changed.

With a systems problem-solving approach, we analyse by seeing the interactions in and between all of the parts. We take a more expansive, holistic approach that involves us looking at complex problems with not too obvious solutions. We are aiming to use systems thinking to give us a total system solution.

Systems thinking

We do tend to take our thinking for granted, as once we have learnt something, we behave habitually. As we have explored more fully in earlier sections, to change behaviour, we may have to look at the attitudes, thinking, values and beliefs that underpin the behaviour.

However, to see something happening, we have to know what to look for and this can be difficult with complex systems.

Systems thinking will therefore help us to look into the complex dynamics that are created by people. Systems thinking will show "the big picture".

Mental Models

The real problem here is that what often prevents us from seeing the big picture is our conditioned thinking. As we have looked at before, we have Mental Models; as shown by the following diagram:

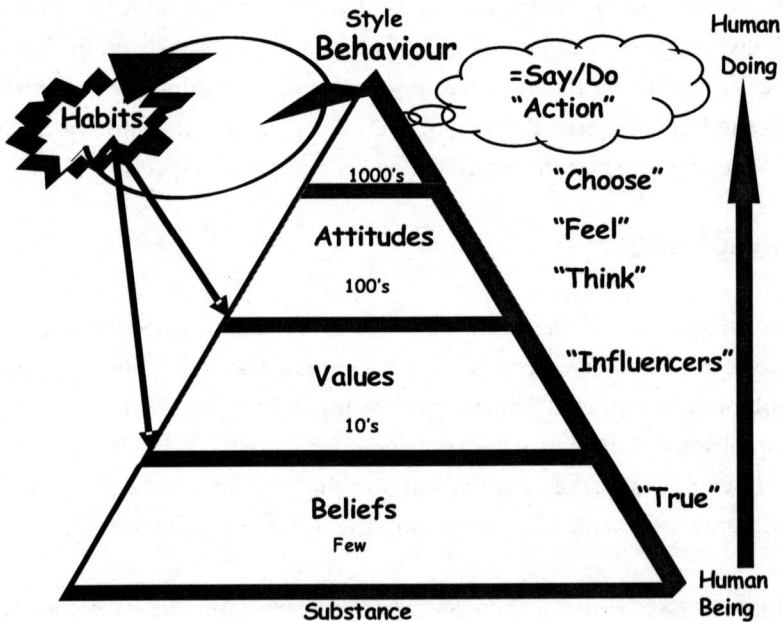

Therefore our "reality" and perspectives come from our attitudes/values/beliefs.
If we get different views, then these views are either rejected or accepted. If these are accepted, then our mental models are changed.

Different perspectives can mean a widened mental model, and our behaviour can become habitual; we can now do things "without thinking" or "automatically."

What we do or say is a visible action that is underpinned by the more invisible attitudes, values and beliefs. Changing our attitudes, values and beliefs may however be difficult and uncomfortable, especially with deep-rooted habits.

We therefore have many shapers to our mental maps, and to our thinking. These include all of the following influences:

- Brain sides: Logical left and creative right
- Mind: Conscious and unconscious
- Memory: Short-working-long terms
- Sight-sound-senses

We can see here that the brain sides shapes our thinking, and are analogous to systems thinking.

The logical left brain is essentially convergent and reductionist "head" thinking that is ordered to think/analyse, then act and then feel. However, the creative right brain is more a divergent "heart" feeler/thinker that is ordered to first feel, then thinks and analyses before acting.

Logical left-brain people will therefore:

- Prefer written, mathematical, science based approaches
- Objective, linear thinking, short-term views
- Breaks things down into parts
- Analytical, step by step "head" thinkers
- Rational "facts" based reasoning that converges

Summary: Analyses-acts-feels

Creative right-brain people will therefore:

- Prefer musical, art/visual approaches
- Subjective, wholes/parallel processing, longer term views
- Sees the "big picture"
- Creative, free flowing "heart" thinkers
- Emotional "feelings" synthesis that diverges

Summary: Feels-analyses-acts

As it is people who operate companies, it is the leaders and managers who in turn will create left- or right-sided brain companies; these are explained below:

Left-brain companies
- Task based/"today"
- Problems often reoccur as only the symptoms are treated ("Band aid" solutions).
- Make profits by making/selling products-services
- Look "inside out"
- The way forward is with science/technology.
- "The numbers speak for themselves."
- Incremental results/parts.
- Functional silo structures, top down

Right-brain companies
- People-based, long-term
- Problems are tackled by looking at the cause/thinking.
- Make people first and before products-services.
- Look "outside in"
- The way forward is by motivating/empowering people.
- "It is how we connect together that is important."
- Holistic results/parts.
- Cross-functional and bottom up

Some of the consequences to these divisions are that in left brain companies, financial decisions may be remote from the actual doing, and are taken "for their own sake" ignoring the implications. There is no effective managing on the right side. There is no effective connection between the inputs-process-outputs.

This often results in short-term financial decisions that cause longer-term instabilities. Problems may be only picked up later, when the figures are available. There is no effective management, as the root causes are hidden and remain unacknowledged.

The right brain organisation however, takes time to set up. With its emphasis on feelings more than facts, proof with objective figures becomes difficult, and with no common financial language, explanations to others are not always going to be easy.

And so we return to the hard and soft values explored earlier. This is not to say that each of these "ideal-typical" brain divisions are mutually exclusive, as the reality is often a balance between the two; what Senge would perhaps call "creative tension."

In trying to find this balance and blend is difficult, and the following are some examples of where this is done:

- Projects are assessed with cost benefit analysis and measurement, but final decisions maybe taken using gut feelings and intuition; a combination of the "head" with the "heart"
- Product demand forecasting that is both statistically and historically based, with also, the sales force market intuition and "gut feel"

The conceptual framework of systems thinking does allow for both objective facts and subjective feelings. It does this by concentrating on the interrelationships that drive the systems behaviour. It recognises that it is people who can leverage and influence the relationships, and therefore the system; such leverage often actually comes from changing the mental models which support the system structure.

In mental models, "perception is realty", or what we see and think about is what we do. And what we do is often reflected and fed back to us.

Thus, what we see within ourselves shapes our reality; we must see our part in changing ourselves. More simply, if it is to be, then it's down to me. If we do not do this, then we are more likely to find ourselves stuck with nothing more than hopeful intentions.

Systems thinking and organisational improvements

The following aspects of a systems thinking should be read with particular attention. By now, you will hopefully have seen that systems thinking is about "mixing the doing and being". It is not about blindly applying tools. It is all about changing our thinking. So, with this in mind, the four important aspects follow:

1) Positive or negative feedback

Systems thinking views the causes of behaviour as coming from circular positive and negative feedback or influences. (It should be noted that the words positive and negative does not mean good or bad). These are:

- Positive and reinforcing feedback. This is where one thing reinforces another thing. Changes to a system come back and amplify and force a change. This change is growth, or collapse/decay, and therefore the system moves away from its initial starting point.
- Negative and balancing feedback gives stability, as it resists attempts to change it.

Importantly, the feedback may be time lagged and delayed. We can also have variability, or unpredictability. As an example, there is complexity theory with its well-known Butterfly Effect: a butterfly today flaps its wings in the Amazon Basin, and that causes a hurricane three days later in Hong Kong.

In relation to dependent and variable process and systems, with feedback, simply put, what happens here may affect what happens there. Unfortunately the here and there may not be seen as being connected, or are seen to be part of "our" system. Here then, we will not have either the knowledge of the dependencies, or we just do not have the visibility of the process.

2) Wholes and not just the parts

Systems thinking sees wholes and not just the parts; i.e. the relationships and connections alluded to above, where small changes in one part of a system area may cause big changes elsewhere. This can then mean, when we look more widely, that greater possibilities are found. An example here is making an overall reduction in costs, whilst the service levels increase; the following shows the changes that were made in one supply chain:

- Raw materials costs fell to 71.5 %
- Production costs increased to 115.6%
- Finished goods stock costs reduced to 66.4 %
- Transport costs increased to 102.8%
- Total costs were reduced to 97.3%
- Service levels increased from 90 to 98%

From a cost base line of 100%, whilst some individual costs increased, the overall costs decreased. Meanwhile, the service was improved. We cannot imagine that the people in change of Production and Transport would have sponsored such a change on their own. So, if a total, more holistic view had not been taken, the double win on cost and service improvements may not have been found.

3) The dynamics of systems thinking are levels and rates.

Levels in systems thinking are levels of resources. Examples of resources that are used as inputs into processes are the 8Ms (2 extra ones are here from our earlier 6Ms):

- Manpower or people
- Motivation levels
- Materials and consumables (for example, energy, water, electric)
- Machinery, plant and equipment

- Money and cash
- Management information
- Minutes; time that most precious infinite resource that one used, has gone, never to return
- Methods of working

These resources may be:
- plentiful or rare
- physical or abstract
- renewable or non renewable, like respectively, profit and oil
- may accumulate, for example, a financial balance sheet that shows the money in the organisation, the raw material stocks held to enable production, the finished goods stocks to facilitate availability to customers

Rates are the flow of resources that cause action; however, we need a decision to cause the action and in turn, we first need information to make the decision.

4) Systems/structure drive behaviour

Systems thinking sees repeatable patterns in a process, and that systems/structure drive behaviour. The behaviour outputs may be growth or decay; goal seeking, variability/ oscillations, or where linked positive and negative feedback respond each to the other and limit growth.

With structure driving behaviour, and in the context of organisational structure, we can see that an organisation is a human activity system of which the structure is just one part. A consultant's overview of an organisation is provided by the McKinsey's 7S Model that shows the following are involved:
- Strategy: the vision and plan
- Systems: the ways of doing things
- Staff: the people
- Skills: the know how and intellectual property
- Style: the management styles and communication
- Shared Values: the culture and ethos
- Structure: the relationships and functions

We have covered all of these 7S aspects in this book.

Improvement methods

For any system to work, it needs a sequence of:

- Information->Decision (Choices made from our Being) –>Action (Doing using Resources).
- Motivation; the drive and push to do things, towards a goal
- Conditions; are what we monitor to see if we have achieved the goal

It is these actions and changes to the structures, which can lead to significant improvements, where leverage often comes from small, but well-focussed changes. Large-scale efforts may not be needed; indeed, Peter Senge has observed that problems are nearly always caused by the way we do things, and that one small policy change may solve many problems easily.

However, the change is usually far away in time and place from where the problem appears, and regrettably, when it is identified often no one believes it is related to the problem. Even if it had been identified, then it is nearly always pushed in the wrong direction, thereby intensifying the problem.

No improvement strategy will ever sustain in the long run due to the ever-changing market dynamics, and external demands. The following diagram emphasises the iterative nature of performance improvement.

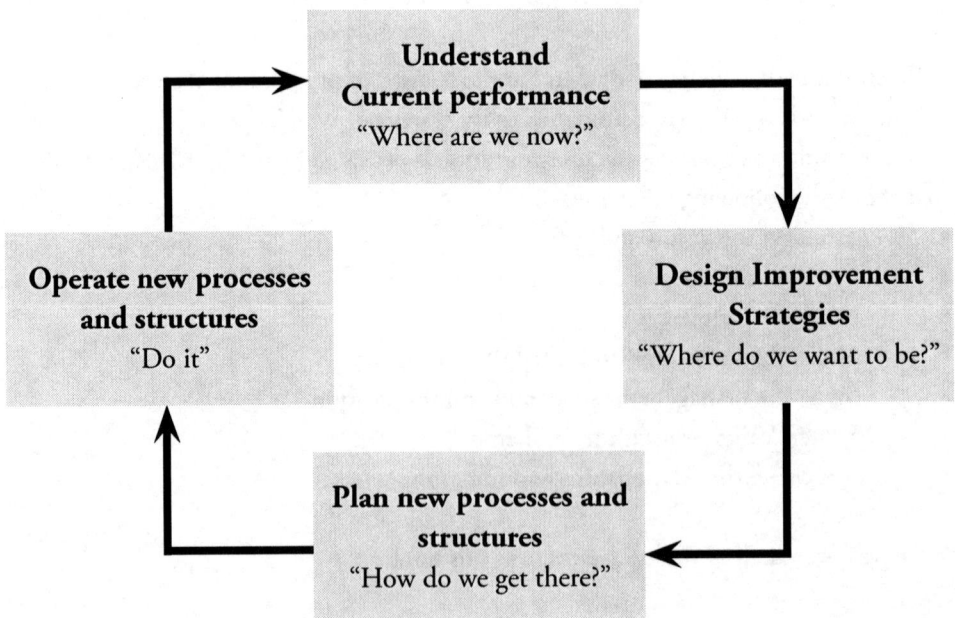

Understand Current performance
"Where are we now?"

Design Improvement Strategies
"Where do we want to be?"

Plan new processes and structures
"How do we get there?"

Operate new processes and structures
"Do it"

Additionally, and critically important in systems thinking, is that a reliance on methods and tools can be dangerous. Indeed, many are unsuccessful in introducing the Toyota Production System, as they concentrate on the explicit tools and not on the implicit principles. They want the easy tools, but not the thinking behind them.

We are back to the earlier section on Mental Models, where "perception is realty", or what we see and think about is what we do. The prime improvement method therefore, is to appreciate that making changes will mean changing both the system and the thinking. Systems thinking is about applying principles, not tools; feedback, wholes, variability, structures and dynamics must be considered. To make continuous improvements, systems principles need to be applied correctly in a continuous series of controlled experiments, that is also an ongoing cycle of learning and change.

Systems Analysis

This is a questioning approach adapted from Balle. It may need several iterations, where at each iteration, deeper detail is revealed:

1) What is the system?
- Can we map the structures and dynamics?
- Are the feedback loops, dependencies, variables and interfaces understood?
- How does the system look, feel, sound?
- What is its history?

2) Who are the players?
- Who is involved?
- Who will be affected by this?
- What is their logic?
- What are their motivation/interests?
- What action do they take?

3) What is the growth engine?
- What positive loop reinforces/drives the system?
- What is in people's minds?
- Where are we now?
- Where do we want to be?
- How are we going to get there?

4) What are the main limiting factors?
- What are the main balancing negative loops?
- Is there some rare resource we are ignoring?

5) Expand the frame
- What is the next link?
- What is the previous one?
- Is there a loop we are not seeing?

6) Operational action points
- Where can we find the leverage?
- Has it been shown by exposing the limiting factors?
- What practical action can we take?

7) Communicate
- Get buy in

Checkland and soft systems

This is a qualitative approach to deal with problem situations in socio-political-human activity systems (also known as soft systems). It gives a structure and specific techniques to look at complex situations and will force a non-technical solution. It uses the following 7 steps; that also may need several iterations:

1) The problem system unstructured

Express (1) by use of rich pictures, these being visual representations and can take many forms like mind maps, combined with flow charts and process charts etc. These show the boundaries, structures, information flows etc. with the human activities.

2) Basic/root definition using CATWOE descriptors

The idea here is to come with a definition of our system. The following descriptors are used to make sure we cover "everything:"
- **C**ustomers; everyone who may gain benefits from the system
- **A**ctors; those who transform inputs into outputs and those who perform the defined activities of the system
- **T**ransformation process; that used to converts inputs to outputs
- **W**eltanschauung; (German: world view), makes the transformation

"meaningful" for someone
- Owner; those that have power start/close/veto the system
- Environmental constraints; external elements to be considered such as policies, legal, ethics etc.

3) Conceptual models
4) Compare (3) with (2)
5) Examine feasible, desirable changes
6) Take action to improve (1)
7) May need several iterations

Lean Service

Systems thinking must be critically applied to organisations, as when "systems thinking is applied to the design and management of work; it is both interesting and profitable." (John Seddon, 2003) The following extract from John Seddon contains many important messages on making improvements, and stresses the importance of using systems thinking to do this.

Change means changing the system

Change for improved performance means changing the system. When features of a traditional management system are left in place, they undermine (or, minimally, compete with) quality principles and practices. If change doesn't change the system, the system doesn't change.

Any intervention in a system which does not change the thinking will produce no change. This is why training in quality techniques fails to improve performance over the medium term (and sometimes even in the short term). The principles and practices of traditional, hierarchical, functional management, which today constitute the accepted norm, are antithetical to quality principles and practices.

This is not just a matter of attitude and belief. The everyday practical matters which managers work with are different in a quality organisation in very real ways. A systems view of the organisation leads to different measures used in a different way. It means designing work according to different principles.

A systems view of an organisation starts from the outside-in. How does this organisation look to its customers? How easy are we to do business with? (One organisation used this as its slogan but was very difficult to do business with. It was the customers who had to manage them to get anything done). The starting place for understanding the organisation as a system is to be able to predict what will happen next week if nothing changes.

Implications for management

It is only when people's view of how to do work changes that their behaviour changes. Changing the system means taking out things which have been limiting or damaging current performance. For example, removing activity measures, arbitrary targets and ceasing to manage performance through budgets; changing structure and processes to enable them to better achieve their purpose. Managers will only take such radical action if and when they appreciate that their traditional means of control in fact give them less control: managing costs cause's costs.

When the organisation is understood as a system, the inappropriateness of such practices becomes stark. It is a major source of motivation for action. Action means "doing the right thing"; putting in place the right "system conditions" to ensure that performance is managed from a strong base of understanding. Deming taught the Japanese to manage their organisations as systems. In four years they out-achieved his expectations. When people work from theory they learn. What Deming gave them was a theory of management which started from the premise that the organisation is a system. Organisations of the future will be learning because their people, the people who do the work, will be learning. But that will only happen as fast as we change the way we run organisations. Without doubt it is the right thing to do.

From: John Seddon: www.lean-service.com; **Systems thinking - management by doing the right thing.**

Perhaps one day, all organisations will continual improve and learn by making improvements in a series of controlled experiments. This is the promise of systems thinking, that is all about applying principles, not tools, and that considers feedback, wholes, variability, structures and dynamics.

Total Quality Management (TQM)

Introduction

Japan's industries and companies dominate many markets, and they use TQM extensively.

It should be normal and expected that no one wants to be associated with poor quality, especially in a changed business world with:

- Customers who are more demanding; for example, travel/trade barriers are removed, the growth of consumerism etc., which create changing demands
- Suppliers are under pressure; for example, reduced supplier bases for consistency, reduced costs, collaboration with only a vital few suppliers
- Employees who become involved and more motivated/productive/effective

TQM will, however, assist with giving adequate responses to such changes.

Additionally, where there is price competition, then differentiation is needed on quality, plus also with the product/service positioning and pricing. This may need a long-term initiative to raise the quality and reduce cost by adding value to those things important to the customer, and by eliminating waste/rework/unnecessary checking etc.

Aspects of Quality

It should also be noted, both practically and philosophically, that quality will not be found with checking alone. For example, it is said, "you cannot design in quality by checking, it is too late".

Checking will:

- Add cost; such as materials, lower morale, space, working capital, delays and longer lead times
- Not add value
- Be done by the wrong people; e.g. a separate QC team.

TQM initiatives ensure this is done by the original workers/users themselves as part of their normal job; "right first time, every time".

For many organisations, TQM is a necessary condition for business, indeed quality is an entry condition for some markets. Whilst there is still need to win business on price, delivery and reliability, because competitors practice "continual improvement", the goal post keeps shifting. This happens globally, as well as locally, therefore "getting better at being better" is the ongoing challenge, and a view that "everyone has two jobs, one as per the job description, two; to improve it" is the challenge facing managers and staff.

Checklist: Qualify defined

- Quality is not necessarily "luxury"; e.g. the quality car, designer clothes etc.
- Quality is that "something" that:
    - meets customer requirements
    - is fit for purpose
    - delights the customer
    - is of value to the customer
- Quality assurance is the total way work is done with systems, procedures, designed into processes and methods with an output performance of consistency and conformance.
- Quality management is therefore the result of what is done, where everyone is responsible for quality of their own work, "right first time every time", using the standard set by the customer.

We can see that by being specific, good quality does not always mean the highest or the best, but that it really means having a predictable degree of uniformity and dependability that is suitable to the market.

Quality is therefore essentially delighting/satisfying the need(s) of the customer, plus adding value at little or no extra cost. With striving to "continually satisfy requirements", quality takes a view that over-engineering is wasteful, when the customer does not want it, or is not prepared to pay for it? Total Quality is therefore continuously improving customer satisfaction, and simultaneously improving margins by gaining everyone's commitment and involvement.

TQM and common sense

It is argued by many that TQM principles are plain common sense, and that often it is not new. But TQM is also all about no longer conditionally doing those bad habits that have "always been done", such as:

- Bad management
- Wrong measurement systems
- Making and buying cheap products/services that no one wants

Clearly here, we can also see that whilst TQM is common sense, and makes sense, it is not very common, because it involves changing habits that have become "wired in" to resist change, points we have discussed already in this book.

Making changes can also take time, and companies so often, especially in the West, want a quick fix, a fixed toolkit "plug in and play", "work in all circumstances" approach. So, superficially, "following the fashion" to implement TQM will just not work or be sustainable in the long-term, and is frankly, doomed to fail if the commitment is not present. Meanwhile, those managers who are active in TQM will:

- Demonstrate what they say
- Gain commitment and earn respect
- Are able to balance individual differences; (e.g. learning styles) with groups/ teams; e.g. collaboration in and between groups of people, internal and external
- Lead individuals towards having their say in "what to do and how to do it"
- Ensure the desired results are achieved
- Love change (and recognise that change can be continuous, radical and evolutionary)
- Know that TQM is all about continuous improvement

Checklist: TQM is/is not

TQM is:
- Customers set the standards
- Reducing total cost
- Continuous improvement
- Strategic change lead by managers
- Doing the right things that add value
- Everyone is involved
- Avoiding waste/eliminating errors

TQM is not:
- Meeting only own standards
- Compromising quality
- Control
- Quality experts checking what is done
- Luxury
- Quality experts only

Successful TQM is also not an automatic overall "catch all" to enable business success. Decline can still happen due to wrong products/poor logistics/weak leadership etc.

Implementing TQM

Clearly implementing TQM has a cost, so, does quality cost an organisation more than previous management methods?

The long-term view of a Quality guru, Crosby, says it is actually free, as Quality will:
- Reduce waste
- Stop re-work
- Stop non-value adders

Meanwhile, whilst the cost levels will depend on the starting point, in the short-term view of costs, there are the potential costs of consultancy, training, new systems/methods, making improvements, taking prevention measures like process controls etc. So whilst there is a cost, following on from Crosby, these will need to be balanced against the reduced costs of:
- Failure e.g. re-work, handling complaints
- Appraisal e.g. checking, testing, inspection

Checklist: TQM: Do/don't

Do:
- Involve people throughout
- Encourage learning by doing and by making mistakes
- Foster collaboration
- Push people to tackle root causes of problems
- Maintain external customer focus

Don't:
- Impose TQM from the top
- Go through the motions
- Incite unhealthy competition
- Solve the symptoms
- Become preoccupied with internal issues

Checklist: TQM Fails/Succeeds

Fails:
- Incremental changes only
- Driven by internal needs
- Training is only in the company

Succeeds:
- After benchmarking a world class performance
- Performance measurement
- Continuous improvement
- Customer value
- Financial returns
- Training is focussed

TQM: Quality models

The key attributes in TQM can be seen by looking at models used for assessment purposes on the effectiveness of a specific TQM approach.

The Baldrige model has the following key attributes:
- Leadership 10%
- HR utilisation 15%
- Information and analysis 7%
- Strategic quality planning 6%
- Quality Assurance systems 14%
- Customer satisfaction 30%
- Quality results 18%

Meanwhile the EFQM model has:
As Enablers:
- Leadership 10%
- People 9%
- Policy/strategy 8%
- Partnerships & resources 9%
- Processes 14%

With Results:

- People 9%
- Customer 20%
- Society 6%
- KPIs 15%

For those who have taken successfully the TQM route, the following checklist shows what a TQM company is.

Checklist: Quality Company

- Profit from customer satisfaction
- Prevent problems
- Cost containment by disciplined approach to internal and external supply chain operations
- People "rule"
- High training spend
- Explicit standards
- Complaints are seen as a chance to learn
- Technology is selective
- Run by people working with other people
- Restless search for improvement and with an holistic and all inclusive inter-linked view

New Culture that has

- Right first time
- Continuous small improvements
- Walk quality
- What do we need to do to improve service?
- "Not rejected here"
- Shows interest in helping others
- Welcomes good/bad feedback
- Both manages and leads people

However, for reasons such as expectations of "quick fixes" that have already alluded to, the majority of TQM initiatives actually fail. This is also connected to the management of change.

9: Management of Change

Change is the one constant of life. The only certain aspect of the future is that it will be different; a future of stable turbulence. It is in the dealing with this uncertainty in the future that managing change becomes a key leadership function.

"In the global marketplace, incremental change is not the answer, instead, large scale, fundamental change is imperative in order to compete and survive."
– Jack Welch

In today's intensively changing world, a central challenge is managing change whilst at the same time ensuring people continue to contribute to organisational goals by being willing participants, with trust and commitment.

Effective change never comes by making small quick fixes; it only happens when the leadership adopts new ways of thinking and then leaps into the unknown.

Sources of change
Most people will have noticed the following trends and resultant changes in recent times:

From Old Ways	Towards New Ways
Technology/product/supply	Customer/Market/Demand
"Push" product flows	"Pull " product flows
Product Sells	Customer Buys
Non TQM	TQM
Manage People	Manage Messages
Specialist Skills	Broad Skills
Bureaucratic control	Empowerment
Instruction/telling	Consulting/Selling
Job for life	Portfolio jobs
Earning a living	Learning a living
Adversarial	Partnership
Fire-fighting	Fire-lighting

The **Dynamics of Change** are found in any situation where there are two forces dynamically involved: the driving and the restraining forces. Examples of the driving forces are:
- Job enrichment
- Upgrading

273

- Broadening
- More Responsibility
- More Reward
- More Status
- Better Conditions
- Easier work

Examples of the restraining forces are:
- De-skilling
- No discretion
- Changed jobs
- More difficult work
- Degrading
- No promotions
- Redundancy

One force represents the "foot on the gas"; the other represents the "foot on the brake".

A key action, therefore, is to identify the driving/backing forces, and the restraining/ blocking forces in any change situation and its context. Next, it is useful to recognise that if we move forward by increasing the driving forces, then there may be an increase in the resistance to maintain the balance.

This means consequently, that the best way to move forward can often be by analysing the restraining forces, and trying to minimise their impact. There is usually some resistance to change, many of the reasons for this are shown below:

50 things that stop change

1. We've never done it before.
2. Nobody else has ever done it.
3. It has never been tried before.
4. We tried it before.
5. Another organisation/person tried it before.
6. We've been doing it this way for 25 years.
7. It won't work in a small organisation.
8. It won't work in a large organisation.

9. It won't work in our organisation.

10. Why change, it's working OK.

11. The boss will never buy it.

12. It needs further investigation.

13. Our competitors are not doing it.

14. Its too much trouble to change.

15. Our organisation is different.

16. The ad department says it can't be done.

17. Sales department says it can't be done.

18. The service department won't like it.

19. The janitor says it can't be done.

20. It can't be done.

21. We don't have the money.

22. We don't have the personnel.

23. We don't have the equipment.

24. The union will scream.

25. It is too visionary.

26. You can't teach old dog new tricks.

27. It is too radical a change.

28. It is beyond my responsibility.

29. It is not my job.

30. We don't have the time.

31. It will obsolete other procedures.

32. Customers won't buy it.

33. it's contrary to policy.

34. It will increase overhead.

35. The employees will never buy it.

36. It is not our problem.

37. I don't like it.

38. You're right, but....

39. We're not ready for it.

40. It needs more thought.

41. Management won't accept it.

42. We can't take the chance.

43. We'd lose money on it.

44. It takes too long to pay out.

45. We're doing all right as it is.
46. It needs committee study.
47. Competition won't like it.
48. It needs sleeping on.
49. It won't work in this department.
50. It is impossible.

Reactions to change

Change can be dramatic, and can, if handled wrongly, be traumatic. Change will always impact on people, and people go through various stages:

Stage one will commence when a person first hears about the change.

Stage	Comments	"Here" to "there"
1. Shock, immobilised	"They can not do it"	Past orientation
2. Denial	"We will never do it"	Past
3. Frustration and defensive	"It is just too difficult"	Past
4. Acceptance and discarding	"I might try"	Past/Future
5. Testing	"Lets try"	Future
6. Search for meaning	"It seems to work"	Future
7. Integration	"I can do it"	Future

The impacts felt will vary. Also, whilst all of the people involved will experience the same stages, it is very likely they will not experience them at the same time or in the same way.

Change will often be resisted because it can mean changing the way things have always been done – a point noted by Peter Drucker:

"Finding and realising the potential of a business is psychologically difficult. It will always be opposed from within, because it means breaking down with old established habits."
– Peter Drucker

People's attitudes to change will vary in any group of individuals, and these attitudes can be very emotional and wide ranging:
- Stimulating to Resisting
- Exciting to Denying
- Dynamic to Fear

- Anticipation to Anger
- Enthusiastic to Stress
- Exciting to Concern
- Challenging to Worry
- Opportunity to Certainty
- Visionary, looking forward, to staying with the current situation

It is critical to appreciate that all people will go through such emotional responses, but they will do it differently and at different times. Leaders and Managers need to be alert to such variations, and manage them effectively. After all, people have to change one at a time.

Resistance to change can however be minimised when the change:
- Is agreed by all
- Is owned by individuals
- Is supported by leadership and management
- Follows culture and values
- Decreases current problems
- Increases new experiences and interests
- Emotions are understood by management
- Reactions are allowed to be discussed with management
- Does not cause personal security to be threatened

Change and communication

Managing change is a skilful process, and a key skill in dealing with change is communication. It has been said that communication and change are synonymous, as people are uncertain during times of change, and thus need to be clearly communicated with. It is critical to involve people, communicate, listen, give people chance to air objections, and to give people time to adapt. This should involve making the following choices in the methods of communication:
- Not "telling" propaganda, but "selling" proper communication
- Inform people at all stages
- Ask them questions to uncover feeling
- Listen carefully to the answers
- Use written communications only where they are appropriate. Concentrate mainly, on face-to-face methods, as these provide for more effective communication (as we shall see shortly)

- Consult wherever possible
- Admit any mistakes and learn from them
- Celebrate individuals and group success
- Be as open as you can

Communication must have the following keys:
"The objective of communication is to prevent misunderstanding"
"It is NOT a one-off exercise but is continual, and needed over and over again"
In change it needs to be: "Communicate - communicate – communicate".

The following represents a most useful overview of change:

Kotter's change hierarchy (How to do it)
- Establish a sense of urgency
- Create a guiding coalition
- Develop a vision and strategy
- Communicate the change vision
- Empower employees
- Generate short-term wins
- Consolidate gains for more change
- Anchor the new approaches

Kotter's errors (What to avoid doing)
- Too much complacency
- Under powered coalition
- Under estimating the real power of vision
- Seriously under communicating the vision
- Permitting obstacles to block change
- Failing to generate short-term wins
- Declaring victory too soon
- Not anchoring changes in the culture

Kotter's consequences of errors (What can go really wrong)
- New strategies are not implemented well
- Gains do not achieve the expected synergies
- Long time-scales and high costs
- Down-sizing does not control the costs

- Anticipated results are not realised

Source: John Kotter **Leading Change** (1995) and **The Heart of Change** (2002)

And finally on change
The following case study shows a practical outworking on some of the above best practice principles:

Case Study: Retailer

The "Problem"
- Not customer focused
- Low quality product
- Family focus ownership of a PLC

The Plan used was:
- Establish a mission statement, e.g. on value for money, customer service, friendly environment in stores
  Establish a set of values, e.g. trust, respect, communication
- Planned the change programme, e.g. current and future cultures identified
- Worked on the top managers behavioural style, e.g. less "tell"
- Work on the mid managers behavioural style, e.g. teams, interactions
- Worked on branch managers/department managers behaviour style, e.g. customer service
- Some communication initiatives were Focus groups, internal cross-functional, external on customer service; Annual conference; Monthly area meetings; Weekly trading meetings

Leading and managing change involves the full and complete leadership and management repertoire. The following checklists are therefore helpful as reminders of the critical aspects involved:

Checklist: Change Levers

Some of the "lessons from experience" are as follows:
- A clear understanding of the need for change

- Quality of leadership
- Commitment of sponsors
- Clear vision for the future change
- Change structured programme
- Educate and train people
- Effective two-way communication
- Aligned infrastructure
- Aligned reward structures
- Aligned organisational structure
- Skilled change agents/leaders

Checklist: Leadership and Management Steps of Consistency

- Develop an awareness of your impact on others
- Try always to involve people
- Believe that teamwork is the best approach
- Have a consistent management style
- Spend time coaching and developing people
- Build a positive climate in the team
- Empower team members rather than control them
- Develop appropriate performance reviews systems and methods
- Set challenging achievable and measurable objectives
- Communicate
- Agree improvements
- Give regular feedback
- Tackle poor performance
- Reward success

Checklist: Change Maxims to be lived by

- Communicate, communicate, communicate
- Survival needs change and continuous improvement
- Keep trying until you get it right
- Celebrate success
- Think outside the box and experiment
- Create ownership and involvement

- Walk the talk
- Let people be responsible and accountable

Checklist: Change Principles for People

- Honesty - so that people can trust.
- Aims - so that people can participate in a clear sense of mission or purpose - the simpler the better.
- Uncertainty is unsettling.
- Participation gives a commitment for results. Getting involved works.
- Recognition of people's effort scores higher, than material rewards.
- Mature individuality is needed - yet traditional cultures often do not like this but they also expect people to behave like adults!
- Full commitment of all those affected or involved with the change.
- Clearly linked values with behaviour promote trust.
- Team working and good inter-personal relationships.
- A shared vision and a defined role in that vision.
- Time is needed to maintain quality.
- Individual attitude and behaviour will have to change.
- Culture and systems changes predispose individual attitude and behaviour change. The "rule book" is unlikely to work in a new situation.
- Team involvement and approaches work.
- People make change therefore, emotional needs are involved.
- Takes time and quick fixes will usually fail.
- Plans are needed to serve and no enslave. So, plan in short intervals with flexible priorities. Be the tortoise and not the hare.
- Performance at the start will suffer before the improvement works through.
- Find people throughout the organisation, who are interested and have relevant skills/high energy levels, and use them as change champions wherever they are in the organisation. Ask for volunteers?
- Risk that as it takes time, then it appears to be, indecisive. Therefore, a person losing their motivation is a risk.

Checklist: A Model for Change

Step one - Reviewing (Why change, type of change, how to go forward)

1. Have you thoroughly understood the drivers for change?
2. What type of change are you facing: incremental (go to question 3) or fundamental (go to question 4)?
3. How should you approach the incremental change, having regard to urgency and the amount of resistance you expect to encounter?
   - High urgency/low resistance. Focused participation
   - Low urgency/low resistance. Extensive participation
   - Low urgency/high resistance. Persuasive
   - High urgency/high resistance. Persuasive/coercive
   (Go to question 5)
4. How should you approach the fundamental change, having regard to the urgency and the degree of resistance you expect to encounter?
   - High urgency/low resistance.   Visionary/charismatic
   - Crisis/low resistance.   Visionary/persuasive
   - High urgency/high resistance. Visionary/coercive
   - Crisis/high resistance.   Dictatorial
5. Modify your choice of change strategy as a result of your answers to the following:
   - Do those you wish to involve those who have the ability to participate?
   - Are they motivated to participate?
   - Does the need for confidentiality affect your ability to involve others?
   - Does involvement (or lack of it) fit the culture of the organisation?
   - How important is the post-change motivation of employees?
6. For all choices of approach, ensure that you understand the reasons for resistance:
   - What threats are those affected likely to feel?
   - Do you understand the basis of their psychological contracts?
   - Will there be resentment at imposed change?
   - Do they have faith in those making the change?
   - Do you understand the emotional hang-ups?
7. How can you reduce resistance? Consider the value of:
   - Participation
   - Communication
   - Training.
8. For all change situations, have you assessed the implications and effects of the change?

9. Have you used force field analysis or other approaches to think through all aspects of the change?

10. Have you considered all aspects of the change to the organisation, as below, and thought through, which elements have to change and how these affect the other elements?

- The desired change
- Tasks
- People
- Structure
- Decision processes
- Culture
- Goodwill
- Information systems
- Control systems
- Reward Systems
- Operational systems
- Intended Results

11. Is your change:

(a) Incremental and with relatively minor impact on the elements of the organisation. If so, move to question 12.

(b) Incremental with a complex impact on the organisation? If so, move to question 14.

(c) Fundamental? If so, move to question 14

12. If your answer to 11 (a) is yes, then:

- Have you gone through all the points so far so that you have a clear definition of the change and the way in which it must be implemented?
- Have you established action plans to implement?
- Have you set up a way of monitoring progress?

Good luck, you should be ready to implement. All other change situations will benefit from a structured approach. Are you ready to use the findings from your analysis so far to modify how you use the approach? Then, continue to Step Two

Step two. Be clear on the vision

Is the vision:

- Credible?

- Challenging?
- Consistent in all parts?
- Clear?
- Providing a bridge from the past to the future?
- Something that you believe in whole-heartedly?
- An integral part of the organisation culture?

Step three. Get the message across

Have you determined how to get going?

- How to demonstrate your own belief in the vision.
- How you will use personal contact to communicate the vision.
- Whether to use workshops and conferences.
- How opportunities for two-way communication can be created.
- What communication media will be used to support the messages?
- How you can use everyday meetings to build the vision.
- The use of external public relations.
- How you will seek out and use examples of success.
- How to check that training is reinforcing the vision?

Step four. Help people through

- Have you thought through a strategy for giving support by:
- Expressing confidence in those working with you to implement the change?
- Providing coaching when it is needed?
- Empowering key people?
- Having empathy with those involved in the change?
- Using praise and thanks when appropriate?
- Helping people through after mistakes and failure-which are all part of learning and therefore of change

Step five. Plan the actions needed

Have you thought through the detailed implementation actions to make the change happen, including:

- Strategies to implement the vision?
- Short-term plans and budgets to turn strategies into action plans?
- Project management for complex situations?

Step six. Monitor and control the change process

- How will you monitor and control the change process?

Step seven. And finally:

- Have you thought how you will motivate by giving recognition to those playing a part in the change process?
- Are you emotionally prepared to deal with all the unexpected things that will crop up, and all the matters you should have thought of but overlooked?
- Have you given thought to how you might reduce the levels of stress that those under you will feel when the change is implemented?
- Have you given attention to the particular problems of the reactions of survivors, if the change has involved people having to leave the organisation?
- Will the change affect departments other than your own in a fundamental way?

And finally, have you:

- A clear understanding of the change?
- Evidence to support the need for the change?
- Assessed the levels of support you are likely to receive from your boss and the top management of the firm?
- Considered the value of finding a champion for the change from the ranks of top management?
- Examined ways that you can get key managers on your side through participative approaches?
- Understood the dangers that face a specialist unit that suggests major change, but is otherwise isolated from the organisation?
- Developed a plan for gaining top management commitment to your vision?

If you have followed the points through, you should have a comprehensive approach mapped out that will enable you to implement in an effective way. Remember that there is a continuous nature to many of the steps, and that some will be repeated. It will be a routine activity in a changing future, which involves learning to learn and to be continuous learners.

Appendix

Fact file – listening

Listening is an important skill to develop. Listening is not just the natural and passive act of hearing. Listening, is more than just hearing, it is more about understanding and then going on to do what has been listened to. (A Chinese proverb says "I hear and I forget", but "I do and I understand").

Listening is not an easy skill to learn. Yet, its importance is immense. How many times has someone criticised us, for not listening?

Always remember that when thinking about listening, that we have two ears and one mouth. So, we should remember to use them in that proportion.

Listening is hard work, which requires concentration. We need to be Active Listeners. Here is the problem – most people think about four times as fast as they speak, therefore each listener has about 75 per cent of each listening minute spare. This spare time is often then used on "own" business.

Concentration demands interest, so any new input must then battle for attention.

One "trick" to help us, is to behave in a way that will help us concentrate, so, by being prepared, acting interested and getting involved, this will then, improve our ability to concentrate.

So don't wait to be "in the mood," get started and act interested, often enthusiasm will grow out of our action.

Active listening in a one to one situation, involves us looking the other person straight in the eye whilst they are speaking. Listen without interrupting. Absorb what they say, try really to understand. When they have finished, repeat it back to them by paraphrasing what was said. For example, "so as I understand it, what you said is X". Only when they agree, can you move forward.

This shows that we have listened and demonstrates we have heard.

Active and productive listening in a group situation, starts by understanding ourselves and then by understanding the listening situation.

Let's expand this further:

1.   Get Ready
- **R**eview what you expect.
- **E**liminate any distractions (for example, uninterested colleagues).
- **A**nticipate what is being said – you then become active.
- **D**etermine why you are there – know why you are listening.
- **Y**ou are there complete – not just the body – but with an active mind to focus on the now and not on yesterdays or tomorrow problems.

2.   Assume the position
- **S**it-up, don't slouch, let your posture speak.
- **W**atch, as well, as listen, to body language, to any visual aids etc.
- **A**cknowledge what you hear by nods and questions as your active involvement completes a feedback loop.
- **T**ake notes.
- **S**quarely face the speaker
- **O**pen posture is to be kept by you, as this shows the speaker you are receptive.
- **L**ean slightly forward as this shows your presence and interest
- **E**ye contact holds interest.
- **R**elaxing shows you are at ease and receptive.

3. During the process
Focus on content and ideas and believe what the person is saying is true for them. Do not focus on their appearance/accent/tone/personality. Focus on why you are there, for example, to gain/refine your knowledge/skills. Focus your attention as you would if you were having a one to one conversation with your best friend.

Abbreviate your notes – it is only you who need to understand them, not anyone else. Also 'Abbreviate" your own ideas so you can understand the speakers' ideas!

Review and revise your notes within 15/20 minutes of the end.

So READY – SWAT/SOLER – FAR, is the mnemonic for listening.

Fact file – memory

To retain information we must actively absorb ourselves in a subject. In turn, we need to make connections in the brain. These connections require us to repeat and review information. ("Use it or lose it'.) So much of learning will mean that we have to Review and Review and Review!

Memory is based on the ability to create links and associations between information. The memory is a store that requires recall to access it; here it is your recall that is the trigger needed, to open up the store. These triggers are known as association techniques:

- Linking ideas to colours, emotions (for example, angry links to the colour red).
- Pegging ideas to rhymes visual cues (for example, I before E except after C).
- Mnemonics or creative sentences (for example, a mnemonic for listening is "Ready – Swat/Soler – Far", as detailed in the Fact File – Listening).
- Remembering to remember (for example, see below).
- Practising using your memory (for example, try using visual cues).
- Putting meaning into it (for example, determining your WIIFM).
- Review/Review/Review (for example, immediately in 24 hours, in one week, in 6 months).
- Being healthy (for example, right combination of rest, food, exercising, and a healthy body equals a healthy mind).
- Breaking when studying (for example, maximum 20/40 minutes' heavy concentration, then a 5-minute review. This will help retention, as we remember more easily the first and the last parts of a learning session).

Remembering to remember is important, because, even when we try to remember, we will forget. New information is rapidly lost, especially in the first 20 minutes. 70 to 90% of new information can be easily lost in one day.

So if you are really serious about wanting to remember, then you must:
- Review it within 20/30 minutes.
- Break long sessions in 20/40 minutes blocks followed by 5-minute reviews.
- Remember that reviewing for 20 minutes a day for 5 days is better than reviewing for two hours at one go.
- Keep information into bite size chunks of seven items or less (as this suits our short-term memory).

Finally let's try and put all these ideas together in the mnemonic, "STOOR USE".

1.   Spread out any heavy memory work (e.g. detailed learning of complicated formula), over several sessions. 20 minutes a day for 5 days is better than 2 hours at one go.
2.   Test and retest yourself by repeating previous learnt material
3.   Organise your material by putting it into patterns or relationships – (this is the idea of Mind Mapping note taking).
4.   Over learn by reviewing material you have learnt several times, as constant repetition does actually work.
5.   Recite material out loud, as Research studies show answering questions aloud, improves recall by at least 80 per cent
6.   Use all your senses for example:
     •   See it (by reading and visualising).
     •   Say it (by reading and hearing).
     •   Feel it (by reading and feeling).
7.   Study before sleeping and upon awakening. Reviewing right before sleep enables you to process while you are sleeping. When you awake, then review it again.
8.   Expect to remember by making it a decision - if you really want to remember, then you will. (Attitude is your secret weapon. Believe in yourself and in your ability to learn, remember that you do need will, to develop a skill).

Fact file – note taking

Note taking is another personal skill which when learnt will enhance the overall learning process. Notes contain key facts and therefore enhance the recall. Note taking also ensures you become active in the learning process.

The format of notes kept is often a very personal and individualistic process. They are kept for us and us alone. Therefore, no two people notes will be identical in every respect. There are however some common aspects, as follows:

1. Get Organised
•   Use a spiral notebook
•   Date and number all pages

2. Set up a format, for example:

- Main ideas in the left margin of right hand page, with recall/review ideas in the right margin. On the left-hand page, write down questions or textbook notes.
- Mind mapping with main ideas and branches containing details

3. Taking Notes

- Include all definitions, lists, formulas, or solutions.
- Leave plenty of space to allow in filling with your later ideas/connections.
- Use symbols, diagrams, abbreviations.

4. If taking notes when listening, it will help if you:

- Watch/Listen for the speakers voice changes, as this usually signifies important points
- Watch/Listen for any repetition of the speaker's, as this is a clue to the importance of the material.
- Stay actively involved.
- Ask questions to clarify what is unclear.
- Keep on thinking, reflecting, and reacting.

5. Review

- Immediately refine any missing areas and rewrite any garbled notes.
- File your notes in a logical order/sequence, and build up your personal library.

Fact file – reading

Reading is a portable, versatile and flexible way to gather information in the learning process.

The key to effective reading is to be mentally active, so we then think about what we read. Remember, reading is thought, guided by print. Writing has been the author's job and that job is done. Reading is the learner's job and that job is now ours.

To read effectively then the following pointers can help:

1. Preview

- Browse the materials to see what's coming.
- Plan your reading into 15/20 minute sections

2. Read One
- Actively ask questions about each section or heading, for example, who, what, when, why where, how?
- Write down what questions you want answering.

3. Read it again
- Actively read not the words, but the ideas.
- Engage your senses by reading out loud, underlining the text, colour coding, drawing pictures etc. Make notes and create interest in what you are reading.

4. Read it again
- Actively check you have "got it".

5. Review
- Reread the sections and review your notes.

Fact file – writing

Writing is within us all. It is part of our desire to communicate and tell others. But it is probably the last thing we learnt as a child. First, we learnt to listen, then from this, to speak. Next, we started reading, which then lead us finally to writing.

The starting point is to get clear objectives or purpose about our writing. Identify the objectives before starting, which include considering the audience. Who are we writing to, who is the reader? If you don't know where you are going, then any road will take you there, so, clear objectives will give you the focus. So, why are you writing and what is the purpose and expected outcome?

There are two main keys to effective writing; Grouping and Looping.
Grouping takes us into getting ideas onto a rough plan; Looping takes us through the actual process of writing.

Grouping
The stages in "Grouping" are all about sorting through our thoughts and ideas and then getting them onto paper; it's like a written "brainstorm," with no judgements, just a paper dump. The steps are:
- Put down the ideas in a box or a circle.

- Visualise what you see.
- Imagine hearing what someone would say about the ideas.
- Feel the subject and write down your feelings.
- Expand on these inputs and ideas.
- Make connections and link these ideas.
- Start to see the content forming.
- Experience the delight as the structure starts to form into a rough plan.

Looping

- We then take this rough plan into the next step, "Looping". The steps here (5*R with 2*E) are as follows:
- Rough draft is prepared (from the "Grouping" stage).
- Review with others.
- Revise the draft with the feedback received.
- Review again with others
- Edit for spelling, grammar etc.
- Rewrite with final content and with edited changes.
- Evaluate.
- Now all of these steps in Looping (5*R with 2*E), are themselves a Loop, for after the rough draft step, you keep going around the loop until it is finalised; i.e. when you are happy with it.

Bibliography

Adair, John. (2004). *The John Adair Handbook of Management and Leadership*. London: Thorogood.

Adebanjo and Kehoe. (2001). **An evaluation of factors influencing teamwork and customer focus** in *Managing Service Quality* Vol. 11 No. 1 pp49-56.

Audit Commission. (1998). A *Fruitful Partnership: effective partnership working*.

Balle, Michael. (1994). *Managing with Systems Thinking*. London: McGraw Hill.

Balle, Michael. (1995). *The Business Process Re-engineering Action Toolkit*. London: Kogan Page.

Belbin, Meredith. (1981). *Management Teams*. USA: Butterworth and Heinemann.

Business Age. February 1999.

Checkland, Peter. (1981). *Systems Thinking, Systems Practice*. Wiley & Sons.

Chartered Management Institute and Adecco. (2004). *Motivation Matters*.

Covey, Stephen. (1989). *The 7 Habits of Highly Effective People*. London: Simon & Schuster.

Drucker, Peter. (2004). *The Daily Drucker*. London: Harper Business.

Emmett, Stuart and Granville, David. (2007). *Excellence in Inventory Management* Cambridge: Cambridge Academic.

Emmett, Stuart. (2005). *Excellence in Warehouse Management*. London: Wiley & Sons.

Emmett, Stuart and Crocker, Barry. (2006). *The Relationship Driven Supply Chain*. London: Gower Press.

Emmett, Stuart. (2008). *The Toolkit Series*. London: Management Books.

Harvey Jones, John. (1995). *All Together Now*. London: William Heinemann

Herzberg, Frederick and Mausner B, Snyderman B. (1959). *The Motivation at Work.* Wiley & Sons.

Herzberg, Frederick. (1968). **One More Time: How do you motivate employees?** in *Harvard Business Review.*

Independent on Sunday, 11 April 1993.

Kotter, John. (1995). *Leading Change.* Boston: Harvard Business School Press.

Kotter, John and and Cohen, Dan. (2002). *The Heart of Change.* Boston: Harvard Business School Press.

Leighton, Alan. (2002). Quoted in *Motor Transport,* 28 November 2002.

Pagonis , William (former senior US Army Officer) and Cruikshank, Jeffrey. (1994). *Moving Mountains: Lessons in Leadership and Logistics from the Gulf War.* Boston: Harvard Business School Press.

Maslow, Abraham. (1943). **A Theory of Human Motivation** in *Psychological Review;* <www.all-about-psychology.com>

McGregor, Douglas. (1960). *The Human Side of Enterprise.* London: McGraw-Hill.

Mckinsey Quarterly, The, 2003, number 4.

McNamara, Richard. (2002). *The Human Resources Toolkit.* London: Management Books 2000.

Read, Nick (CEO Vodaphone UK) quoted in *The Sunday Times*, 1 April 2007.

Seddon, John. Systems thinking – management by doing the right thing <www.lean-service.com>

Seddon, John. (2003). *Freedom from Command & Control.* London: Vanguard Education Limited.

Senge, Pete. (1990). *The Fifth Discipline.* London: Century.

Van Hoek R.I. and Mitchell A. J. (2006). **The Challenge of Internal Misalignment** in *IJLRA*, Volume 9, issue 3, September 2006.

Welch, Jack, with John Byrne. (2001) and (2003). *Jack, straight from the cut.* <www.ukhrd.co.uk>

Index

Lightning Source UK Ltd.
Milton Keynes UK
UKOW021050131011

180202UK00001BA/16/P